The King of Western Swing

BOB WILLS REMEMBERED

The King of Western Swing

BOB WILLS REMEMBERED

Rosetta Wills

BillboardBooks

An imprint of Watson-Guptill Publications/New York

To Chad, my "Brown-Eyed Handsome Man"
and
Reneé, my "Brown-Eyed Girl"

Senior Editor: Bob Nirkind
Edited by: Amy Handy
Book and cover design: Jay Anning, Thumb Print
Production Manager: Hector Campbell

First published 1998 by Billboard Books, an imprint of Watson-Guptill Publications,
a division of Billboard Productions, Inc., at 1515 Broadway, New York, NY 10036

Library of Congress Cataloging-in-Publication Data

Wills, Rosetta.
    The king of western swing : Bob Wills remembered / Rosetta Wills.
        p.   cm.
    Includes bibliographical references (p.   ) and index.
    ISBN 0-8230-7744-6
    1. Wills, Bob, 1905-1975.   2. Country musicians--United States--
    Biography.   I. Title.
ML422.W6W55   1998
781.642'092--dc21
[B]   97-46113
        CIP
        MN
Manufactured in the United States of America

First printing, 1998

1 2 3 4 5 6 7 8 9 / 06 05 04 03 02 01 00 99 98 97

We would come in from the fields at noon and gather around an old battery-powered radio to hear Bob's music. It gave us hope during those hard times that the words of politicians could never equal. The music made us feel good, feel happy.

FORMER U.S. CONGRESSMAN CLEM MCSPADDEN
From the eulogy delivered at Bob Wills's funeral
May 15, 1975

Acknowledgments

When you begin a project as immense as writing a book, it is impossible to succeed without the support of the people closest to you. I am grateful to my husband, Michael, for his editing skills and tremendous patience. I am also grateful to my mother for telling me her story. I appreciate Wills family members and close friends of my father who shared their special memories with me. All of the former Texas Playboys I interviewed were extremely helpful. Their fond recollections communicate the devotion and love they continue to feel for my father. My Austin writer friends Nancy Bell and Michael Point gave me guidance during a crucial period by editing my first draft. Many thanks to New York attorney Bill Krasilovsky, who put me in touch with Bob Nirkind, Senior Editor of Billboard Books, along with editor Amy Handy, both of whom have worked closely with me on this project.

Dr. Charles Townsend's biography *San Antonio Rose,* containing Bob Pinson's discography, was invaluable in my research, along with the many other books and articles listed in my bibliography. Steve Hathaway's numerous *Western Swing* newsletters also contained great resource information.

I would like to share a few experiences that helped sustain my motivation while writing this book. In 1995 Fern and Ernie James guided me to the old house where my father was born on March 6, 1905. Ten years earlier these longtime Wills followers, who lived in Houston at the time, had searched for the birthplace near Kosse, Texas, Ernie's hometown. After learning the general vicinity, they walked several miles before locating it. Fern said, "I was wearin' a dress and high heels, but I wouldn't give up till we found it." They commissioned an artist to sketch the house from a photograph they took that day. (They also sent me a copy of the photograph.)

Collectors Johnnie Burnett (of Ponca City, Oklahoma) and Harvey Tedford (of Chepota, Kansas) prepared audio and video tapes for me. One contains a clip from an early sixties Glen Campbell television show when Bob fiddled while Campbell sang "San Antonio Rose." Harvey is proud that my father called out his name on two recordings. At the end of "Gone Indian" on *From the Heart of Texas* recorded for Kapp (1966), Bob bellows, "Brother Harvey, how'd you like that?" And after "Bob Wills Waltz," recorded on a rare Longhorn album, Bob says, "Come on there, Brother Harvey, you know you like to dance them old-time waltzes." But Harvey's biggest thrill happened in 1965 when my father gave him an autographed copy of

Hubbin' It inscribed, "From An Old Pal, Bob Wills." On a version of "Panhandle Rag" (Kapp, 1969), Bob also mentions two other fans, Mr. Frank Hughes and his wife, May, from Odessa, Texas. They received so many calls after this record was released, they switched to an unlisted number.

Bill Gibson (of Lakewood, California) sent me quality reproductions of Bob's old movies from the forties and shorts made in the fifties. Watching these movies reminded me of an eerie experience when I set my VCR timer and turned off the sound to tape one of the old movies scheduled for three A.M. on cable. When I sleepily stumbled to the kitchen for a glass of water in the middle of the night, my father's face silently peered at me from the darkened room's TV set. For a split second, I thought it was his ghost!

Hometown native Phillip Fortune's comprehensive collection includes all Bob's 78s (except for five he has on tape), 45s, and LPs. He sent me reel-to-reel tapes along with a complete discography and a video tape of the first Pawhuska, Oklahoma, Western Swing event that included off-the-cuff Playboy conversations in his home. Phillip remembers my father as "a fine gentleman with a cowboy hat and fancy, handmade boots" whom he first met in 1953. After interviewing over two hundred musicians who worked for Bob, Phillip commented, "Not a single person spoke an unkind word about Bob."

Bill Hall, a fan since 1939, sent me two photos he had taken of my father at Cain's in June 1962. "I remember how hot it was that night I took those pictures at Cain's. Sweat was runnin' down your daddy's left cheek. He played a Paul Jones number where the people are supposed to change partners when the whistle blows, but the people weren't changin' so Bob just stopped the music and told the dancers, 'Now, you people know how to do the Paul Jones. If you don't want to do it, then we'll just stop and go back to somethin' else, but let's try to get it right.' As soon as they finally started changin' partners, he smiled and hollered, 'See, I told you that you could do it right!' He played until eleven P.M., picked up a double handful of cigars people gave him, and left."

Lloyd and Erma Lee Curtis faithfully videotape the annual Bob Wills Day show in Turkey, Texas, each year. Tom Holmes sent me a videotape of a segment from Jody Nix's Texas Western Swing Hall of Fame show, when Jody persuaded me to come onstage with him while he sang "Rosetta."

Former disc jockey, band leader, and promoter Buck Wayne Johnston sent me a tape of an interview he conducted with Bob in El Cajon, California, in 1962. His accompanying letter expressed his admiration for my father when he wrote, "I truly loved your dad. . . . He was my hero. On May 13, 1975, I had just come out of cancer surgery when they told me Bob Wills was dead. I could hardly wait for them to get out of the hospital room so I could let the tears flow freely."

During a visit to collector Glenn White's home in Oklahoma City, he gave me a cardboard fan with a printed appeal on the back: "If You Enjoy our Program, Give the Boys a Hand. Feel Free to Applaud After Each Number." During the late thirties these were handed out to the sweaty noontime crowd attending the KVOO radio broadcasts in the non-air-conditioned Cain's Ballroom. He also gave me a tape of the 1944 Warner Bros. film about Bob's life, *Bob Wills and His Texas Playboys.*

I extend my sincere thanks to the many Bob Wills fans who provided the inspiration to write this book. A newspaper interview with Glenn White sums up how they all feel. When he told a reporter he had a picture of Bob riding a horse and playing a fiddle, the response was, "Why, nobody can do that."

Glenn replied, "Bob Wills can."

Contents

Chapter 1

Daddy Bob and My Mary

I take a trip every evening,
Journey down memory's lane,
Strolling along those familiar paths,
Living those days again.

—STUART HAMBLEN, "MY MARY"

Loud fiddle music blasted "San Antonio Rose" into the hot night air when the cowboys staggered out the back door. Noisy cars and rowdy people filled the dusty parking lot when Fairfax folks turned Jump's Roller Rink into a dance hall on Saturday nights. Next door the All Night Cafe & Motel advertised cheap, convenient rooms. These sights and sounds aroused my bright-eyed curiosity as I sat quietly in the car between my grandparents. I stared at the big white bus with BOB WILLS AND HIS TEXAS PLAYBOYS painted in black letters on the side. The band's steel guitarist wailed a spirited "Steel Guitar Rag," but the maestro had not yet arrived to holler, "Take it away, Leon." The longer we waited, the more my anticipation grew.

"Okay, Rosie, there he is." Grandma broke the silence in the car when his long yellow Cadillac convertible glided into the Sinclair gas station across the highway. "You just run over there and tell him who you are." As I darted across that dark road, my skinny legs shook in rhythm with my churning stomach. I desperately longed to run the other direction, but I never defied Grandma. I halted, took a deep breath, and then slowly crept closer to the driver's side. "Hi, I'm Rosetta Wills."

The startled man wearing a big white hat and chomping on a cigar gasped as he stared at me in disbelief. Then he suddenly opened the door and climbed out with outstretched arms. He spoke in the softest, kindest voice I had ever heard. "Well, God bless you, honey." As he hugged me, he asked, "Where in the world did you come from? Where's your mama?"

"Grandma's 'cross the street."

"Well now, honey, you just get in the car with me and we'll go see her."

Since Grandma had warned me about accepting rides with strangers, I hesitated before I scrambled through the door and slid into the passenger seat. Even though I knew this stranger was my daddy, I didn't remember him. But I remembered what Grandma always said. "Your daddy's a good man with a magnetic personality who wanted to be a preacher."

Grandma Parker's fondness for drama inspired our surprise visit. My daddy had recently moved to Oklahoma after living in California for the previous seven years. Nine years earlier my teenage mother had divorced him when I was eleven months old and moved home to Pawhuska. Grandma became my mother figure due to her passion for nurturing and to my own mother's youth.

We found a table in the back of the bustling cafe next to the dance hall. My daddy smiled the whole time while that cigar bobbed in his mouth. He shook Grandpa's hand over and over as he perpetually patted him on the arm. I had never seen such a friendly stranger. Maybe this was what magnetic meant. He hugged Grandma and carried on as if she was the most wonderful person in the world. His dancing dark eyes sparkled when he asked me, "Honey, do you know how to fiddle?"

"No, I sure don't."

"Do you know the difference between a fiddle and a violin?"

"No. Aren't they the same thing?"

"Oh, no! You carry your fiddle in a flour sack and a violin in a case. If I sent you a fiddle, would you learn how to play it?"

"Oh, I don't think so. I'm already takin' piano lessons and dancin' lessons." For years I thought his fiddle and violin definitions came straight from *Webster's* dictionary.

Some guy kept poking his head in the back door. "Hey, Bob, aren't you gonna play that fiddle? That damn crowd's yellin' for ya!" My daddy seemed reluctant to leave and dismissed the man's urging until the third time, when the guy gruffly growled, "Bob, hey, I'm sorry, man, but you gotta git goin' with that fiddle 'cause that crowd's gettin' out of control."

He gave me a good-bye hug before he turned to Grandma. "Miz Parker, she's a real sweet little girl. You're doin' a mighty fine job of raisin' her." Then he disappeared.

September 2, 1950

Dear Diary,

Last night I saw my real daddy. He was so nice to me. He is wonderful no matter what my mother says. I love him. He liked me

too. I played the record Rosetta and I had to cry. I wish my daddy
and I could live by each other. I love him.

A few days after our meeting he sent me a gold identification bracelet engraved with ROSETTA on one side and DADDY BOB on the other. Birthday and Christmas gifts arrived each year after that.

As I rocked in the front porch swing, I overheard my mother talking to Grandma through the open windows. "Well! Can you believe he sent her a bracelet with his name on it? He probably got drunk and felt guilty." I covered my ears to shut out her disturbing words as I rocked faster and faster. I hated to hear her talk about his drinking. Didn't she have any happy memories? I stroked my gold bracelet lovingly and vowed never to get divorced if I had children.

Back in 1909 William Blackhawk Parker had married Grace Belle Jackson three days after her nineteenth birthday. Her mother's death when she was four years old had instilled an ache to raise a large family, but Grandpa's deception shattered her dreams. He didn't tell her before their marriage that a bout with the mumps as a young boy had left him barren. She yearned for a baby ten years before she convinced Grandpa that they should adopt a child.

Grandma's tender heart almost burst when she solemnly walked down the long rows of stark beds filled with crying children, all pleading with her to take them. When she looked into two-year-old David's sad brown eyes, she couldn't resist him. With outstretched arms he begged, "Me. Me. Please." The stern nurse at the orphanage warned her about his poor health, but she couldn't walk away from him. He died from pneumonia two years later at age four. All her love and devotion couldn't save little David.

Grandma's grief engulfed her for months until she dreamed an infant waited for her in Oklahoma City. The next morning she took the train to a home for unwed mothers. She caught a glimpse of the sixteen-year-old mother lying in a bed when the nurse took her child away. "I'll never forget the forlorn look on the young girl's face." Grandma returned home that evening with a baby girl she named Mary Louise.

Strangely enough, in 1939 Mary Louise met Irene O'Neil, her teenage mother who had given her up for adoption seventeen years earlier. Irene's Catholic family had forbidden her to marry Clarence Crowley, the non-Catholic father. In 1922 a decent bank account met the easy requirements of the uncomplicated adoption laws. Even the names of the biological parents were disclosed to the adoptive parents. Clarence and Irene had grown up in Calumet near Oklahoma City, but coincidentally Clarence's sister and her children lived across the street from Grandma Parker in Pawhuska. Since one of the boys was the same age as Mary Lou,

Grandma feared she could unknowingly marry a cousin. When she turned fifteen, Grandma revealed her father's identity to her. My mother couldn't keep the secret that her childhood friends were her cousins.

Soon Clarence, a tall slender man, appeared at Grandma's door and demanded to see his teenage daughter. He told Grandma that he and Irene had kept in touch for the past fifteen years and asked if Mary Lou would write to Irene. They corresponded for the next two years. After my mother married Bob, he arranged a face-to-face meeting for them in an Oklahoma City hotel. Irene, an attractive Irish redhead, charmed Mary Lou. Grandma said, "I was so scared for her to meet her real mother, but I knew it was the right thing to do." Each time the band played Oklahoma City, Bob rented a hotel room so she and Irene could visit. They continued to keep in touch until Irene joined the WACS during World War II and went overseas. Eventually the two lost contact and my mother never located her again.

Despite my mother's opinion of him, my interest in my daddy increased as I pieced together their story. She had saved his frayed letters and some old, yellowed newspaper clippings in her small cedar chest. I learned that Mary Lou Parker had married Bob Wills on July 22, 1939, when she was seventeen and he was thirty-four, twice her age.

I also discovered that Bob Wills and His Texas Playboys were the most popular band in the five-state area, playing for dances, fairs, rodeos, and political events. They even played for Oklahoma governor Leon Phillips's 1939 inaugural ball. In 1937 Phil Harris, a famous singer and bandleader, had broken attendance records in Amarillo when he played to seventeen hundred. But my daddy drew twenty-four hundred the next night in the same club.

My daddy may have been a cotton picker from Texas who learned his grammar in the fields, but he became the greatest entertainer in the entire Southwest. People drove hundreds of miles to enjoy the charismatic Bob Wills. He hired his band members for their personality and character, not just their musical abilities, even though he expected them to play everything from fiddle breakdowns to popular big-band songs. He demanded appreciation for their fans. "You boys be nice to each other and to the public. Shake hands and find out their names. We owe them folks. I don't care how dirty a man looks, if he's paid his money to come see us, then I'm grateful to him. If it wasn't for them payin' to see us, we'd be eatin' day-old corn bread with our grease gravy."

In 1938 Joe Frank Ferguson had played bass in the band for the previous two years. His father, a butcher, and his mother, a bookkeeper, both worked for Pawhuska's downtown Packing House Market, the busiest grocery store in town. When the band came to town, they first stopped at the store to say hello to Joe Frank's parents, drink pop, eat candy bars, and promote the dance before heading out to the Pig Stand diner on the edge of town. My mother was close to the Fergusons so she had an opportunity to meet Bob and other band members. "It was like being part of an inner circle. Bob knew who I was long before I was old enough to go to the dances."

One night Charlie Laughton, Bob's young saxophone player, met my mother at the Pig Stand. He asked her for a date the next time they played Pawhuska. Later that evening Bob spotted her and strolled over to chat. "Mary Louise, are you comin' out to our next dance?"

"Yeah, I've got a coke date with Charlie after the dance."

"How nice. Hope to see you there."

When time for the dance arrived, Grandma reluctantly allowed my mother to attend with her girlfriends while Mrs. Ferguson went along as the chaperon. As soon as my mother got out of Grandma's sight, she applied thick layers of lipstick to complement her bright red dress. The giggling girls sprinted up the steep stairs to Whiting Hall, a large, open room over a downtown furniture store. Folks overflowed into the dark corridor for illegal swigs from their pint bottles. Filled with excitement, she held her breath as she eagerly searched for Charlie, but she couldn't see him. The large crowd jamming the dance floor made it difficult to see the bandstand. She gradually moved closer to the bandstand through the boisterous crowd, stretching and straining her neck to locate Charlie.

Bob spied her red dress in the audience as soon as the band burst into a rousing "Take Me Back to Tulsa." He pointed his fiddle bow and winked at her as Tommy Duncan sang about the gal with the red dress on. When Tommy finished singing, Bob stepped up to the microphone. "This next little tune is for you, Mary Louise." He then sang, "Big brown eyes, curly hair/Can't you tell that's Mary?/Rosy cheeks, ruby lips/Can't you tell that's Mary?" Embarrassed by such attention, she blushed and smiled back at him. He motioned for her to come closer to the stage. As she shyly approached the bandstand, he knelt down and reached for her hand. His piercing, dark eyes peered into hers with a flirtatious gleam. "I'm so sorry, Mary Louise, but Charlie just up and quit today. I know you had a date, so I hope you're not too disappointed and have a good time anyway." He continued smiling as he stood up and turned to his steel guitarist, Leon McAullife. "Hey, Leon, you see that pretty little girl out there with the coke-bottle figure? I'm gonna marry her one of these days."

After the dance Bob happened to appear nearby when her friends discovered they had a flat tire. He immediately offered her a ride home so her parents wouldn't worry. Simple coincidences? A friend whispered, "Mary Lou, you better not do that! I heard he gets fresh with the girls." The other girls bristled with green-eyed jealousy as they sped away in his shiny black Buick, but she shivered with fright. She sat as close to the passenger door as possible and hardly said a word.

"Mary Louise, did you enjoy the dance?" he asked.

"Yes."

"Can I buy you a coke?"

"No, I gotta go straight home."

"Honey, how old are you?"

"Sixteen."

"Would you write me a letter?"

Mustering her courage, she coyly answered, "I don't write letters. I just answer them."

"All right, then. Will you answer my letter?"

"Maybe."

As he walked her to the front door, he asked, "Could I drive up here and visit with you some Sunday afternoon? That is, if it's all right with you."

"I guess." Then she added, "But only if Mama says it's okay."

She kept the ride home and his promised letter a secret from Grandma until a few days later, when the postman confronted her. "Hey, Mary Lou, what are you doin' gettin' a letter from ole Bob Wills! What did he have to say?"

"I didn't get a letter from Bob Wills."

"Oh, yes, you did. I delivered it yesterday."

Grandma reluctantly admitted she had hid the unopened letter. She felt uneasy about her young daughter receiving mail from an older man. But after my mother's tearful pleading, she let her read his letter. The first of seventeen letters typed on Bob Wills and His Texas Playboys letterhead read like a message for a pen pal rather than a future wife. However, the complimentary closings progressed from "As Ever, Your Friend, Bob Wills" to "Sincerely, Bob Wills" to "As Always, Bob," and finally "With Love, Bob." Since he had no formal education, he dictated his letters to his secretary, Ada Perry, who then typed them for him. He never found out that Mary Lou dictated her letters to Cousin Gerry, whose superior penmanship outshone hers.

The letter postmarked February 24, 1939, laid the groundwork for their new relationship:

> *This letter may surprise you, but I usually try to keep my word. Mary Louise, I'm not very much of a letter writer, but would like to have a friendly "chat" with you sometime. We are going to have to speak to someone about your "growing up,"—that is, in years, I mean. You act the part already. Remember, that Sunday date, one of these days!*

"Oh, Mama, please, can he come visit me? I met him at the dance the other night and he's such a nice man. I know you would like him. You know, he's famous!"

His courtship through his daily programs shocked Pawhuskans who had listened to him on Tulsa's KVOO the past five years. He dedicated "My Mary," "Mexicalli Rose," or "Rosetta" (her three favorite songs) to Miss Mary Lou Parker in Pawhuska. "Honey, I hope you're listenin'."

In a typical month the band averaged sixteen dances throughout the state along with ten dances at Cain's, totaling twenty-six dates in thirty days. Only sacred Sundays were available for courtship. He lived 45 miles south of Pawhuska in "The Big House" on 265 acres, where he stabled horses. He provided horses for every band member, dramatizing their western image, even though several didn't know how to ride. Other family members, sometimes band members, lived in the smaller house in the back.

March 7, 1939

I've been spending most of my spare time riding my horse. Most of the boys have horses now, and we usually get together every Sunday, but one of these Sundays real soon, I'm going to take the day "off" and make that promised visit to Pawhuska—that is, if it's alright with you.

March 17, 1939

I received your letter today. . . . Mary Louise, I don't know whether you'd be interested or not, but since you say that you have a horse and like to ride, I would like to drive up there some Saturday evening, say maybe a week from tomorrow, and get you. I would like to have you get acquainted with my mother, sisters, and all the folks, and we would be glad to have you spend the weekend with us.

We could attend the dance on Saturday night and spend Sunday riding the horses, and I could take you home Sunday evening. Maybe this is a bit sudden, Mary Louise, but if you think you would be interested in such plans, I wish you would write me real soon and let me know. I am sure that we would have an enjoyable Sunday. We have now about 14 horses, so have quite a time on Sundays.

My mother knew how to ride because she had grown up around rodeos, but she didn't own the phantom horse she had described in her letters. She had led a sheltered life as Grace and Bill Parker's adopted daughter. Daddy Parker had grown up in the midst of Kentucky's family feuds, toting a gun long before he became Pawhuska's police chief. A handsome man over six feet tall, he cut an impressive figure in his blue uniform. Yet his protectiveness of his petite young daughter was no match for the impulsive Bob Wills, who had already sworn he would marry her.

Mary Louise's formal courtship consisted mostly of visits in her home. When Bob began courting her, he shrewdly brought more presents for Grandma than for my mother. He called on her a month after his first letter had arrived. In awe of him, Grandma carefully wrapped waxed paper around his half-smoked cigar in the ashtray and tied a pink bow around it with a note: "Bob's cigar—March 27, 1939." Fifty years later the cigar still rested in her antique trunk with other keepsakes. Grandma, a hopeless romantic only fifteen years older than Bob, talked about him in a way that made me wonder if she wasn't in love with him herself.

My grandparents allowed my mother to sit next to Bob on the living room sofa. When the weather turned warm, they all sat on the porch, with Grandma and Grandpa in chairs and my mother next to Bob on the porch swing nearby. Since Pawhuskans considered Bob a celebrity, his expensive car parked outside the Parkers' modest home on Sundays created a steady traffic flow during those early spring months. Few cars ever traveled Ninth Street—except on Sundays when Bob visited Mary Lou. He didn't seem to notice since he was used to more traffic in Tulsa and didn't know about Ninth Street's lack of traffic. Stories proliferated about the numbers that assembled along the highway into town and on the steps of a Barnsdall building to wave at him on Sundays. My mother admitted, "Our courtship involved everybody."

The next day after his first Sunday visit he wrote a letter expressing high regard for my grandparents. He mentioned them in every letter he wrote. He had a habit of always acknowledging people and making them feel important.

March 28, 1939

Well, Mary Louise, I suppose that you will be surprised to hear from me so soon, but I had such a wonderful and nice time in your home Sunday afternoon, that I feel I just have to write and tell you so.

I am awfully glad that I had the opportunity to meet your Mother and Dad and think they are two of the "swellest" people that I've ever talked with, and I am not fooling. Give them my regards and tell them again for me that I surely enjoyed meeting them and my visit there with them.

April 4, 1939

*I have really felt happier than usual all week. Everything seems
mighty "real" when I am with you.*

As I looked at a photo of my mother clutching her clarinet while she wore a
PHS band uniform, I couldn't imagine this teenager—who looked about twelve—
together with the glamorous Bob Wills. When she attended a marching band contest in Enid, her friends teased her about Bob. One of the boys taunted, "I don't
believe Bob Wills has really been to your house. I think you're makin' the whole
thing up." She accepted the challenge and reached Bob at Cain's, asking him to
please pick her up in Enid and drive her back to Pawhuska (a round trip of several hundred miles) . "I thought that boy was gonna faint when Bob drove up in his
fancy car!"

Back then, Grandma responded to the telephone operator's "Number, please?"
with three digits. The operator sometimes said, "Grace, Mildred's not home. Her
car's 'cross the street at the Packin' House Market." When Bob added phone calls
(averaging over $150 a month) to his courtship practices, the delirious operators
made sure Mary Lou Parker did not miss any calls from Bob Wills. If she didn't
answer, the operators put him on hold and phoned around town until they located her at a friend's house, J. C. Penney's, or the Rexall Drugstore.

April 26, 1939

*We're getting pretty busy now, getting ready for the Rodeo and all.
I'm sure you're going to enjoy it, if you like rodeos, but of course
that's several weeks off yet.*

May 3, 1939

*I surely enjoyed your visit down here and hope you can come
again soon. I've been thinking about you. . . . As the song goes
"Wishing Will Make It So."*

May 10, 1939

*I hope you enjoyed yourself at the dance last Monday night. We
had a very nice crowd at Elmwood Park last night and we have
another long trip for tonight. I don't know just when we will be
playing in Hominy again. We're looking forward to opening the*

Blue Moon, and I believe it will really be nice out there. I'll come after you some night, if that will be alright, when we start playing out there for dancing.

May 23, 1939

Mary Lou, the folks were awfully glad to have you down for a visit, and hope that you can visit again real soon. And, of course, those are my wishes too. Hope that you really had a nice time at the dance. It's really going to be nice out there at the Blue Moon this summer. . . . By the way, we are going to be playing in Pawhuska Monday night, June 5th. . . . I'm looking forward to seeing you next Sunday. This week surely seems long, as it seems ages since I've seen you. In the meantime, write to me, and until I see you, bye.

May 31, 1939

Just received word from Ruby who is visiting my sister Olga down in Texas, that Olga and Kelly [her husband] have a baby girl, which makes me an uncle again. Well, Mary Louise, I miss you alot, and am looking forward to seeing you Sunday. Still, it's a long time until Sunday, so why not sit down and write me a long letter to make the time seem shorter.

June 13, 1939

I love to read your letters, even though I'm not very good at this letter writing business. . . . I've been "wheeling and dealing" so much today I'm pretty tired. This rodeo business is sure keeping us all busy. We've been working on some songs for the rodeo again today. I'm really enthused about the show and believe it is going to be a real one. . . . By the way, we will be back up in your territory next Monday night, as we are playing in Hominy. Well, Mary Lou, I don't know anything else to write about, except that I have been thinking about you alot this week and wishing that Pawhuska wasn't quite so far from Tulsa. I sure have missed you alot and am looking forward to seeing you real soon. I'll be looking for a letter from you!

In 1939 Bob produced the first Bob Wills Rodeo at the Tulsa Fairgrounds Arena. Running Thursday through Sunday, it had a general admission ticket costing fifty-six cents. During the Sunday night event, a Brahma bull threw its rider, bellowed shrilly, and headed straight for the chutes, getting as far as the escape hatch before becoming stuck. Working his head through the barrier, the bull smashed a two-by-eight support, vaulted a seven-foot wall, and charged up the catwalk to the top bleachers and methodically began circling the entire arena. Bob's brother Johnnie Lee and his wife, Irene, along with my terrified mother, were sitting in the top arena bleachers when the bull went right past them. Irene recalled, "Johnnie Lee had a broken leg and was on crutches, but when he saw that big bull comin' toward us, he just dropped them in my lap and ran."

The screaming, fainting masses panicked and scrambled for safety as rodeo attendants attempted to corral the bull. The bull made three deliberate rounds before the cowboys were able to rope him. Due to the slick concrete, every time a cowboy managed to latch a rope onto the bull, the animal dragged his pursuer a few feet and then shook the rope off. Finally a cowboy threw a jacket over the bull's head and, with help, tied the animal down. Some people were taken to the hospital, although the bull did not attack anyone. The Bob Wills Rodeo was renamed the "Bob Wills Stampede."

June 20, 1939

Well, Honey, after talking with you last night, I am going to keep my promise about writing. . . . Mary Lou, I will try to be up there sometime Thursday afternoon, and if anything comes up to cause me to be very late in getting up there, I will be sure and call you. Take care of yourself for me and I will be seeing you Thursday.

Cousin Gerry from Shidler, a small community twenty miles from Pawhuska, was the one person besides Bob's sister Ruby allowed to accompany my mother on her dates with Bob. Big Beaver, a brick oil pumping station on the Arkansas River near Beaver Creek outside of Shidler, became a popular dance location after it was no longer in use. Bob recorded an instrumental called "Big Beaver" that came from a melody he learned as a boy working in the cotton fields: "As I worked the row next to an old Negro man who hummed the same tune over and over, I learned the tune from him." The first time they played Big Beaver (described by guitarist Eldon Shamblin as "way out in the brush without a soul around"), they worried that nobody would come to hear them, but by nightfall the locals overran the place. They also packed them in at Buttermilk Hall above the Midway Creamery in nearby Ponca City.

One hot Sunday afternoon Grandma let Mary Lou and Gerry drive with Bob to Sunset Lake, where they rented a canoe. Grandma's overprotectiveness always prevented my mother from going in the water. "She would let me watch, but never get wet." Bob rowed clear out into the middle of the large blue lake. Hefty Cousin Gerry kept rocking the boat when she shifted her weight, making my mother and father both nervous. "Gerry, be still, you're gonna tip the boat over and I can't swim," Mary Lou scolded.

Nodding agreement, Bob added, "She's right, honey. Be careful 'cause I can't swim either."

Fearful Gerry cried, "Oh, my gosh, neither can I. Get this thing back to shore as soon as possible!" My mother swore never to get in a boat again and she never even learned to swim until she was fifty years old.

June 28, 1939

Mary Lou, I surely enjoyed your visit up here this past week, but it has made me miss you that much more since you went home. It sure has been lonesome around here without you. How are you liking the little radio by this time? Of course, I don't suppose that you ever tune in around 12:30 on KVOO! Well, Mary Lou, Honey, it's time for me to go again. . . . Take care of yourself for me.

July 5, 1939

How was your Fourth of July? I'm sure that you had a grand time, but wish you could have been here for the day. We were in Claremore most of the day, in connection with their rodeo. We had a nice crowd at the Blue Moon for the dance. . . . I will be looking for a letter from you real soon, and will be seeing you.

July 12, 1939

I'm thinking about you. . . . This has sure been a tough week for us, several long trips, with several more in store for us. We had a very nice crowd in Stonewall last night, as well as at Big Beaver Monday night. The crowds are really holding up well during this warm weather [alluding to the fifteen hundred in attendance each night on the road and the thousand every Thursday and Saturday at Cain's]. I'm looking forward to our dance in Pawhuska next Monday night. . . . I will call or see you soon and we can have a nice long "visit," which will be much better than a letter anyway. Write to me. Be sweet, and take care of yourself for me.

Bob's last letter, postmarked July 18, 1939, declared, "Well, Honey, I think everything is going to turn out okay, as far as what we were talking about last night is concerned, I will call you soon and tell you more about it." Amazingly, these remarks were his only reference to their planned wedding four days later. As I read the letters, looked at the old photo album, and listened to the stories my mother told me, their marriage baffled me. He was a handsome man and she was a pretty girl, but what did they have in common? I suppose 1939 societal mores dictated matrimony when sexual attraction blossomed. The attention their relationship created affected her more than anything else. Hundreds of women envied her.

When Bob was a young boy growing up on a farm down between Big Red and Little Red rivers in West Texas, he loved to break young mules, 35 or 40 "Mexico" mules each spring. Perhaps his compelling desire to tame wild animals influenced his relationships with women. This seductive man with the beguiling smile could conquer any woman. But he still searched for the innocent girl he could mold into the fantasy wife he had failed to find three times.

My mother was only seven years older than his daughter Robbie Jo from his first marriage to Edna Posey, whom he divorced in 1935 after nine years. He never could shake his guilt feelings for leaving them. Edna had endured tough financial times and helped him overcome his fears about his lack of education. However, after their divorce, he continued an open, friendly relationship with Edna and helped her purchase several cars and a home. He married briefly two more times in the four years following his divorce from Edna, first to Ruth McMaster, his violin teacher and herself a concert violinist, and then Mary Helen Brown, the former wife of western swing Milton Brown.

In the beginning Mary Lou responded to Bob's interest primarily to make her high school crush envious, but his irresistible charm won her over. Although the letters don't reflect it, he talked about marriage early in his courtship, even voicing his intentions to her parents after his first visit. Grandma's concern that my mother wouldn't make a good wife because she didn't know how to cook or clean did not bother my infatuated father. He assured Grandma it didn't matter because he would hire a full-time housekeeper (and he did).

My mother had little input into their wedding plans. She picked out an exquisite white lace dress and Grandma ordered pink silk lingerie for her trousseau from the Sears & Roebuck catalog; however, Bob picked out the wedding rings, acquired an Oklahoma marriage license, and arranged for the nuptials to be held in Edmond, in the home of a friend she had never met. On the way Bob stopped in Bristow to visit his good friend George, making them two hours late for the planned eight o'clock ceremony. By the time they arrived, even the Presbyterian minister had gone home, but he returned to pronounce them husband and wife.

Afterward they drove to the Skirvin Hotel in Oklahoma City for their three-day honeymoon (a wedding gift from George).

Bob lived on a ranch with his parents, John and Emma Wills, his younger brothers and sisters, and other relatives. He had moved his family from a farm in Muleshoe, Texas, and added seventeen-year-old brother Luther J. to brother Johnnie Lee's band, the Rhythmaires. He repeatedly assured them they could live on the ranch after the wedding. He and my mother planned to live in the house he owned in town. But on their honeymoon he changed his mind.

Without my mother's knowledge, he phoned his parents with instructions for them to move immediately from "The Big House" into the small house in back and move Johnnie Lee and Irene into the "The Big House" to help Mary Lou with the housework. He then directed his father to rent an apartment for his sisters Olga and Ruby and Ruby's two children, allowing John Wills only three days to uproot and resettle four families into new homes. Bob's money had bought the ranch and supported the family, but his whim spelled a bad beginning for my mother's relationship with her new in-laws, introducing her to his ruling role in the family. "I was disappointed," she admitted, "'cause I had no desire to run the house and loved bein' with all those people."

She received elegant wedding gifts at a shower the band members' wives hosted at Tulsa's Blue Moon Club. The crumbling newspaper clipping in her cedar chest read "Mrs. Bob Wills Complimented" and listed the Texas Playboys' wives and family members who honored her at the shower (Mrs. Son Lansford; Mrs. Johnnie Lee Wills; Mrs. Herman Arnspiger; Mrs. Tommy Duncan; Mrs. Everett Stover; Mrs. Roy McKey, Bob's sister Helen; Mrs. Ruby Sullivan, Bob's sister Ruby; and Mrs. John Tompkins Wills, my paternal grandmother). While listening to a noon broadcast, my mother was surprised when station manager Bill Way presented Bob with a chest of sterling silver. She waited impatiently for him to bring the extravagant gift home. An engraved plaque on the lid read "Congratulations from KVOO, William B. Way, Manager, 1939." She rushed out and bought a complete set of fine bone china to complement her new silverware.

An antique white clock with a golden pendulum perched on a pedestal and a bronze incense burner shaped like Cleopatra were two gifts he brought her from road trips. He even bought her a red sequined designer dress from a California tour. But, she told me, "Your daddy wouldn't take me any place where I could wear it."

Chapter 2

"Let's Ride With Bob"

In the Southwest, Bob Wills and others were creating Western Swing, a blend of country and big-band jazz that was as musically progressive as it was danceable—the first fusion, the first crossover.

—TAD RICHARDS,
THE NEW COUNTRY MUSIC ENCYCLOPEDIA

"The best damn fiddle player in the world" played his first fiddle tune at age nine after he grew weary listening to his thirty-five-year-old cousin struggle for hours to play a simple melody. "Cousin Olford, I can play that tune better than you can."

"Jim Bob, if you can, I'll never touch no fiddle again as long as I live!" After seizing the fiddle, Bob played it flawlessly—a natural like his father and grandfathers. Poor Cousin Olford never picked up a fiddle again.

Bob accompanied his father, John, on the mandolin at ranch dances lasting until after midnight—grueling work for a youngster who had to pick cotton the next day. The ritualistic gathering at a neighbor's ranch on Saturday night provided a social activity important to Texans in those days. Ranch dances spread a dance style consisting of German polkas, Mexican waltzes, Scottish round dances, and Texas square dances.

"It was real tough on me when I was a little fella. When we would come in from the fields and wash up, Papa would say, 'Come on now. We're goin' over and play for a dance tonight.' I knew it was gonna be all night. We would stop at midnight and have supper. I played so long and hard that blood from my fingers ran down on my little ole round "Tater Bug" mandolin. I went cryin' to my mother one day saying, 'When I grow up to be a boss of my own, I'll never step my foot in a dance hall again.'" Then he added with a wink, "It don't pay to say what you'll never do 'cause you're liable to wind up doin' that very thing."

The first time Bob played the fiddle for a ranch dance he was only ten years old. His father had a reputation as a drinking man as well as a damn good fiddler. One night the drinking became more prominent than the fiddling. John's absence unsettled the eager dancers, especially the men indulging in the corn liquor, so Bob scrambled up on a high box, collected the fiddle, and began playing the only six tunes he knew. He repeated them all night long as the dancers pranced to his peppy rhythm. From then on, his fiddle playing supplemented their small farming income in the twenties.

The tumbling-down walls of the small house where my father was born on March 6, 1905, still stand in a remote pasture in east Texas. In 1995 Ernie James's old blue pickup truck took me down a road thick with scrub oaks, looking once again for what was left of the house. We began to fear the house had completely fallen to the ground, but then, all at once, we saw it in the distance—still standing. We parked the truck and tromped to the front door through the knee-high grass and ragweed in the hot September sun.

I peeked through the window at the rotted floor and partially caved-in roof in front of the living room fireplace. My eyes wandered to the bedroom where I imagined my frightened, eighteen-year-old grandmother Emma's face after she had given birth to my father ninety years before. My mind's ear heard my grandfather John joyfully shouting at the aging country doctor who had ridden horseback for miles to deliver the baby. "It's a boy! I knew we'd get us a boy." He then wrapped his first-born in a blanket and whispered in his ear, "I'll make a fiddler out of you, son."

My great-great-grandfather Saladin Wills, of English-Irish descent, had moved to east Texas in 1845, along with three brothers. All four had graduated from college and taken up careers in the medical profession. Saladin became a successful country doctor in Groesbeck and married Nancy Hunter. He hired Amos Foley, a young man the same age as his son Tom, to help him run his large cotton plantation. Tom Wills married Mary Lou Tompkins (of French-Cherokee descent) about the same time Amos Foley married Amanda Ainsworth. Thus, the twelve Wills children and the thirteen Foley children grew up together.

In 1904 my grandfather John Tompkins Wills married my grandmother Emmaline Foley, who had been in love with him since childhood. No fiddler in Limestone County played her favorite fiddle tune "Sugar in the Coffee" like Johnnie could. The two families spawned the best fiddlers in the Brazos River country, famous for their frontier breakdowns and waltzes. To my grandparents' dismay, their eldest son did not initially show any interest in the fiddle and preferred to play the mandolin even though the fiddle later became his dominant instrument. Bob often said, "Both of my grandfathers, nine of my uncles, and five aunts, mostly on the Foley side, were all fiddlers. Imagine that. Looked like I had to play a little fiddle music. It was kinda a "have-to" case with me 'cause it runs in our blood."

Unfortunately, my great-grandfather "Uncle Tom" Wills was not the business-man his father had been. He had lost the plantation and all his money by the time my grandfather was grown. Thus my father was born into a tenant farmer's family with barely enough rented land to harvest a small cotton crop in Limestone County. Harsh times forced my grandparents to labor long hours to keep food on the table. Ruby, Eloise, and Johnnie Lee were also born in that tiny house on that unfriendly soil. Since Bob was the oldest child, he was picking cotton by the age of five. He had to watch after his two younger sisters while his parents picked cotton, so he raced between the cotton plants and the blanket where the babies rested, desperately trying to fill his small sack with as many pods as possible.

At an early age he listened to trumpets wail late at night from the shacks of their black neighbors. The sound of horns and the lonesome blues moved him and helped him develop a jazzy, blues sound to his fiddle. Many black families in the cotton camps sang the blues by day as they worked the rows and more blues at night after the children were sleeping. The music that helped soothe their souls inspired Bob. He danced the jig with black children, learning unrestrained ways to express his soul through music. Years later he declared, "I slurred my fiddle in order to play the blues."

When Bob turned eight and his mother was expecting a fifth child (Olga), the family relocated five hundred miles away to west Texas, still struggling to earn a living from the earth. Two covered wagons journeyed almost three months to make the trip. They picked cotton at farms along the way and played the fiddle for money whenever possible. In the early part Bob followed on a donkey named Little Joe, but he finally had to give up riding the mule and ride with the family.

John Wills settled the family on a stretch of crimson soil between the Little Red and Big Red Rivers nine miles from Memphis. Olga, Helen, Luther J., Lorene, Billy Jack, and Jessie (their tenth child who died at eighteen months) were all born in Hall County. Bob attended school in nearby Turkey but abandoned his education after the seventh grade to help out in the fields. He loved the cowboy life, taking part in bronc riding and steer roping at local rodeos.

His father harvested a hundred cotton bales bringing $200 a bale in 1919 and escaped the tenant farmer's life when he purchased 600 acres of ranch land near the Red Rivers. But the money disappeared as quickly as it came. Their land produced a bigger crop the next year, but the bottom fell out of the market. Sadly, they couldn't sell their cotton for what it cost to pick it. Bob knew his father always took the easy way out, borrowing from others and letting things drift.

Bob recalled, "Ole man Bridges worked for my daddy. He was a fine old man. His feet was so tough he could strike a match on them 'cause he always worked barefooted. He was a big man with a fine, big head who would have amounted to somethin' if he had ever had a chance.

"When he was plowin' the fields," Bob continued, "he would yell at me, 'Jim Rob, look at this old head—bald as a rat! Look at these feet, tough as whip leather from bumpin' clods all my life. Don't you stay here on the farm or it'll happen to you. Don't tell your Pappy I'm tellin' you this, but go away!"

When Bob turned sixteen, he hopped a freight train headed east. Cold and hungry, he finally made it to Ferrar, where the hospitality of some relatives restored his spirits. With a borrowed fiddle he made five dollars playing a dance at the town depot. Traveling on down the road, he found work harvesting wheat but was fired when he passed out from exhaustion, lack of food, and the extreme heat. He roamed around east Texas doing odds jobs until a man named Roscoe Partridge hired him to work on his farm. The Partridges were a religious couple with no children and treated Bob like their son. Roscoe Partridge encouraged him to become a minister and offered to send him to a seminary. He declined the offer, though later he occasionally seemed to regret that he hadn't pursued it.

Eventually he became homesick and caught a ride to Wichita Falls, jumped another train where he shared the bare floor with more than sixty destitute men, and leaped off when they reached Childress, forty miles from his home. After a brief, joyous reunion with his parents, more crop failures and lack of work thrust him into deep depression again. This time he moved to Amarillo, where he shined shoes in a barbershop until he found a job at the local smelter. When he turned twenty years old, he went back "down between the rivers."

He strived to live the Christian life he had learned from the Partridges, but gradually his old friends and habits took control. Irresistibly drawn to fiddle music and nightlife, he accepted that he could never be a preacher. No matter what other jobs he had, he continued to fiddle. "I always had some sort of a little band I could put my finger on ever since I was ten or twelve years old. Usually a guitar and a mandolin, a so-called band that I'd call up when we got a little job and we'd go play it." His reputation as a fiddler spread and soon he was playing ranch dances everywhere within the farm's sixty-mile radius.

Then he rambled out to east Texas where his family's status as champion fiddlers preceded him. He wasn't more talented, but he had a novel technique that thrilled the audience. His soft notes often became loud and then soft again depending on his mood. His smooth bowing fascinated and pleased the audience. He often said, "When I find a note I like, I hang on to it." He always stood when he fiddled so his body swayed with the melody's rhythm. Holding the fiddle under his chin for long, hard hours bruised his neck and left a lifelong scar. He played breakdowns with a heavily bowed fiddle that sounded more pop than country and had a flawless beat for dancing.

When he returned to west Texas, he learned he had lost his childhood sweetheart to a man who had won her father's approval. "Bob, please don't blame me," she pleaded. "You don't never seem to settle down and make any money. I love you, but I couldn't wait forever." His pain and disillusionment unleashed a wild side of him.

His insecure childhood had forced him to work hard and assume tremendous burdens at a young age. Embarrassed because his father owed money to everyone in town, he became uncomfortable around his boyhood friends. He formed new friendships with hard, fast teenagers branded as hoodlums, rebelled against his father, and ignored his mother's pleas. Out of spite, he traded his father's two mortgaged milk cows for a racehorse. He entered the horse in several races but lost all his bets, the saddle, and the horse. Lovable Jim Rob had turned into the family's black sheep. After a few brushes with the law in the uncivilized oil boomtown of Borger, he deserted his reckless friends and sought solitude back on the farm. (A few years later young Woody Guthrie experienced his restless years thirty miles away in Pampa.) Eventually the shortage of money compelled Bob to turn to the fiddle again.

Bob's divorce from his third wife became final only one month prior to his marrying my mother. In 1937, when he began dating Mary Helen Brown, his covetousness caused problems even before they married. He felt resentful of her former husband, Milton Brown, a musician he fondly called "my pal." Milton and Mary Helen were already divorced when Milton died from pneumonia following a car accident in April 1936. Nevertheless, references to her as "Milton's widow" caused Bob pain, while her beauty fueled his paranoia. To combat these feelings, he dominated her at every opportunity. Their brief marriage lasted from New Year's Day to the end of June. He penned the melancholy "I Wonder If You Feel the Way I Do" for her shortly after their 1938 divorce. But their passionate feelings did not die, and after many tearful phone calls they remarried, only to part again a few weeks later. She moved to her mother's home in Fort Worth but waited eight months before filing for the second divorce.

Even though Bob and Mary Helen were separated while he courted my mother, they were still legally married. He received an angry letter from Mary Helen after she learned he was dating a young girl. Knowing Grandma would be disturbed if she discovered Bob was not divorced, my mother confronted him.

Though only sixteen at the time, Mary Lou had a keen mind. "Bob, if you love me, why don't you get a divorce?"

"Well, I thought Mary Helen would go ahead and file again."

"Maybe she wants money. Or maybe she wants you back."

"No, I don't think so."

"Okay, then, you call her up and tell her how you don't care nothin' about me and you still love her and you'll come down to Texas to bring her back home."

Bob made the call while Mary Lou snuggled next to him, listening to every word. Within a few days Mary Helen officially filed for the divorce that paved the way for his fourth marriage. However, his same apprehension continued in his marriage to my mother. "Mary Lou, honey, you're only seventeen and I'm already thirty-four. In ten years you'll be twenty-seven and I'll be forty-four. I'll be old and you'll still be young. You won't love me anymore." Nothing she said helped. When he took a nap, she stayed in the bedroom with him even if family or friends were visiting. Tommy Duncan declared, "Mary, I've seen you in bed more than I've seen you out."

Grandma's pampered only child, now barely seventeen years old, became a prisoner on the ranch far from town with nothing to do. Her live-in German housekeeper did all the cooking and cleaning. My mother complained, "I was so lonely. The maid just went to her room and shut the door. She wouldn't socialize with me." My father forbid Mary Lou to attend Cain's dances after they married, which was a big disappointment for her. He didn't want his wife or even his band members' wives there. Johnnie Lee said, "Bob was easily swayed to somethin'. One or two of his wives thought there would always be bright lights."

Bored and lonely, my mother phoned Grandma every day and spent time in Pawhuska when Bob was on the road. Sometimes his sister Ruby, who taught her how to make Texas-style biscuits, stayed with her when Bob played out-of-town. She adored Ruby, but she didn't understand her desire to be in charge. When my mother returned from a Pawhuska visit and found the master bedroom furniture had been rearranged, she grilled the maid about why she had moved the furniture. "I didn't," replied the maid. "Bob's sister did." My mother moved it back and never said a word to Ruby about it.

One evening a young couple unexpectedly arrived near dinnertime. Motivated by her craving for company, she asked them to stay for dinner. After they left, she said, "Bob, honey, we need to do that more often. I get so lonely out here by myself. Why don't you ask more of your friends to visit us?"

"My friends? I never saw them before. I thought they were your friends."

"We're gonna go to Texas. I'm takin' you to my hometown where we're gonna visit some old friends and family." Bob's slurred speech confirmed his inebriated condition—the first time in their four-month marriage she had even seen him take a drink. She felt panicky and unprepared for the two-week escapade she termed a running drunk. They journeyed through the harsh west Texas terrain of red dirt and fierce winds as they drove from Lubbock to Lakeview to Memphis to Quitaque before they finally arrived in Turkey. She said, "Rosetta, I think you were conceived on that trip to Turkey 'cause you were born nine months later." When they spent the night with Bob's aunt, an attractive young woman knocked on the door and asked for Bob. "He just up and left with her. Stayed gone for hours. I think she was an old girlfriend but he never explained it to me. I was so nervous 'cause I didn't know those people we were stayin' with."

Since she didn't know how to drive, Bob drove all the way—drinking the whole trip. His father's unbridled anger over Bob's untimely disappearance resulted in a fistfight between them upon his return. "I was so afraid Bob's daddy was gonna kill him. He was so mad he just kept hittin' Bob. I'd never seen two men fight like that before. The whole thing scared me so much I thought about leavin' right then."

This misadventure prodded her quickly to learn how to drive. Even though she took lessons from a Tulsa instructor, she mastered only the basics. Dressed in her best navy suit and red-feathered hat, she drove Bob's new 1940 LaSalle to the testing office. When the patrolman opened the car door on the passenger side, she blurted out, "I gotta have a license so I can drive my husband's brand new car, but I can't back up." In response to his stony stare and silence, she added, "I'm married to Bob Wills." The loyal fan walked around to the driver's side and asked her to please move over so he could back the car out for her. Another patrolman standing nearby observed, "If that young gal gits a license, it'll be 'cause of that red hat."

The next month Bob's attorney, David Milsten, came to the house announcing, "Mary Lou, Bob doesn't wanna be married any longer." Shock and anger provoked her impetuous response. "Fine! If he doesn't want to be married, I don't want to be married!"

Extreme confusion surrounded the annulment granted on November 8, 1939. Newspaper stories alleged that her joining the First Baptist Church without his knowledge incited Bob's wrath. A faded article in her cedar chest read, "Wills was so opposed to her joining the church, she had to either withdraw her membership or get an annulment."

Yet this was not the real story. My mother knew he respected churches and often discussed his desire to preach. He told Grandma, "When I was livin' with the Partridges, that was the best time of my life. I even joined the Baptist Church." He later dedicated his Wednesday KVOO radio show to sacred music, but he didn't play it in dance halls. Record buyers did not connect him with religious music the way his radio audience did. Bob often sang his favorite, "No Disappointment in Heaven," an old Billy Sunday classic, while Tommy Duncan performed standards like "In the Sweet Bye and Bye," "When the Roll Is Called Up Yonder," "Farther Along," and "God Be with You Until We Meet Again." Years later Bob rented the Memorial Auditorium in Wichita Falls and played a free show as a tribute to the Partridges.

Bob often spoke with Grandma about his unfulfilled need to preach and constant uneasiness about leading people astray in the dance halls. His nagging guilt doggedly followed him into the honky-tonks. "You know, Miz Parker, I love people. I never let myself think about money or how many is out there. I can go into a dance feelin' so low, so low, I don't think I can even pick up a fiddle, but when I see those smilin' faces out there, just wantin' to have a good time, it brings me up. I just hope I ain't keepin' 'em out of the churches." Grandma, a good Baptist who never missed a service, felt he had missed his calling. However, she briskly walked out the church door one night when a visiting evangelist preaching Hell, Fire, and Damnation railed about sinners dancing at a Bob Wills dance.

Since my mother had been raised in the Baptist Church, she encouraged his interest in religion, hoping to save him from his drinking problem. When he told his father and his manager he wanted to quit the music business to preach, they emphatically reminded him about his responsibility for the livelihood of family and friends. He never mentioned it again. In those years before televised superstar evangelists, nobody realized just how lucrative spreading the gospel could be.

My mother suspected the presence of a loosely woven conspiracy after she urged my father to preach. Grandma never forgot how sad Bob sounded when he put his arms around her and cried. "I love Mary Louise, Miz Parker, but they're tryin' to break us up. They want me to leave this little girl." Twelve years later when John Wills was on his deathbed, he asked my mother to forgive him for not supporting Bob's call to preach.

Five weeks after the granted annulment, Bob did a live Christmas broadcast from a specially constructed platform at the Triangle Building's north end in Pawhuska. The caption beneath his photo in the Pawhuska *Daily Journal Capital* read, "Bob Wills, genial orchestra leader of the Southwest, who enjoys the zenith of popularity, is pictured above, standing beside his new 1940 LaSalle." But Mary Lou didn't want to see him standing on the Pawhuska bandstand smiling at the gossips. Barely six months earlier the same newspaper had run happy headlines like "Bob Wills Takes Pawhuska Bride as His Fourth Wife" with such flattering comments as "Mrs. Wills, daughter of the William Parkers, is described as a beautiful brunette by friends."

The annulment would have ended the marriage, but one week later my mother discovered she was pregnant. After this alarming news, her lawyer declared the annulment must be set aside and a divorce petition filed in order for me to have a legal name. But Bob surprised her when he became excited about becoming a father again and asked her to come back to him. She was prepared for a divorce, but his sincerity prompted their reconciliation. After sharing the news with his family, my mother drove to Pawhuska expecting him to come for her the next week. But miscommunication arose again.

His lawyers had been pleased with the quick $500 annulment settlement. My mother felt they convinced Bob she wasn't expecting a child. "She's just after your money, Bob." He lacked financial acumen and relied on others to make the business decisions. He never wrote checks and preferred to deal strictly in cash. My mother once explained, "When he was short on cash to pay the delivery man for the dry cleaning, he gave the man a horse that was probably worth a lot more than the bill he owed."

Five powerful attorneys filed a suit to contest setting the annulment aside, while lone Pawhuska attorney Floyd Yarbrough represented Mary Lou. The latest Tulsa headline, "Former Wife of Bob Wills Seeks New Settlement," produced even more publicity for the highly anticipated hearing.

On April 2, 1940, scandal-seekers jammed the Osage County Court House. Dr. Roscoe Walker testified that six-months-pregnant Mary Lou was indeed expecting a baby. Bob's attorney then called her to the stand and commenced to badger her. In a few minutes, Bob couldn't endure it and leaped up shouting, "Shut up! You can't talk to Mary Lou like that. I won't have it." He spun around and yelled at his lawyers. "She's really gonna have a baby. Call this whole damn thing off."

The judge convened a recess and after only fifteen minutes' consultation, they agreed on another reconciliation. This time the Tulsa headline read, "Unborn Child Reunites Wills and His Bride." The local paper ran a full-page story:

> Judge Hugh Jones gave a brief lecture on the foundation of the American home and the love of one man for one woman and ordered that the annulment be set aside. . . . The hearing ended shortly after noon with Mr. and Mrs. Wills and Mr. and Mrs. Parker reunited in a happy family group.

In less than two weeks, on April 15, 1940, my father recorded his biggest hit, "San Antonio Rose."

Later that year, my mother took me, as an infant, to the Tulsa airport to greet my father when he returned from filming the movie *Take Me Back to Oklahoma* (originally titled *Oklahoma Bound*). To laud the Rialto Theater opening, Bob rode Punkin, his fine bloodline Palomino stallion, in the biggest parade in the Midwest for a cowboy star. More than a thousand expert horsemen in their most colorful riding outfits, along with Lieutenant Governor James Berry and movie star Tex Ritter (who introduced the classic "You Are My Sunshine" in the movie) rode down Main Street. The band made appearances between showings while thousands turned out for the movie. The initial audience broke all house records.

My mother kept the penny postcard response (postmarked October 15, 1940) to a letter she wrote to him (which he obviously didn't get and they didn't read) while shooting the movie in Hollywood. The postcard advertised the movie, which starred Tex Ritter and Bob Wills:

Dear Friend:

Bob Wills showed us the greeting you sent him in Hollywood. We offered to answer it so that he could spend all his time appearing with Tex Ritter in "Oklahoma Bound," or seeing Hollywood. Thanks from both of us for your interest in Bob's movie debut. We hope you'll have as much fun watching him in "Oklahoma Bound" as we did having him in it.

W. Ray Johnston,
President, Monogram Pictures

Bob's next film, *Go West, Young Lady,* flopped on the East Coast but scored high in California, Nevada, Oklahoma, and Texas. The producer said, "Bob, your song 'Ida Red' saved my picture." Cindy Walker composed several songs (including the popular "Blue Bonnet Lane," "Miss Molly," and "Dreamy Eyes Waltz") for their first eight movies (often referred to as "Seven Day Wonders" since it took only a week to shoot one) starring various popular movie stars such as Tex Ritter, Ann Miller, Penney Singleton (who portrayed Blondie in the Dagwood movies), Glenn Ford, and Sterling Hayden. The eight movies were *The Lone Prairie, A Tornado in the Saddle, Riders of the Northwest Mounted, Saddles and Sagebrush, Silver City Raiders, The Vigilante's Ride, Wyoming Hurricane,* and *The Last Horseman.* Walker's "Dusty Skies" painted a vivid portrait of the Oklahoma Dust Bowl days when the dreadful storms forced folks to abandon their homes and move on. The lyrics brought tears to Tommy Duncan's eyes the first time he sang it.

Cindy Walker (inducted into the Country Music Hall of Fame in 1997) told an interviewer, "The really important phase in my life was when Bob Wills recorded five of my songs at one time, which really set me up in the country and western field of music. This was after he had 'San Antonio Rose.' In fact, he was the biggest thing in the world." She had contacted his manager, O. W. Mayo, when Bob came to Hollywood and asked if Bob would listen to her songs.

The band stayed at the Hollywood Plaza Hotel during the two weeks it took to complete a movie. "It's the easiest work I've ever done," said Bob. "I was always afraid of pictures thinkin' that maybe I couldn't remember the lines. But they can cut the picture after every line if necessary so you don't have to memorize much at one time. I never knew what I was gonna say until five minutes before I said it."

The movie poster for *The Lone Prairie* read "HARD HITTIN HE-MEN ON THE LOOK-OUT FOR OUTLAWS . . . AND DEEP IN THE GROOVE FOR YOU!" and *Tornado in the Saddle* listed "A HURRICANE OF ACTION! A WHIRLWIND OF SONG!" while *Wyoming Hurricane* was billed as "RIP ROARING RANGERS VERSUS RUSTLERS. ROUGH RIDING AND ROMANCE!"

During the fifties Bob also filmed shorts. Between the two genres he made twenty-six full-length movies and shorts. (Many collectors are still searching for 1947's *Rhythm Roundup*.) The cowboy movies led to a "singing cowboy" image even though his music reflected jazz and blues at the time.

Amazingly, Bob's huge success didn't seem to affect him. Adoring followers steadily showered him with gifts of colorful pillows, rugs, handmade shirts, embroidered dish towels, and knick-knacks they made for him. One woman, hoping I would be a Bob Wills, Jr., even embroidered "Bob Wills" on an infant shirt pocket. Bob stayed indebted to the fans who loved him. His humbleness probably resulted from his early childhood training when his father taught him to respect other fiddlers. John Wills cautioned the young, impressionable Bob, "Never go up to a fiddler and ask him if you can play a tune. In fact, never ever push yourself in on nobody."

Ruth Thomason, an avid fan from Enid, Oklahoma, became obsessed with Bob Wills and His Texas Playboys after a car accident left her paralyzed and bedridden. She listened to all their broadcasts from 1934 through 1941. She entered comments and listed songs they played in yearly radio diaries that she presented to Bob each year. The 1940 diary my mother saved is the only one that has survived. On Thursday, July 25, 1940, Ruth wrote that Bob was missing from the noon broadcast. My birth certificate announced my arrival into this world on that day at 11:45 A.M., 45 minutes before the daily 12:30 broadcast that began when Everett Stover announced, "The Texas Playboys are on the air!" The band then sang, "Now listen everybody from near and far/If you want to know who we are/We're the Texas Playboys from the Lone Star State."

My father and Ruby were at the Pawhuska City Hospital, but he returned for the midnight broadcast and sang "My Mary" for my mother and "Rosetta" for me. The band closed the Saturday night dances with everybody joining in on "Good Old Oklahoma."

Rosetta, my Rosetta,
In my heart, dear, there's no one but you.
You made my whole life a dream,
and I pray you'll make it come true.
God bless you, honey.

God bless you, honey. The phrase he spoke to me the night Grandma took me to his dance in Fairfax came naturally to him. I memorized the lyrics of my name-sake song, written by Earl "Fatha" Hines, after listening to my father's old scratched 78 rpm record for hours.

The following excerpts are from Ruth's 1940 radio diary:

April 2, 1940

Bob missing. On the new's broadcast to day I heard the annulment of your Marriage was set aside. I do hope every things works out alright. Anyone who strives to make other's happy should be entitled to happiness. Bob you make lots of people happy and I know things will work out right for you.

April 15, 1940

Bob and band in Dallas making records. Uncle John and His Musical Buddies filled in for the band.

Thursday, June 6, 1940

Interuption [sic] from NBC for the speech of Primer [sic] Minister of France.

July 19, 1940:

Hitler had to, of all times, pick 12:30 to do his poppin' off. Who wants to hear him? NOT ME!

September 26, 1940:

Bob, Eldon, Son, Wayne, Johnnie Lee, and Leon leave right after the broadcast for Hollywood to make a picture with Tex Ritter. I wish you every success, and a safe journey. Good-bye, good luck, and God bless you all.

I was almost four months old when Ruth made the following entry about me:

November 5, 1940

I heard today you had a little baby girl named Rosetta, a beautiful name, and I know she is a beautiful baby. I have never seen her mother, but I bet she looks just like her mother and will have her father's wonderful personality.

Saturday, November 16, 1940

12:30 P.M.—Bob missing. Big parade and opening of Bob's picture "Take Me Back To Oklahoma". Tex Ritter there.

   Midnight broadcast—I don't like Tex Ritter's singing near as well as you boys on "You Are My Sunshine."

December 31, 1940

Reminiscening (sic) the past six years:

- *The change of sponsors, from Crazy water crystal to Playboy Flour in '35*
- *"The mustache-growing spree" and interviews in '36*
- *In the summer of '36 Son Lansford and Tiny Mott went to Texas, and organized Bands of their own. Joe Ferguson took up the bass fiddle. Everett started announcing.*
- *"The Birthday Spankings" and "Oil nightclub" broadcasts of '37*
- *On Monday November 8th 1937 Eldon Shamblin (electric Guitar) joined Bob.*
- *"The famous horse races of '38"*
- *On November 8, 1938, four days after Johnnie Lee and his Rhythmaires disbanded, Johnnie Lee, Luther J. Wills, and Son Lansford joined Bob.*
- *Christmas Day, 1938, Bob and Boys opened Glenn Condon's new radio station KOME in Tulsa.*
- *January 10, 1939—Junior Barnard joined Band.*
- *February 9, 1939—Bob and Boys celebrated their 5th anniversary on KVOO. Mr. Wm. B. Way came to the Broadcast.*
- *"The Big Rodeo of '39"*
- *March 25, 1939—Leon's 4th anniversary with Bob*
- *May 20, 1939, opened the Blue Moon on north Cincinnati.*
- *September 21, 1939, it was 7 years since Tommy Duncan sang his first song with Bob. "I Ain't Got Nobody"*

In April 1940 the band had traveled to Texas for a Dallas recording session. On Wednesday, April 17, Ruth Thomason listened to a 4:00 P.M. broadcast and recorded comments made by the studio announcer, Gordon Fitzgerald, who inadvertently called the band "The Texas Cowboys."

"Forgive me, Bob, forgive me. I had better turn things over to your capable announcer, Everett Stover." Everett thanked Ocie Stockard, who had played banjo with Milton Brown's Musical Brownies, for giving his half-hour show over to the Texas Playboys. Milton's brother Durwood played guitar in Ocie's current band.

Bob chimed in with his thanks and asked, "Where is Ocie anyway?" After calling Ocie onstage, Bob continued, "Come on up to Tulsa and visit us sometime, but, of course, we won't give you our half-hour on the air! But we'll try to be good to you, just not near as good as you've been to us. By the way, how many have you got in your band these days?"

"Nine, countin' myself," Ocie replied.

"Nine! You don't count old Durwood Brown a whole one, do you?

"No, we count him one and a half."

"Lord, Lord, how that young fella has grown up. He used to skip school after he learned his F, C, and G cords on his little guitar."

"That's all he knows now."

"Well, when he first learned them, he'd come over to my house and ask if he could play somethin'. I'd tell him, my boy, you had better get on back to school before Mrs. Brown comes over and kills me."

After a few more numbers, Bob continued, "Well, folks, you know that when I first started out, I used to have lots of hair, but look at me now. That's what years of hard studyin' to be a big orchestra leader like me costs. Yes, sir, it took long years of hard work to become a big orchestra leader like me."

"Oh, yeah, Bob?" Jesse Ashlock shouted as all the guys in the band started laughing.

"Sure. It takes a lot of work to learn how to handle one of those, uh, those things. Everett, what do you call those things?'

"A baton."

"Oh, those batons."

"Bob, I saw you start one number with a baton and then you stuck it under the piano and never touched it again. That's what you learned."

In keeping with her devotion to Bob, Ruth Thomason composed the following guidelines for a Bob Wills fan:

Dear Friend,

So you are a Bob Wills Fan and you are not wholly satisfied with the way he acted? Perhaps you are not well acquainted with the duties and qualifications of a Bob Wills fan. In that case, let me enlighten you with a definition to serve you from now on and for all time! A BOB WILLS FAN.

1. Is preferably a girl, but may be a man.

2. Never knocks, but always boosts Mr. Wills.

3. Is faithful to the end.

4. Attends every dance possible and always listens to the broadcasts, careful to memorize momentous bits of conversation so that she may say to her friends, wasn't he swell when he said this or that.

5. Is one whose room is completely lined with Bob Wills pictures, even though your folks say its going to ruin the wall paper.

6. Never says cruel things about his wife, envies her at first, then admires her for winning out.

7. Never ridicules a Kyser or a Wayne King fan, simply pities her for not knowing enough to be a Bob Wills fan.

8. Is always ready to jump to his defense, even at the risk of losing a friend who just can't understand what she sees in him.

9. Knows that it is her mission in life to convince all her friends that he is the Man of the Hour.

10. Above all, believe in everything he says and try to make her friends believe it too.

11. Lives with the hope that someday she will see him again, just to be able to shake his hand and say in a reasonably calm tone of voice, "Hell, Bob, sure glad to see you."

That, my friend, is a Bob Wills fan. Let's hope you don't worry about him any more and realize how lucky you are to be able to go see him.

Many people thought Bob's success depended on luck, but actually his determination and nerve made it happen. Making sure his image met his fans' expectations required his continual concentration. His struggle to keep a high energy level flowing to his public admirers caused him to let down at home. But when he walked on that bandstand, he was in another world—totally confident. By closely observing people, he intuitively knew what they wanted to hear and called a tune depending on how he read the crowd, keeping the selections spontaneous. Guitarist Eldon Shamblin said, "He just lit a fire under you when he came on that bandstand." His drummer Smoky Dacus referred to him as a master psychologist who developed an uncommon connection with the public. "If the people weren't dancin' by the time we reached the bridge, Bob changed the tune. We never played anythin' the same way twice. We didn't even know what he was gonna play before he started, but I learned to figure out the tempo by the way he picked up the fiddle and the direction he took with his bow."

My mother loved our home on East Archer, the new addition's first finished model. That November when Ruby turned thirty-three, my mother bought Ruby a red dress and invited the whole Wills family over for a party. My mother remembers Ruby said, "This is the first real birthday party I've ever had." But soon Bob's drinking and their resulting fights began again.

"If he was five minutes late comin' home from a dance," my mother said, "I knew to just pack up and go to Pawhuska 'cause I probably wouldn't see him for days." When he started drinking, he usually didn't stop anytime soon, often staying at either the Mayo or Tulsa Hotel rather than coming home. Late at night she received a phone call from a First Street bar owner who asked her to "please fetch Bob from his bar." She asked a man who worked for them to take her into town. They went into the bar together and found Bob at a table in the back, but he refused to leave. Bob then ordered Mary Lou to sit down and eat something. Embarrassed, she responded, "No! I wanna get out of here. It's too dirty." On the way home he agreed to stop at Bishop's, a fine Tulsa restaurant. After she ordered a steak, she asked him if he wanted to order something. "Hell, no! It's too clean in here." But he usually wasn't humorous when he was drinking, and he even assumed responsibility for the accident that killed Oce Sullivan, Ruby's husband, because he was driving the car.

My mother even made a feeble attempt to win him back after their divorce. She wore a beautiful silver fox fur draped over her shoulders to attract his attention at a Pawhuska dance. "Every time I tried to get where he could see me, he put Leon between us. Leon just kept movin' back and forth. I later found out Bill Newport had told Bob I had a gun under my fur and was gonna shoot him. Bob said, 'Leon, you stay between me and Mary Lou 'cause she won't shoot you. She likes you.'"

Chapter 3

Those Oklahoma Hills Where I Was Born

*Only after the group crossed the Red River did Wills, with
ever increasing swagger, audaciously add the Texas to the
Playboy name. The Okies ate it up.*

—JOE NICK PATOSKI,
"WILLS' TESTAMENT," *TEXAS MONTHLY*

Back in 1926 when Bob met Edna, it was love at first sight. He said, "She's the girl
I've been waitin' for." And she told her brother, "That's the man I'm gonna marry."
However, her brother refused to let her date Bob due to his reputation for such
excesses as drinking, gambling, fighting, and womanizing. So the pair slipped
around. She finally left Lakeview, Texas, where she had been staying with her brother, and found a job in nearby Canadian. They married in 1926 and moved to the
Wills family farm near Turkey.

Hard times weren't getting any better. Work in the fields was rough on the
hands, which were important to a fiddler, so Bob became a barber to protect his
hands. After Bob finished Dendy's Barber College in Amarillo, they moved to Roy,
New Mexico, a thriving boom town in the twenties, where he barbered two years
but never missed a chance to fiddle. They returned to Turkey three months before
their daughter, Robbie Jo, was born in 1929. Ham's Barbershop (still a business in
Turkey today) hired him, but he kept his fiddle close by to play tunes for the cus-
tomers—too close for his career as a barber. One Saturday night a man ran into
the shop and told Bob he had better go down to the fiddling contest at the end of
the block. Bob rushed down the street, played a breakdown that won him the $5

first prize, and then returned to the shop. Saturday nights were prime time for fiddle contests and dances, but they were also when everyone came to town for a haircut. In farming country, dances could only be held on Saturday nights in plentiful seasons, since farmers rarely had extra cash. Cutting hair provided a more steady income than fiddling. "Barbering was a sure way to eat a hamburger," Bob said.

His only serious contender for "Best Fiddle Player in Turkey" was his father, who was often in the finals with him. The winner depended on the judge's age; the elder Wills was famous for playing the old tunes while young Jim Rob naturally favored the newer ones. In the larger contests that encompassed West Texas, Oklahoma, and New Mexico, the stiff competition included A. C. "Eck" Robertson from Amarillo. In 1922 Eck had wrangled a recording contract with Victor that released four of his tunes. However, no effort was made to pursue the music's commercial potential. "Eck was good and very hard to beat. I never could beat him, but Papa beat him lots of times."

At a contest in Munday, Texas, Eck and John competed in the finals for prize money worth two months' work. Eck opened with "Beaumont Rag," leaving John a tough act to follow. But the contest was over when John started hollering a harmonizing octave above his fiddle on "Gone Indian." When asked if John had out-fiddled him, Eck replied, "Hell, no, he out-hollered me!"

Tired of barbering and eager to play his fiddle, Bob left Turkey to work as a blackface comic for Doc's Medicine Show in Fort Worth. "When haircuts went down to ten cents, I couldn't make a livin' so I set out with a medicine show." The show used music and comedy to sell so-called miracle drugs to cure whatever ailed you. His versatility in playing a fiddle, telling jokes, and dancing the buck 'n' wing made him popular with the people. "I was popular 'cause I could do so many little things, none of them so good. I got lucky and after six months I was rated number one in Texas, even beatin' out ole Gassoway." His modest comments about himself always played down his talent.

Guitarist Herman Arnspiger first discovered Bob doing blackface comedy for a medicine show set up on a vacant lot. Duly impressed with Bob's performance, Herman went backstage and invited Bob to a jam session at his apartment. Herman then teamed up with Bob on the show. After the medicine show closed, he and Herman, known as the Wills Fiddle Band, played area house parties (these were actually drinking parties during prohibition) and on Fort Worth radio stations. They played "Cotton-Eyed Joe" for the old folks and a raunchy "St. Louis Blues" for the young ones.

On November 1, 1929, they recorded "Gulf Coast Blues" (a Bessie Smith song) and "Wills Breakdown" (a fiddle tune) for Brunswick Records, but they were never released. "On some pop tunes that come out," Bob said, "strings can play just as good as horns. I had a good friend named Armstrong who had another band in town who tried to do everything, all the pop stuff. His big trouble was he really wasn't qualified to lay it on top shelf. Some of them tunes, strings can't touch because they're too complicated."

One night a flamboyant young man wearing a black overcoat, white scarf, and derby hat sauntered into a Fort Worth house dance. Bob told Herman, "Here come a bunch of smart alecs. They think they're gonna make fun of us country folks." But he soon noticed that the sociable man and his friends danced and talked with everyone. The stylish cigar salesman named Milton Brown flipped the ashes off his stogie, sprightly stepped onstage, and joined them in a chorus of "St. Louis Blues." To quote Dan Jenkins, "A cowboy grinned at his lady as he said, 'Them Benny Goodmans don't have to play St. Louis Blues no more. It just got done!'"

Milton's dauntless move spawned a third member of the Wills Fiddle Band that evolved into the Aladdin Laddies and eventually emerged as the popular Light Crust Doughboys. "Milton had never sang in a dance hall, only a quartet," Bob recalled. "After we started playin' together, Milton sang through one of those deals, uh, a megaphone. I'd tear up two or three bows a night tryin' to make all those people hear us."

"Boys, what kinda music do you play?" asked the staff pianist at KFJZ in Fort Worth.

"Different," said Bob. "The Wills Fiddle Band plays different."

Al Stricklin, then working for KFJZ, said when they auditioned for him in 1931, they looked like bad hombres in need of a shave, with Bob carrying his fiddle in a flour sack. "I thought they were doin' a comedy routine when they cut loose on 'Who Broke the Lock on the Henhouse Door?' but then I figured out they were playin' straight from the heart." The station hired them to play six days a week for $15 a week. They received more fan mail than all the station's other entertainers put together. They had to pick up the mail because the postman refused to deliver the hundreds of letters that deluged the post office. Four years later Bob recruited Al Stricklin to play piano with the Texas Playboys.

Milton's brother Durwood, a youngster still learning how to play guitar, joined the Wills Fiddle Band before they auditioned for a program sponsored by the Aladdin Lamp Company. They were hired for the new radio show on WBAP as the Aladdin Laddies. Fan letters came pouring in once again. After their radio triumph they added Sleepy Johnson on banjo and played weekly at Crystal Springs, where they "entertained the cowboys and their ladies from nine till Fist Fight." Bob said, "We didn't figure on too many people showin' up at that big hall in Crystal Springs, but we had quite a few friends around town since we'd been playin' private dances. We was just tryin' to make a livin' back in those hard days."

In early 1931 Bob persuaded the Burrus Mill and Elevator Company to let the band play an early morning program to help sell flour, but W. Lee O'Daniel, the company's general manager, refused to pay them a salary despite the growing fan mail. One morning Bob confronted O'Daniel.

"The boys in the band need money. We want jobs," Bob insisted.

"So you want to work?" O'Daniel asked. "It's out of the ordinary for a musician to want to work, isn't it?"

O'Daniel finally agreed to pay them $7.50 a week and sponsor them as the Light Crust Doughboys if they worked for the company forty hours, but he would pay nothing over that wage for the daily seven A.M. broadcasts on KFJZ. So Bob drove a truck, Herman Arnspiger loaded sacks, and Milton sold flour. (O'Daniel probably had no notion that over the next sixty-five years 175 musicians would call themselves the Light Crust Doughboys. In 1977 a Texas Senate Resolution honored the many Doughboys for their contribution to the musical history of Texas.) The original Doughboys on KFJZ consisted of Bob on fiddle, Herman on guitar, Milton Brown on vocals, and Truett Kimzey as the announcer. The early Doughboys' string band consisted of a fiddle and a guitar; later they added a banjo. On their daily morning programs they played mostly hillbilly music, with an occasional hot jazz number sandwiched in. In a later interview Bob stated that O'Daniel objected to his hollering and stopped him from doing it for a few months. "We got better than a thousand letters wantin' to know what become of the little animal that was on the show. The one that was sayin' 'Ahh Haa!' Put him back on!"

O'Daniel closely monitored their broadcasts and eventually took over as their announcer, writing poems and songs for them to perform. As the show became more popular, O'Daniel moved them to 12:30 in the afternoon (prime time) on WBAP and later broadcast over the Southwest Quality Network (Fort Worth, San Antonio, Houston, and Oklahoma City). This radio exposure initiated Bob's big break. "We were the first band to hit a lick on that network. We had to go through the mail we received from day to day. Most of my mail, or rather 'our mail' I should say, came from Oklahoma, so I had a desire to go there."

After Jimmie Rodgers, "The Singing Brakeman," died of tuberculosis at age thirty-five in 1933, the Light Crust Doughboys originated a successful tribute show. The Fort Worth *Star Telegram* reported that they carried out over fifty thousand letters in ninety-eight-pound flour sacks. Thirty years later my father said, "Think of that, over fifty thousand letters. I shoulda been thrilled, but I don't think I was smart enough at the time." After that O'Daniel raised their salaries to $25 a week.

Disputes with O'Daniel, the Bible-thumpin' Do-Gooder who "forbid" them to play for dances where their pay exceeded their weekly Burrus Mill salaries, prompted Milton to leave and form his own group by 1932. Bob and Milton remained friendly rivals even after they parted ways musically. Almost twenty years after Milton's death, Bob recorded Cindy Walker's "Good-bye Old Pal" as a salute to "His Pal Milton."

In the mid-thirties, Bob's manager, O. W. Mayo, arranged a Battle of the Bands at the Green Terrace on Lake Waco: Bob Wills & His Playboys (Station WACO) versus Milton Brown & His Musical Brownies (Station KTAT). The Musical Brownies featured Cecil Brower and Jesse Ashlock on fiddles, Wanna Coffman on bass, Durwood Brown on guitar, and Fred "Papa" Calhoun on piano; Bob Dunn on steel was probably added later. Mayo recalled, "Milton had a full band with two fiddles, a bass fiddle, a guitar, and a piano player. May have even had a steel guitar player, too. Bob only had his fiddle, a guitar, a banjo, and a bass fiddle. Milton had that group's attention until Bob jumped up on the stage and did a little buck 'n' wing shuffle. When Bob started hollerin', the crowd went wild! Milton started cussin'. 'Oh, hell, I knew that 'so and so' would steal the show!'"

Perhaps it was Bob Wills's charisma that brought him the crown of King of Western Swing. In *Milton Brown and the Founding of Western Swing*, authors Cary Ginell with Roy Lee Brown (Milton's brother) challenge the widely held belief that Bob is the "father" of western swing but do not question his position as "king." (Ginell also produced a ten-hour documentary on Bob Wills syndicated for radio in 1981.) Speculating on Brown's impact on western swing's history seems futile, although the Brownies had released over fifty records by his untimely death in 1936. At best the book suggests a controversy surrounding the credit for founding this musical genre but does not resolve the issue. Many sources agree that Brown has not received adequate recognition for his contributions, but they hesitate to bestow the title "Father" on him. In *Texas Rhythm, Texas Rhyme*, Larry Willoughby observes:

> In 1932 Milton Brown created his own swing band, the Musical Brownies. Various members of the band joined or left it at different times between 1932 and 1936, but they were all instrumental in moving the Texas dance band tradition toward the more experimental jazz sounds they had learned under Bob Wills's tutelage.

In addition to O'Daniel's pesky interference with the band's dance gigs, he didn't want brother Johnnie Lee in the band, he berated Bob's father, who rented farm land from him, and he spoke to Bob in a condescending manner. Finally, all these problems, along with Bob's drinking, provoked O'Daniel to fire Bob. The next year Burrus Mills fired O'Daniel, who then formed his own Hillbilly Flour Company and pilfered Bob's idea to use music on the radio to sell flour.

A 1938 Texas tour with the Hillbilly Boys singing "Pass the Biscuits, Pappy" essentially elected O'Daniel governor for two consecutive terms. (Rumor had it that the song "Beautiful Texas" won the election.) O'Daniel scored a repeat performance in 1941 and beat out Lyndon Johnson for the United States Senate. And Bob had his own foray into politics. In 1940, "the boys in the political know" approached him about entering the Democratic primary against Senator Josh Lee. "Ten thousand people in Oklahoma have urged me to run for governor, but I think they just want to hear some free music." A Tulsa newspaper article quoted a man interested in Lee's reelection:

> There's no doubt but what Bob Wills would get lots of votes. He's got a band and a good personality. But I really think he would run better for governor.

And from one interested in a gubernatorial candidate:

> No, the people would go for him quicker for senator. It's true that W. Lee "Pappy" O'Daniel was elected governor twice and won the U.S. senate race recently in Texas, but times are changing. Oklahomans expect more from their governor than from a senator. I think Wills would run better for senator.

A few boys in the first Doughboys band followed Bob to Waco, where Everett Stover, then radio WACO station manager, gave them a noon spot for a short time (the same time slot as the Light Crust Doughboys in Fort Worth). During their stay in Waco they began to call the band Bob Wills and His Playboys. The band consisted of Bob, Tommy Duncan, Johnnie Lee Wills, Kermit Whalin, and June Whalin. Most band members were in their early to mid-twenties and dressed like preppy college students, wearing pullover sweaters and slacks rather than cowboy outfits. This was at a time that the adventures of Howard Hughes, the epitome of a cool society playboy, dominated the newspapers.

O'Daniel and Burrus Mills immediately brought a $10,000 lawsuit against the band for advertising that they were "formerly" the Light Crust Doughboys. Four months later a team of expensive and influential Fort Worth and Waco attorneys challenged Bob's two inexperienced lawyers fresh out of Baylor Law School. But the band beat the lawsuit when Judge Scott ruled in their favor.

Bob added his cousin Son Lansford, who played fiddle, guitar, and bass, along with pianist Don Ivey to the band. Son switched to playing only the bass and within two years was voted by *Variety* magazine "one of the top two bass players in the United States." With Everett Stover as their announcer and O. W. Mayo as their manager, they all headed for Oklahoma City, where they became known as Bob Wills and His Texas Playboys.

Mayo temporarily managed Bob and the band while he was between jobs in Waco. He rented a dance hall in Cameron for $5 on a Saturday night. He then approached a school in nearby Sharp and arranged for the band to play there first. They charged ten cents per person from the four hundred people in attendance. After they gave the school 25 percent of the gross take, they netted $5 apiece. They divided the net from the Cameron dance six ways, earning each one $27.50—enough to purchase some new clothes and strings! Only Bob had earned that much money weekly at Burrus Mills. When Mayo told Bob he was taking a position with Phillips Petroleum, Bob pleaded with him to stay on as their manager. "Oh, no, please don't do that. Let's go to Oklahoma." So they did.

Oklahoma City's WKY put the band on the air, but O'Daniel's vendetta persisted. After O'Daniel learned about WKY, he hinted to the station's management that he might move his well-liked Light Crust Doughboys program from KOMA to WKY if they fired Bob Wills. Upper management ordered program director Daryl McAllister to drop Bob from the station (in my father's words, "O'Daniel had us throwed off the station"). The vengeful O'Daniel never followed through and kept his program on KOMA. Bob said, "Some of the guys wanted to head down to San Antone, but I just kept on pullin' for Tulsa."

Tulsa's KVOO 25,000-watt radio station had pioneered western country music in 1924 when Otto Gray's Oklahoma Cowboys performed on the air followed by Jimmie Wilson and His Catfish Band, Jimmy Wakely, Johnny Bond, and a host of others. In 1929 Gene Autry, a colorful country singer, began his first radio job on KVOO. Will Rogers had suggested he try his luck with a radio show after he heard him sing in Chelsea, Oklahoma. Hollywood eventually made Autry a western singing cowboy star along with sidekick Smiley Burnett, who also had appeared on KVOO.

Bob Wills contacted William B. Way, KVOO station manager, who took a chance on February 9, 1934, that resulted in the Texas Playboys playing on KVOO for the next eight years under Bob's leadership. My uncle Johnnie Lee Wills continued the noon broadcast for another sixteen years. As Bob predicted, his nemesis O'Daniel soon came calling on KVOO management, but he lost the final round. Bill Way made it clear that KVOO management hired whom they wished. "We are not gonna let O'Daniel tell us what we should or should not do."

The first midnight show offered the band's photo to the person in the radio audience who sent a letter from the remotest distance. A woman in Oakland, California, won that prize. Fan mail eventually came from every state and as far away as Hawaii. One night someone named Hugh called them from Canada near where the Dionne quintuplets lived and asked them to play "Nobody's Darlin' But Mine" for his mother. In 1937 the *Tulsa Tribune* reported that they received a letter from a fellow who was within two hundred miles of the Antarctic Circle. The only way out was by sled and the letter had taken thirty days to get to Tulsa. A bio-discography released in the sixties noted that the show's fame was definitely not limited to the Southwest since the "Bob Wills Night Club of the Air" began in Iron River, Wisconsin. The townspeople acquired membership cards and gathered in C. A. Peterson's home to listen to the Thursday night broadcasts. Guitarist Eldon Shamblin recalled, "I remember when a bunch of people up in Wisconsin chartered a rail coach and came to Tulsa. Just to a dance. Can you imagine that?"

The show advertised Playboy Flour and the band's dance schedule. After Bob learned that his announcer Everett Stover played trumpet, it satisfied his vision to add a horn to the band. He later added Zeb McNally on saxophone and Art Haines on trombone, creating what would become known as the Tulsa Band. They tied their instruments on top of an old seven-passenger Lincoln sedan (originally owned by former Texas governor Pat Neff), and the fans helped push-start it after every dance. As the dance attendance increased, profits allowed them to purchase a new Chevrolet sedan. They christened it the "stretched-out Chevrolet" after they sliced it in half and welded in a new section that lengthened it for extra seats.

As their prosperity continued, Bob ordered a new $10,000 bus in 1937 with a pair of longhorns in full display. When asked if his new bus had a lavatory, he replied, "Well, it's supposed to have all the latest trimmings, and if that's one, it's got it." But he began to travel separately by car with one of the guys riding with him, while the others traveled by bus. Close but separate, he remained the "Father Figure," the "Ole Man," "Their Leader." Steel guitarist Leon McAullife said, "Us guys would play golf and fish together, but Bob didn't go with us."

The sizable gatherings in Tulsa and the surrounding towns made Bob's gate receipts his major income, although a contract with Red Star Milling Company, who manufactured Play Boy Flour, paid him a royalty for each barrel sold. The flour sacks sold in the local grocery stores contained pictures and recipes for Ginger Creams needing four cups of Play Boy Flour, country breakfast muffins calling for two cups of Play Boy Flour, and a Bob Wills's Devil's Food Cake requiring two cups of Play Boy Flour. His flour commercials on the air made him the first musician to buy his own radio time. A Play Boy bread wrapper and a willingness to clap loudly when the "Applause" light came on paid your admission into the noon broadcasts, while Cain's Saturday night dance tickets cost a whopping $1.50.

Guy Logsdon, University of Tulsa professor, claimed that Oklahoma had more dance halls than any other state. "You couldn't drive twenty-five miles without running into a dance hall. And since dancing was not an accepted Bible Belt activity, Oklahomans danced all Saturday night and prayed all Sunday morning."

Logsdon maintained that bands like the Playboys were responsible for the development of the electric Fender solid-body bass and solid-body rhythm guitars. In the late forties Bob became friends with Californian Leo Fender, who built steel guitars and amplifiers. Bob refused to use any other brand. Fender gave amps and prototypes to Eldon Shamblin and Herb Remington to road-test on tour. Years later rock 'n' roll bands picked up the amplified sound created for these early dance halls and went from there.

In a mid-sixties interview, Bob told Buck Wayne Johnston, "I think so-called western swing or whatever you want to call it would have caught on years before if amplifiers had been around so people could hear it. Everybody liked string music, but they couldn't hear it at those old country dances. They made so much noise with their feet dancin' in those two rooms of a house, they couldn't hear my fiddle, you know. It fell just right for us to get some amplification in a big hall. So, I think that was the secret really."

The years 1937 through 1941 had brought radical changes in my mother's life. At fifteen she met her biological father for the first time; at sixteen a famous personality courted her; at seventeen she married him and met her biological mother for the first time; at eighteen she gave birth to her first child. And at nineteen she filed for divorce: by early 1941 my father's drinking and deep depression demanded too much from her. "I was on the edge of a nervous breakdown" she admitted. "The mood swings were gettin' too hard to handle, not knowin' whether we were goin' up or comin' down. We were either completely happy or completely unhappy." While he was in Dallas for a recording session, she packed everything in the house except his clothes and moved to Pawhuska. Although he phoned her every night, she did not tell him she had left him. His return to their barren house brought their turbulent marriage to an abrupt ending. The latest Tulsa newspaper headline read "Crooner Hits Another Sour Note/Wife Sues Bob Wills."

On June 3, 1941, Bob's attorneys were surely pleased with my mother's $4,000 alimony and $50 per month child support compensation. (He had paid $60 per month for Robbie Jo since 1935.) Her original separate maintenance suit (later changed to divorce) had asked for $200 per month temporary support, custody of their daughter, possession of their Tulsa home, their furniture, a 1940 LaSalle automobile, and payment of court costs and attorney's fees. But the final divorce restitution did not award her the house or the car. Although not a vengeful person, Bob probably wasn't feeling too generous during these proceedings, although shortly after the divorce, he did offer to give her the Tulsa home, but she turned it down. My naive mother probably wasn't thinking about her financial future, only her immediate need to end the marriage.

Bob's recording of "San Antonio Rose" had already reached number eleven on the Billboard charts and eventually sold over a million that year. Bing Crosby's version had reached number seven and sold well over a million by 1942. I can't help but wonder why my mother's lawyer didn't ask for royalty rights to "San Antonio Rose" or any other compositions. What about other assets? Even though Bob had completed his first Hollywood movie in November 1940 and signed a Columbia contract to film eight more, her lawyer didn't ask for this major income either. Was my mother's small-town lawyer as satisfied with the settlement as my father's big-city attorneys?

Hedda Hopper reported in her L.A. column that Bob turned down $5,000 for one day's work in the movie *Girl Rush*. Bob said, "My boys need sleep. We've come from Seattle, had to change buses and trains so often we didn't get a wink. You keep the cash, we'll take the sleep." In 1944 it was reported that he grossed $36,000 for three dances in Portland, Oregon; $15,000 for two nights in San Diego; $19,000 for two nights in Oakland; $21,000 for two nights in Venice, California; and $16,000 for one night at the Tulsa Coliseum.

My mother used her divorce settlement to buy a rambling, two-story white frame house two blocks off Pawhuska's sleepy Main Street. My grandparents moved in with us so Grandma could care for me while my mother worked as a beautician at Vera's Beauty Shop in the Triangle Building. In 1945 Grandma saved a *Time* magazine with an article stating that Bob earned $340,000 that year.

My mother's youth fostered a younger sister-older sister relationship between us. I cried when she left with her boyfriends, but I liked the presents they brought me. I quietly laid on the floor outside her bedroom and peeked through the cracked door while she dressed for her dates. She spent hours each evening in front of the tall dresser mirror, rolling and unrolling pin curls before she brushed and fluffed her long, curly brown hair around her shoulders. The strong Evening in Paris perfume she splashed behind her ears made my nose itch, but the dark blue and silver bottle fascinated me. Once I dressed up in her black lace slip and pulled her sheer nylons over my shoes. They shredded into a million tiny spider webs. When she discovered what I had done, her ferocious explosion sent me reeling down the stairs seeking shelter in Grandma's arms. Four-year-olds didn't know nylons were as rare during World War II as nuggets after the Gold Rush.

While Grandpa's shadowy presence trailed in the background, dominant Grandma offered me unconditional love. I became her raison d'être. I slept with her until I was old enough to plead for my own room. She unknowingly traumatized me when she sat on the edge of the bed late at night crying. "Oh, Rosie, what if I don't live long enough to raise you? What will happen to you if something happens to me?" Did she think my mother too reckless to raise me? Kind, loving Grandma never perceived the panic she created for me with her spoken fears.

Grandma always dressed and undressed in the closet, but sometimes I peeked and watched her lace up her stiff corset before she put on her freshly starched dress. Each morning she powdered her face, applied her pale lipstick sparingly, and stuffed her silvery hair into a whisper-thin hairnet, even if all she did was listen to Fibber McGee and Molly on the radio. I thought she wore an apron because she was always in the kitchen, but when I noticed how often she dabbed her misty eyes when anything sentimental occurred, I knew the real reason.

Her oven turned out fresh-baked pies daily, as well as the world's best sugar cookies, filling the kitchen with divine smells. Her luscious grape dumplings, an Osage Indian dish, simmered peacefully on the seasoned gas stove while outside she violently wrung the chicken's neck for Sunday's after-church meal. She refused help in her kitchen because nobody could wash her dishes to suit her. If you challenged her and washed them anyway, she washed them again.

In the mornings I patiently sat on a tall stool while Grandma, smelling like Jergens Lotion, combed my dark waist-length hair into long curls. On cold winter mornings I sat on the kitchen floor watching the gas heater's red-hot flames while she cooked breakfast. She scrubbed our clothes in an antiquated wringer-type washer and hung them out to dry on the line next to the vegetable garden by the chicken coop. After school she brought me snacks in the car and even scrambled some eggs in the middle of the night when I woke up hungry. "Rosie, I read somewhere a little girl starved to death 'cause her mama wouldn't cook for her."

After Grandpa retired from the police force, he consistently lost the Republican bid for Osage County sheriff, but he kept on running. (Osage County probably never elected a Republican in its history.) When he wasn't running for sheriff, he played dominoes at the parlor on Main Street. Grandpa liked to drink, but Grandma hated it. She poured his bottles down the drain whenever she found them in his countless hiding places. One night after an argument I crept upstairs and found Grandpa passed out at his desk next to an empty whiskey bottle. Nearby lay his loaded gun. I read his good-bye letter to Grandma that expressed his love even though he knew she wouldn't believe him. I picked up the gun, balanced it across my open palms, and slowly descended the stairs. Probably a bluff, I thought. But I was relieved he had passed out and eager to pass the gun to Grandma.

November 22, 1951

Dear Diary,
My daddy called me Thanksgiving from Dallas.

Grandma made me play "San Antonio Rose" for my daddy while she held the phone next to the piano. The tattered sheet music had sat on our piano as long as I could remember. Stacks of his sheet music and his Irving Berlin song books were crammed into the black piano bench. Grandma exerted subtle pressure on me to excel at playing the piano, but it only weighed me down. Even though I practiced for hours, no brilliance emerged. Surely I had natural talent and didn't have to practice.

Many mementos of my mother's marriage infiltrated the rooms of our house. A crystal ice bucket with sterling silver tongs sat next to her fine china in the china cabinet. Dining room buffet drawers held embroidered dish towels, place mats, and pot holders with "Bob Wills" stitched on them. Souvenirs such as ceramic figurines, ashtrays, and various other objects rested on our end tables. An oak twin bedroom set with a log cabin carved on the chest of drawers filled the guest bedroom, while their blond master bedroom set now resided in my mother's bedroom. The exquisite Navajo rug in our living room had once been in the Tulsa ranch house living room. My father's pictures sat on Grandma's bedroom dresser as if he was still a family member. When Grandma finally let me have my own bedroom, she put his pictures in there, but I wasn't sure if these keepsakes throughout the house were there for me or for her.

Pawhuska, the Osage County seat, had a substantial Osage Indian population. My next door neighbors, Francie and Steve, descended from a noble Osage Indian Chief whose picture hung in their living room. Mary Kennedy, their full-blood Osage grandmother, intrigued my other childhood neighbor John and me. She rocked in her chair for hours, spitting tobacco in an empty Folger's coffee can while mumbling in her native tongue.

Steve and I started kindergarten at the same time and later walked down the aisle together during our high school graduation ceremony. On warm summer evenings Steve, Francie, and I played outside until dark, catching lightning bugs we saved in glass Mason jars with holes in the lid so they could breathe. Grandma threatened to switch my legs all the way home if I ran off to Francie's house after supper when she told me not to. Mickey, Francie's daddy, laughed when Grandma rapidly approached his front porch with a switch in her hand. "Uh, oh, Rosie, here comes Miz Parker after you." I didn't think it was funny. And it wasn't funny when Grandma's rooster chased me either, but he laughed at that, too.

From my preschool days all the way through high school, I followed Francie around, imitating her gestures and mimicking her voice. I worshipped my Indian princess, whose olive complexion and black eyes made me feel pale and washed-out.

December 25, 1951

Dear Diary,
My daddy sent me a saddle bag purse for Christmas. Francie got a
new leather purse. It's pretty but I don't like it as well as mine.
There are lots of purses made like hers but not like mine and
besides I like my purse better than any in the world because my
daddy sent me mine. That means something to me.

My mother remarried when I was eight and moved to Pennsylvania. Large packages stuffed with toys, carmel corn candy, and new dresses arrived weekly. My stepfather, Donald Carl Cloud, known as Rainbo, traveled extensively for a pipeline company. His marriage at age forty-two to a woman sixteen years younger was his first. My half-sister, Donna Lou Cloud, was born in 1949; my half-brother, Billy Carl Cloud, was born in 1954. In the early fifties Pawhuska again became my mother's home base while my stepfather worked in other states. He loved to hunt and fish and hang out with his pipeline buddies when in town. Nobody dared to suggest that "Grandma's little girl" could now live with her "real mother." Our extended family lived in the same town but in separate dwellings, attended the First Baptist Church together, and ate fried chicken at Grandma's house on Sundays.

I spent summers with my mother and Rainbo in various parts of the United States, including Michigan's upper peninsula and later several southern states. Just breathing the same air as Muddy Waters and Jimmy Reed exhilarated me. I had discovered rhythm and blues on late-night radio stations long before I journeyed to the heart of R&B country. When I was fifteen Rainbo took me to a club in Opelousas, Louisiana, to hear Clifton Chenier's authentic Zydeco music. I didn't know what they called it then, but I begged to hear more. The next year I discovered rockabilly when Rainbo sent me Carl Perkins's "Blue Suede Shoes," making me the first one in town to have the hit 45 rpm record.

Rainbo's generosity filled a tall, glass cabinet with storybook dolls from airports across the United States He always tucked money inside the cards and letters he sent me. If my mother said, "Rosie, you don't need that," he would buy it anyway. At age ten I begged for Cinderella, an expensive Madame Alexander doll I saw in a Tulsa department store window. He bought it. At age twelve I fell in love with a 14-carat-gold mesh purse I saw in downtown Henry's jewelry store window. He bought it. And when I turned sixteen and pleaded for the most expensive bathing suit in Lowry's dress shop, he bought that, too.

When he was working in Nashville, we attended Grand Ole Opry shows at the Ryman Auditorium. My mother, the unmistakable country music fan, had to drag me with her, although I enjoyed Marty Robbins and Johnny Cash. My friend Lou

Ann and I begged her to take us to a real rock 'n' roll show. My adventurous mother decided to please us, but nothing prepared her for the erotic opening act of scantily dressed twin females shaking every body part. She even feared a surge of the tremendous multitude would crush us, but we were overjoyed to see the untamed Bo Diddley in person.

November 12, 1953

Dear Diary,
My daddy came to see me and brought me a dress. I can't explain
the way I felt.

My father had not played in Pawhuska for eleven years. Less than two years after his divorce from my teenage mother, he married nineteen-year-old Betty Lou Anderson, eighteen years his junior, and moved to California. During my childhood he only played a few Oklahoma dance halls on his cross-country tours. Now when I was an awkward thirteen-year-old, he was booked at Whiting Hall again.

My friends' questions about him took me back to my first day in kindergarten. I once again felt the hot air rush through the heavy double doors as squealing youngsters banged them loudly. My terrified eyes searched for Grandma as the children ran past me in various directions, but she was nowhere to be found. I cringed each time the shrill bell buzzed and another classroom door slammed shut. I finally stood alone, frozen to the large hallway's floor. Soon Mrs. Coble, the soft-spoken kindergarten teacher, opened the door and walked toward me. She smiled warmly and patted me on the back as she guided me to her classroom. When recess finally came, we scrambled outside to the playground.

"Hey, Rosie, what'd your daddy say from the top of that tall ladder?" the children taunted.

"I dunno," I mumbled.

"Take it away, Leon!" They ran away giggling.

Mrs. Schirmer, my fifth-grade teacher, told the class my father was starring in a western movie at the downtown Osage Theater. Grandma took me to the movie, but singing "Good Old Oklahoma" from a stage coach didn't appeal to me the way my hero Roy Rogers did when he sang "Happy Trails" astride Trigger. I felt too embarrassed to return to school.

The posters advertising the upcoming dance appeared in Irby's Drug Store windows and the Manhattan Cafe. I grew more nervous as the days drew closer. If my daddy didn't visit me, Grandpa might tote his gun to Whiting Hall and escort him to our house. After all, the judge had fined Grandpa $25 when he punched Bill Newport for making disparaging remarks about my mother at the annulment hearing.

Around seven o'clock that evening my daddy and his manager Sam Gibbs knocked on our door. When I opened it, wonderment swept over me. The absence of his physical presence hadn't diminished his power over me. Underneath his arm was a big gift-wrapped package that proved he planned to visit me. The Neiman Marcus box held a red-and-white square dance dress with red tassels around the bottom of the full skirt.

Grandma and Grandpa fussed over him, making sure he had the most comfortable chair in the living room, as they bombarded him with questions. He looked just like the picture Grandma kept in her bedroom, the one where a diagonal crack in the glass created a wrinkle across his face, only without the wrinkle. He arched his bushy black eyebrows when he smiled. A white hat rested on his broad face and high forehead, but when he took it off, his baldness surprised me. He had more hair in those heavy eyebrows.

His open, friendly nature warmed the whole room as he softly spoke to Grandma, "You know, Miz Parker, it's important folks keep on talkin' 'bout you even if it's bad. The main thing is they keep talkin'. The crowds are a little small these days, but I'll work just as hard, play just as hard, if there's only three or four enjoyin' it. Don't kid yourself, can't nobody say they ain't had bad nights. The fans, that's what you live for. The people, the folks, keep me goin'. You know, I started so young."

Grandma chattered on and on that evening as I sat quietly in the background, dreading the moment she would ask me to play the piano. Just thinking about it made me shudder with crippling fear, terrified I'd hit the wrong notes and embarrass her. But I played "San Antonio Rose" perfectly.

Three years later, in 1956, Bob moved back to Tulsa to help my uncle Johnnie Lee revive the dance attendance at Cain's. Television, the undoing of the dance business, kept the population home-bound. Their combined bands operated from Tulsa with daily KVOO broadcasts similar to the late thirties and early forties. Grandma and I huddled next to the small bedroom radio in the dark listening to "Lone Star Rag" while the chattering mob at his midnight broadcast whooped it up in the background. Johnnie Lee and his announcer, also named Johnnie, kidded around, discussing new band members. Finally Johnnie Lee reminded the announcer about the special occasion. "You remember what we have been talkin' about for the past ten days or so?"

"Oh, yeah, I think I see a new man and smell a new aroma there in the back."

Bob bellowed out, "Now, let me tell both of you Johns somethin'. You done my introduction so gradual, I don't know whether I'm here myself or not." The audience roared when they heard his voice. "Alright now, Mr. Billy Bowman is rarin' to go on a little tune called "Boot Hill Drag!" His continuous off-the-cuff remarks and compelling laughter throughout the broadcast convinced you he was your best friend.

Dance posters once again sprung up in downtown store windows and the clerks asked, "Are you gonna go to your daddy's dance?" The night of the dance Grandma paced the floor downstairs while I walked the floor upstairs. Even though my sixteen years on this planet could now get me past Whiting Hall's doorman, surely my daddy would knock on my door again. But he didn't. How humiliating. Would Grandpa go after him with his gun this time? Later friends told me that my daddy had asked them why I wasn't at the dance.

Letters addressed to me simply at Pawhuska, Oklahoma (no address necessary and long before zip codes), had no problems reaching me. Our enthusiastic postman would say, "Hey, you got another picture from Hollywood." Back then Hollywood responded to fan mail with 5x7-inch autographed, black-and-white, glossy movie star photos. My collection included Vera Ellen, Gloria DeHaven, Maureen O'Hara, Lana Turner, and Marilyn Monroe. My expanding interest in music, as well as movie stars, led to the purchase of country hits such as "Don't Just Stand There" and "Don't Let The Stars Get in Your Eyes" as early as the sixth grade.

The most exciting event at the downtown Kihekah Theater occurred when Ben Johnson (known as Son Johnson to locals) and Harry Carey, Jr., came to town for their premier of *She Wore a Yellow Ribbon* that also starred everyone's hero John Wayne. Ben Johnson, Sr., had long been my special friend who bought me candy every time he saw me grocery shopping with Grandma at the Packin' House Market.

Unlike Barbara Mandrell, I wasn't into country when country wasn't cool. How boring to have a father who played fiddle in a country band instead of lead guitar in a rock and roll band. However, I loved Ray Price's "Crazy Arms" almost as much as "Heartbreak Hotel." And then, of course, there was Hank Thompson and His Brazos Valley Boys. I flipped over Hank's "Wild Side of Life" and "Girl in the Night." My friends and I often sat in the alley below Whiting Hall listening to Hank's version of "San Antonio Rose" flow from the open, screenless windows. Tottering drunks weaved their way across the street to the Dairy Queen for another coke to mix with their cheap bourbon. We scaled the fire escape and peeked in at the dripping wet dancers. Hank played the fast-beat "Six Pack to Go" and other danceable spin-offs like those by Ernie Fields, the black Tulsa bluesman. After I was able to get past doorman Woody Winton, I never missed a Hank Thompson dance, especially if I could dance with Max, my ultimate high school crush, whose virtues and vices filled the pages of my diary. I dreamed about white bridal gowns and white picket fences. After all, my mother met my father at Whiting Hall.

Chapter 4

Way Down Yonder in the Indian Nation

To fully appreciate Western Swing, the listener must erase from his mind every preconception concerning the nature and sound of country music which he might entertain. . . . Western Swing, above all, is dance music . . . imagine a crowded dance hall in Texas or Oklahoma on a Saturday night: lots of noise, perhaps a fight or two, and a band onstage capable of dominating this chaotic scene.

—WILLIAM IVEY,
LINER NOTES FOR *THE BOB WILLS ANTHOLOGY*

Precious Grandma, my daddy's biggest fan, always said, "You know who this little girl is, don't you? She's Bob Wills's daughter." She made it sound so special, but if it was so special, why didn't he spend time with me? At an early age I subconsciously planned my quest to win his love. "Rosie, when you're all grown up, you just put on your prettiest dress and go to your daddy's dance. You'll look just like your mama did when she married him."

My chance to do Grandma's bidding came in 1957, when I turned seventeen. After agonizing for hours over what to wear, I chose my peach-colored cotton dress with white lace on the sleeves. As I nervously rolled my long locks in giant curlers and stuck plastic picks through them, I wondered if my daddy would like my hair. I kept thinking that if only I was pretty enough, he'd pay attention to me. If only I could get rid of my ugly braces. If only . . . if only. My friend Tommy drove my friend Judy and me to Tulsa, the big city fifty miles from home.

Once again, the familiar "San Antonio Rose" melody soared from the Cain's stage. Cain's limestone structure hasn't changed much since it was built in 1924. The ticket booth and long bar still look the same. The framed portraits of stars from C&W's golden age give it the feel of a country music hall of fame. The primitive dressing room behind the stage resembles a narrow crawlspace. The spring-loaded maple dance floor actually shakes from the heavy automobile springs that were installed under the center sections. Originally called the Louvre, it is even referred to as "Western Swing's Alamo." The name changed to Cain's Dancing Academy when Madison "Daddy" Cain bought the building to instruct citizens how to do the Charleston properly. O. W. Mayo took over management in 1940 and purchased it four years later.

I gawked at the bottles on the tables and under the tables—more alcohol in one place than I had ever seen in my young Baptist life. "Cain's—the home of Bob Wills" decorated the center of the red velvet curtain above the stage while my daddy's giant portrait hung on the right and Uncle Johnnie Lee's hung on the left. The sepia images of two other uncles, Billy Jack and Luther J., also framed in knotty pine, graced the other walls. Men in cowboy boots and women in high heels squeezed together on the packed wooden dance floor.

My first Cain's dance—my first time to see my daddy perform in person. He wore an expensive, tailored western suit, white shirt, dark tie, and custom-made cowboy boots, along with the ever-present white Stetson and cigar. No flashy rhinestone suits for him. He worked his way through the throng from the back of Cain's to the stage. He affectionately greeted everyone along the way, shook hands, and nodded recognition to others farther away. He was one of 'em—the kind who told a good story and swallowed a stiff drink. As he approached the bandstand, he fought off the mob. How remarkable, I thought, the way this man inspired others after playing for over thirty years. When he drew his bow across his fiddle, the people roared. He glided in and out of notes with powerful feeling. And when he shuffled around onstage pointing his fiddle bow and hollering his lively Ahh-haas, they yelled louder. His magic bewitched the audience for hours.

Judy literally dragged me up to the bandstand. My daddy's perplexed look expressed his surprise about my presence. He stooped down, leaned toward me from the stage, and clasped my hands in his. Warm energy radiated from his hands and attentive eyes, but I wasn't prepared for his casual conversation. "Honey, how are you? Is this your little friend? I hope you kids enjoy the dance." Bewilderment settled over me when he soon left the bandstand and never returned. I knew he would hate my ugly braces.

A few months later my daddy and my uncle Johnnie Lee teamed up on the Cain's broadcasts again. Grandma tuned in every day at noon.

January 2, 1958

Dear Diary,
Listened to my daddy's noon broadcast from Cain's. It was great! I
just love to listen to him! Grandma thought we should call him up
at Cain's. So we did. He was so nice. Grandma let me stay up and
listen to the midnight broadcast too. Sounded like a big crowd.
How exciting!

After much urging from Grandma, my mother agreed to take me to a noon broadcast. Uncle Johnnie Lee smiled and waved at her from the stage, but the other band members she recognized ignored her. After they finished playing, my daddy came down from the stage and walked over to us. He firmly shook my mother's hand as he gazed into her eyes. I felt ignored. I had worn my chocolate brown mouton jacket especially for him, but I still had those unsightly braces. She had dressed up for him, too, showing off her new mink stole over her pale green silk suit. However, at the time I didn't think about this being their first face-to-face encounter since the bitter divorce sixteen years ago. After my daddy left Cain's, other band members joined us at our table. They told her Bob had forbidden them to ever mention her name. But perhaps "Time Changes Everything."

May 15, 1958

Dear Diary,
Got a beautiful gold watch from my daddy today for graduation.

I attended an Oklahoma State rush week party dressed in my tight, straight skirt with a kick pleat, my broad-brimmed hat, white gloves, and three-inch heels. A sorority member whispered, "I heard her daddy's some kind of a hillbilly singer and her parents are divorced. I don't think she's [sorority] material." In the Eisenhower days, country music and children of divorce were unacceptable on campus. Twenty years later I saw the same snickering Theta's photo plastered on the *Tulsa World*'s society page as the chair of a fund-raising event. The accompanying article applauded Bob's musical accomplishments. Even the Tulsa Philharmonic Symphony, along with Roy Clark, planned to salute his well-known songs at the celebrity event.

Grandma's starched apron couldn't hold all her tears when I left for college. Oblivious to Grandma's suffering, I relished sorority life, boys, and parties. Ungrateful youth that I was, I took my dirty laundry home and let her wash, starch, and iron all my clothes with possibly a "Thanks, Grandma" as an afterthought as I rushed off again. A consistent postscript appeared at the bottom of all her letters: "P.S. Rosie, honey, don't you let none of your college friends read my letters cause I can't write good or spell good."

My desire to marry Philip Ray Arnett, a cool Tulsa guy who quoted Lawrence Ferlinghetti's beat poetry and recited Hamlet's soliloquy, upstaged my crusade to win my father's love. After Phil introduced me to the Beat Generation, I longed to ponder philosophical questions with Allen Ginsberg in the City Lights Bookstore. Phil, the alluring nonconformist who broke all the rules, appealed to my rule-bound, straight-A-student personality. He took me to the Rose Room, a Tulsa black nightclub, to see Ray Charles in person. We two white folks swayed joyfully with the large congregation of black folks as Ray sang "What'd I Say."

We fell asleep in Phil's car parked next to the Alpha Delta Pi house and didn't wake up until three o'clock in the morning. Nobody believed our innocent, true-to-life "Wake Up, Little Susie" experience. The sorority officers' committee punished me for my misconduct by taking away special privileges for a month. The fraternity boys laughed and congratulated Phil. In 1960 strictly enforced curfews and other rigid rules existed for girls only. Sorority houses even dictated dress codes, and you committed a sacrilege if you wore pants in the campus library.

My immature attitude knew marriage would settle Phil down. But the summer before our junior year he panicked at the prospect of settling down and asked for his Sigma Chi pin back. In a dramatic gesture, I dropped out of college and boarded a flight to California. Touché. My friend Lou Ann had a summer job at Disneyland, and after it ended she landed a position with the prestigious J. Walter Thompson Agency in Los Angeles. Primed for "Angel Town," my nineteen-year-old logic launched my job search from the well-known corner of Hollywood and Vine. When I stepped off the bus, a Kelly Girl Employment sign beckoned me to become a Pacific Finance employee.

Sunny California's colorful paradise of manicured flower gardens and leafy green bushes beat out those Oklahoma hills where I was born. Rows of palm trees encircled the walkways leading into the courtyard next to the swimming pool at the Palms Apartments. Lou Ann and I met Susan there, another girl our age looking for some roommates, and moved in with her. Her handsome brother Dick and his friends, all students at the Art Institute, lived next door.

We rode street cars and buses, quickly learning our way around L.A. When we could borrow a car, we drove over Mulholland Drive in the Hollywood Hills or visited the Griffith Park Observatory, where closing scenes from *Rebel Without a Cause* were shot. But when our friend Sam died in a terrible freeway accident, California became a bit frightening after all.

October 9, 1960

Dear Diary,
We saw Jayne Mansfield in a store in Hollywood today.

Taking advantage of the city's cultural opportunities, we enjoyed the Royal Ballet's *Swan Lake* with Margot Fonteyn as Princess Aurora, *The Threepenney Opera* at the Music Box Theatre ($4.30 per ticket), and Sammy Davis, Jr.'s one-man show at the Huntington Hartford Theatre ($5.40 per ticket). The Kingston Trio, George Shearing, Peggy Lee, and Ray Coniff performed under the stars on the impressive Hollywood Bowl stage.

On Friday nights we imbibed a few beers during happy hour at our favorite haunt, the downtown West Seventh Street Bar. My office buddy Niki, a single parent struggling to feed her two children on her meager wages, constantly fought with her ex-husband over child support. Her outrageous attire, as well as tales of her North Hollywood exploits, fascinated me. After discovering "Bubbles in My Beer" on the juke box, I told her about my father. After a few more beers, I sang verses from "There Stands the Glass," a Webb Pierce classic, and Hank Thompson's "Wild Side of Life." She particularly liked the lyrics "I shoulda known you'd never make a wife." Then I found a pay phone and called my father at Vegas's Golden Nugget, where he played the lounge show regularly. He was probably shocked to hear from me, but his warm and friendly voice made it sound as if this was an everyday occurrence.

In November my mother phoned with the disturbing news that Johnny Horton was killed in an automobile crash in Texas. In the mid-fifties she had become acquainted with him when he appeared on the Louisiana Hayride, the KWKH radio show broadcast from Shreveport's Municipal Auditorium. She often tried to persuade me, "an uninterested teenager," to attend the shows with her. One evening Johnny told her he wished I had come along because he wanted to introduce me to a newcomer on the show. The next year after I discovered Elvis, I moaned and cried for my missed opportunity.

However, my opportunity to die in a car crash arrived later that November. After four months of separation from Phil, my ploy worked. His promised engagement ring lured me away from stimulating California. "Take Me Back to Tulsa, I'm Not Too Young to Marry." Some California friends offered me a ride to Oklahoma. Just before dawn on a wintry morning outside Winslow, a slight tap on the brakes spun our car out of control. It careened sideways down the middle of the icy highway until it flipped over and landed upside down in a ditch. The slick, treacherous roads, quite unfamiliar to our Hawaiian driver, surprised him. Miraculously—especially in the days prior to seatbelts—we were not injured. An Arizona highway patrolman soon arrived to help us out of the overturned car. After the body shop man pronounced my friend's auto totaled, she and her boyfriend abandoned me in a lonely bus terminal and boarded a bus back to California.

The chilly wind howled around the creaky old door as I waited for a Route 66 Trailways bus. I stared at the strangers who stared back at me while a military drum roll marched in my head. Horton's familiar words reverberated to the fixed cadence, conjuring up visions of the British retreating "so fast the hounds couldn't catch them." The second-story Student Union dance floor had "shook, rattled, and rolled" when we danced to his patriotic prattling about "The Battle of New Orleans." I couldn't believe Johnny Horton was dead.

After my return to Tulsa, I became better acquainted with my Wills relatives through Sue Keeling, a friend where I worked. She introduced me to Sue House, the daughter of my father's sister Eloise (known as Weezie). We visited Eloise's home, where I met Sue's older sister Corky, and two other aunts, Olga and Ruby. My cousin Sue recalled my father's advice when she was young. "Girls, don't you go 'round tellin' who you are related to 'cause they may say things to hurt your feelings. They'll expect you to do things for them 'cause you're related." She wasn't clear about his meaning at the time, but her early programming had been effective. She continued, "When we were little, we lived with Daddy Papa and Big Ma a lot, so we were around Uncle Bob during that time. We could do anythin' around Big Ma, but when Uncle Bob was home, we had to be quiet. He was Big Ma's baby, I mean when he was there, Big Ma waited on him hand and foot and the other kids were out."

Corky had similar memories even though she was almost eight years older than Sue. Their father drove a bus for Bob when she was young. "I remember goin' to the dances at Cain's and sleepin' on those benches around the wall. A lot of people would take their kids back then. Sometimes they put me up on the bandstand and let Leon McAuliffe watch me. When we were teenagers and went to the dances, we were always very well guarded by Uncle Bob from the bandstand. I was amazed at how many people, sometimes thirty people deep, would stand around the bandstand just watchin' him. Also Robbie Jo and I'd go to his dances in Fort Worth and meet him out at the bus away from the crowds. He had such big crowds back then."

Corky also recalled when she and her cousin Bobbie Nell attended a dance at the Ranch House in Dallas. Bob was warm and friendly as usual and bent down from the bandstand to give them a hug and kiss. Then he asked Corky, "Where's your husband, Jack?" When Corky told him Jack was out of town, he indignantly asked, "Well then, what are you doin' here?" Corky said, "I tried to tell him we had just come to see him, but it didn't seem to matter."

Bob didn't like Robbie Jo to attend his dances, but she showed up occasionally. "When he came to town, he expected me to make all the moves. But I think he was afraid of rejection 'cause he told my mother, 'Thank you for not teachin' her to hate me. You could have so easily.'" Edna told Robbie Jo, "The divorce was bound to happen 'cause Bob just wasn't true." When Edna saw Bob and his third wife at a movie theater, he pushed Mary Helen away as if he was afraid for Edna to see him with another woman.

When she was sixteen, Robbie Jo went to a dance at a wild joint out on the highway somewhere between Wichita Falls and the Oklahoma border. She wanted Bob to help pay for surgery her mother needed. "The band couldn't take intermissions 'cause so many fights started when they stopped playin'." She noticed a woman in front of the bandstand who moved her hand close to Bob's stomach like she was rubbing it, even though she wasn't actually touching him. Bob later told Edna, "I kept cuttin' my eyes over to Robbie Jo. I thought, Oh, God, I hope that woman doesn't touch me 'cause if she does, I'll have to get off this bandstand real quick!"

All three aunts warmly welcomed me into their lives. Aunt Olga also had two daughters, Karen (known as Junie) and Shyrl Ann. Olga had dated Leon McAuliffe in her younger years despite Bob's warning. "My sisters are not allowed to date boys in the band." After Bob reminded Leon, "My sister or your job," Leon lost interest.

Aunt Ruby, the second Wills child, often referred to as "Daddy's Pretty Girl," had two children, Robbie Lee and Bobbie Nell. After Ruby became a widow at age twenty-one, she lived with Bob and his wife, Edna. My mother had felt closer to Ruby than any of Bob's other sisters and spent many hours with her when Bob was away. Even after the divorce, my mother still visited Ruby and Eloise in Tulsa. "We loved to party and go to Johnnie Lee's dances at Cain's." High-spirited Ruby fancied the night life and worked the bar business after her divorce from The Corner Bar owner. The night Phil and I became engaged, we stopped by where she worked to show her my diamond ring. As I watched her play pool with the guys, I wanted to be exactly like Aunt Ruby.

In the early sixties my father's conversations often focused on the Bob Wills's Ranch House—a gigantic club he opened in Dallas in 1950. Dallas proclaimed a "Bob Wills Day" with a downtown parade for the grand opening. The lieutenant governors of both Oklahoma and Texas rode in the parade led by Bob on his beautiful black horse, Diamond. Bob purchased thirty-five hundred boxed luncheons from the local fried chicken establishment to feed the parade participants.

"It won't work," Snuffy Smith said. Filling carts with beer cans to construct a traveling bar for opening night did not appeal to him. But they built the carts anyway, filled them up with beer, and then found out they were so heavy it took three employees to push one. Snuffy lined them up in the corner and fabricated a bar. "Since I didn't have a register," Snuffy recalled, "I walked around 'bout every thirty minutes and collected their drink money in a cigar box. After the dance I took the stash back to the office to count. 'Well, Bob, looks like I got a little money for you. About $4,000 to be exact.'"

Ramona Reed, then only nineteen years old, crashed the parade in order to meet Bob and hopefully land a singing tryout. The stage audition, nine days later, was an ordeal for Ramona, who sang every song she knew while Bob sat in a chair on the dance floor, smoking a cigar. "I sang so long that my feet hurt so I took off my shoes." Bob told her, "I knew you was real people when you took off your shoes." She sang at the Ranch House and toured with the band for the next two years. "Bob was a strict disciplinarian. You loved him, but you feared him. He was very magnetic. Every time you worked with him it was special." She kindled Bob's ire when she wore blue jeans on the bus and quickly learned he did not consider jeans suitable attire for a woman.

The promising club venture in Dallas failed when Bob discovered his accountant hadn't paid the social security or withholding taxes for Ranch House employees. He hadn't even paid Bob's personal income taxes. The detected situation threatened a possible jail sentence so he sold his valuable property in California and his music company to pay the back taxes (a situation ironically similar to the unfortunate circumstances Willie Nelson faced thirty-five years later).

"I've made a lot of deals. I'm a dealer, but I'm not a dealer. I'm not a businessman. I lost over half a million dollars on the Ranch House deal." My immature mind didn't fathom the energy needed to build back the colossal losses he had suffered. "Bob's word was his bond," Eldon Shamblin said. "Trusting people cost him thousands. But this was his way of life."

Bob finally sold the Ranch House to Jack Ruby, a notorious Dallas racketeer now famous for shooting Lee Harvey Oswald while live TV cameras rolled. In 1952 Bob moved back to Wills Point in California to property he had kept despite the income tax fiasco. Until I read Dr. Charles Townsend's biography *San Antonio Rose* in 1976, I didn't realize Bob had sold the copyright to "San Antonio Rose" during that crisis.

My father's warm feelings toward me seemed too real to be false, even though it seemed he had forgotten me while I was growing up—out of sight and out of mind. His sincere manner made me feel loved despite his sins of omission. My experiences with him were few in number, but they were tender and loving. We never spent enough time together to have a disagreement. But how did he make everyone feel loved without genuinely loving people? His warmhearted temperament touched his family, friends, and fans, making him so believable.

I didn't know how to get to know him better, particularly since he stayed on the road the majority of the time. My intuition told me I would never be accepted unless my stepmother Betty liked me. I had only talked with her on the phone and never met her face to face. She apparently picked out the feminine gifts I received from my father, like the green angora sweater and the pink lounging pajamas. Aunt Olga shocked me when she told me Bob's older daughter Robbie Jo had a fight with Betty and slapped her. That ended their relationship.

November 20, 1961
I called the hospital. I talked to his wife Betty. They haven't found out what the problem is yet. I wonder why she wouldn't let me talk to him.

I prayed he would be alone as I gently knocked on his hospital room door. Time alone with him was rare. Phil and I had ventured down to Cain's earlier that Saturday night, hoping to visit with him after the dance. But Uncle Johnnie Lee announced that Bob had been taken to Hillcrest Hospital. I insisted upon going to the hospital immediately even though it was almost eleven o'clock.

The antiseptic atmosphere chilled me as I slowly opened the door of his dimly lit room to discover an aging man sprouting a sparse beard. Looking extremely vulnerable in his polka dot hospital gown, he didn't look like the King of Western Swing that thousands worshipped from afar. He motioned for us to come in and stretched out his arms to hug and kiss me affectionately. He cautioned me about his sore jaw. "Sweetheart, I've got a terrible pain in my jaw. The doctors don't know what's causin' it. I used to be scared to death of hospitals and wouldn't go near one, but now I feel this is where I need to be." Unfortunately, he spent many months in hospitals during the next few years.

Betty's omnipotence emerged shortly after that when Aunt Olga phoned. "Betty asked me to tell you that your daddy doesn't want you to use his name in the newspaper to announce your engagement. Oh, gosh, they just never got 'round to tellin' their kids about you and Robbie Jo. Their kids don't even know he's been married before."

Her words stunned me. I stormed out my office door and walked swiftly toward Main Street, choking back my tears as I paced up and down. Was this what he wanted? I couldn't believe he asked his wife to tell my aunt any such thing! My head reeled with unanswered questions about this bombshell. Surely their children—James, Carolyn, Diane, and Cindy—knew about Robbie Jo and me. How could he keep four marriages and two older children a secret when he was in the public eye? Were they ever going to tell them? No explanations for eighteen years made explaining difficult, like telling your grown children they were adopted at birth.

Evidently Bob's embarrassment prevented him from even mentioning his four former wives without perceiving the upset it would cause for all his children later. Or perhaps, I thought, Betty's desire to be his only wife—with her children his only children—created their reality. Thus her illusion created their reality. Too timid to confront him, I made sure only my stepfather's name appeared on the wedding invitations. Tall, lanky Rainbo with his prematurely white hair walked me down the wedding aisle with misty eyes. He stuffed a hundred dollar bill in my hand when we left on our honeymoon.

When Phil learned my father had not told his younger children about Robbie Jo and me, he resolved that Bob Wills would never charm him the way he had so many others. But I defended my father against the slightest criticism. Still—was the charm bona fide or contrived? Bob consistently asked me, "How's your mother?" Did he care? Next he asked, "How's Miz Parker?" Did he care? If Phil wasn't with me, he asked, "How's Phil?" Despite Phil's suspicions, I wanted to believe in my father's sincerity.

In 1959 during a two-week gig at Las Vegas's Showboat (during which time Laura Lee Owens and Darla Daret sang with the band), the management from the Golden Nugget critiqued Bob's show and offered him a lucrative contract. By early 1960 he had moved his family to Las Vegas. The headliners at that time—such as Wanda Jackson (with Roy Clark as an opening act), Hank Thompson, and Jimmy Wakely—played from nine o'clock until two in the morning while the lesser-known acts filled in the off hours. Bob never liked playing music for listening. He particularly disliked people wandering off to gamble when he was fiddling. Often people danced in the aisles, but the worrisome personnel made them stop.

When Bob first played the lounge act, an employee walked up to him while the band set up onstage. "Hey, you can't be smokin' no cigar on this stage. No ifs, ands, or buts." This demand evoked Bob's characteristic response, "Okay, boys, let's pack 'em up." As soon as Casino Manager Bob Green heard the rumblings, he rushed to the stage to calm things down.

Bob shouted as he waved his fiddle bow at the culprit. "This little ole Elmer you got over here tells me I can't smoke my cigar onstage."

Green turned to the accused party and emphatically stated, "Bob Wills can do anything he wants to do onstage."

So the band unpacked and set up again. When the curtains opened twenty minutes late to a standing-room-only house, Bob took a deep draw on his cigar and stepped up to the microphone. "Sorry we're a little bit late, folks, but we're not here to stay, we're here to play!"

His Vegas popularity attracted additional Lake Tahoe engagements that lasted from four to five weeks each, with both venues taking up seven months, along with his cross-country tours between dates. "We have wonderful crowds, just stack 'em in at the Golden Nugget, but no western music is being played on the radio stations these days. But I'm really proud of our crowds. That's proof enough our music isn't dead."

Later that summer Phil and I made a trip to California and stopped in Las Vegas on the way. When we checked into the Dunes, I picked up the current *Your Host International* with Bob's photo on the cover. Newspapers covering his casino appearances sported headlines such as "The Go-Go Man of Yesteryear," "The Greatest in the Country and Western Field, Bob Wills and His Texas Playboys, now billed as The Bob Wills Show," and "Mr. Western Showmanship Himself, Leading the Band."

I sprayed and teased my hair to new heights before I lined my eyes with heavy black eyeliner. My then-size-five figure slithered into a rubbery girdle, the unnecessary undergarment that held up my suntan hose, before I slipped into my pink chiffon dress with the wide satin belt. Next I added the dyed-to-match high heels to complete my sixties ensemble. Phil donned his white shirt with the button-down tab collar before he put on his only suit. After he carefully knotted his narrow red silk tie, we were ready for our first Las Vegas show. We drove around downtown until we came upon my father's name glittering in the giant marquee's glowing lights.

The backstage security guard asked fiddler Frankie McWhorter to tell Bob we were there. Bob ran down the stairs wearing suspenders over his widening stomach, with his pants tucked into his boots. "Rosetta!" he bellowed excitedly. "My little Rosetta is here." Once again he seemed delighted to see me. He escorted us upstairs to the dressing rooms and proudly introduced us to all the guys in the band before they went onstage.

The Nugget's Keno girls wore skimpy costumes while the floormen were dressed in conservative suits. Noisy casino commotion assailed us when we entered the open lounge area where the band would perform. We chose a small table close to the stage in the dark, smoke-filled room and savored complimentary goldfish crackers as we waited for our drinks. The slot machine's loud buzzer signaling a jackpot winner felt like an intrusion.

When Bob stepped into the spotlight, the band broke loose on "San Antonio Rose." The people crammed into the packed room roared with excitement. He soon told the audience in his soft Texas drawl, "Now, folks, I'm gonna do somethin' special I haven't done in a long, long time. Please bear with me if I forget the words." He sang "Rosetta." I cried.

Casey Dickens, Bob's drummer in Vegas, recalled that night at the Golden Nugget. "Bob had been talkin' to me about you and was real anxious for us to meet. He was disappointed when he heard you got married 'cause he wanted us to get together. We're about the same age and he thought we'd be a perfect match." Uncle Luke was playing with him during that time also. "You sure surprised Bob that night. I thought it was appropriate for him to sing 'Rosetta' for you even if he didn't remember the words and had to hum it."

"Ah, Rosetta, my little Rosetta. Yes, just you, honey, just you"—new words my father added at the beginning of his 1963 version of "Rosetta" on his *Bob Wills Sings and Plays* album. After he returned from the Liberty session in Hollywood, he told me, "I recorded 'Rosetta' for you on our new album. While I was singin' it, I was thinkin' 'bout you the whole time."

Since Cliff Garrett, a pop album producer, thought "Rosetta" would be a hit, they released it as a single. "But," Tommy Allsup said, "just 'bout then was when the Beatles were hittin' and there wasn't nothin' else gettin' played." Tommy had produced two Willie Nelson albums on Liberty that had started to move until Beatlemania smothered the interest. Crash Stewart had scheduled Willie Nelson to tour with Ray Price when Ray backed out. Willie asked if he could take Ray's place, but Crash did not feel he was equal to Ray at this point. However, he took his suggestion to hire Marty Robbins as the headliner but refused to call it "The Willie Nelson Show" despite Willie's pleading.

Two Phoenix promoters had once asked Bob if he would audition Marty Robbins. "Well, after the dance, bring him on down to the motel." Bob courteously listened to a few songs. "Well, you know, you don't fit our band, but I'll tell you what. You tell these two guys to get ten thousand dollars together and take you to Nashville. Kiss everybody's ass down there, and you'll be a star."

When Tommy decided to produce *Bob Wills Sings and Plays*, he called Bob's manager Sam Gibbs, who suggested Tommy fly to Houston and discuss it with Bob. "Why don't you ride with me tonight?" Bob asked. "We're gonna go to San Angelo tomorrow night and we'll figure out what we're gonna do on this album. I want to do somethin' different this time." It surprised Tommy when Bob asked for background vocals. "I'd like to get a girl that can sing real high, do that soprano thing. Get some church harmony going, some good old-fashioned church harmony." Tommy called Vicki Carr, who was getting started and didn't yet have a record out. Vicki knocked Bob out when she hit G above high C. Vicki remembered, "I'd never been as inspired as I was that night with those bunch of cowboys."

"I played drums on that session," Casey continued. "I remember Bob called all the shots." When Bob recorded in the studio, he set the band up like on a bandstand. They all faced the front in a semicircle so he could direct them and signal whatever he wanted them to do. He wasn't comfortable if he didn't have eye contact with band members. He often referred to himself as "Little Elmer" and told producer Tommy Allsup, "This here album is gonna be what 'Little Elmer' wants even if it don't sell ten copies."

Bob, Louis Tierney, Billy Armstrong, Gene Gasaway, and George Clayborn provided the definitive "fiddle ensemble." When Gene Crownover played a solo, Bob said something nobody had ever heard him say. Gene's Fender guitar had pedals on it, unlike Bob's other steel players, who never had pedals. Tommy said, "I don't know if Bob was gettin' commercial or what, but he said, 'Hey, Gene, hit that money pedal on that thing.'"

In the sixties Ada Perry, Bob's former secretary, still sold tickets at Cain's door and regularly nodded for me and my friends to go on in. The familiar "Take Me Back to Tulsa" and other recognizable songs steadily streamed from the stage. Bob's "Four or Five Times" puzzled me as he added curious "Highty Highty Ho Ho" and "Skittlely Skittlely Boo Boo" gibberish along with normal lyrics. I didn't realize he had first recorded this in 1935 when "glib, foolish talk" was stylish. I wondered why he didn't just sing "Kansas City." After the dance I introduced my friend Kay to my father, who charmed her when he held her hand. "Thanks for bein' my little Rosetta's best friend."

Bob always recognized people in the audience, but I never saw him sign autographs. Many stood stagefront during the entire show, never taking their eyes off him. When he wasn't fiddling, he stooped down from the bandstand and shook hands. He smiled as he made eye contact and waved at familiar faces. Johnnie Lee said, "No one cared any more for the public than Bob did, but he wouldn't sign autographs. It made him nervous. But he could keep them standin' around that bandstand all through the dance. Somethin' I could never do and haven't seen many who could."

In an interview with Terrell Lester, Bob's attorney David Milsten recalled:

Bob couldn't sit down and write you a long letter and tell you how much he cared for you. He just couldn't do that. He wasn't capable of it. I had a particular kind of admiration for him. You cannot bribe the muse and write poetry. Neither can you bribe the music world and become a musician. It's either inborn or it's not there. Here's a man who could pick up that fiddle and, if you hummed a tune, he'd immediately give it back to you. That's a God-given talent. There's no such thing as learnin' that.

To show his appreciation or affection, Bob often gave gifts rather than using the written word. Even though he didn't communicate with a pen, his fiddle communicated like no other. In *Cowboy Fiddler in Bob Wills's Band,* fiddler Frankie McWhorter commented about Bob's style:

> Bob knew he wasn't the greatest fiddle player in the world. Bob couldn't play "Orange Blossom Special," there's no way he could, but he didn't have to. I had to, but he didn't. Bob was the best man with a bow that I was ever associated with. Maybe some of the classical violinists were better, but for what he did, he was the best I ever saw. There's no way to explain it. He just was. He never would show me that bowing. He said, 'That's just somethin' you acquire over the years.'

The band never took breaks, so they didn't mix with the dancers until afterward, when all the musicians talked to everybody. I patiently waited as my father worked his way through his admirers to the door. Then we sat in his black Lincoln Continental and talked. Sometimes, if he wasn't driving, we drove him back to the Adams Hotel. Oh, glory days. He often mentioned Robbie Jo and one night asked me to hold up my hands. "Your little finger's just like Robbie Jo's."

Bob seemed genuinely concerned when I told him about my stepfather's death in 1963. "I'm so sorry your mother's alone again." At age fifty-six Rainbo had suffered a fatal heart attack the day before my twenty-third birthday, making my mother a widow at age forty with two children to raise. Donna turned fourteen the next month and Billy was eight. Rainbo often asked, "Rosie, do you kids need anything?" (meaning "Do you and Phil need some money?"). A few months after his death, I broke down and sobbed to Phil, "I don't think I ever told Rainbo I loved him."

Bob Wills and His Texas Playboys in 1946. *Left on horse:* Tommy Duncan; *kneeling left to right:* Junior Barnard, Millard Kelso, John Wills, Billy Bowman (steel guitar), and unidentified man; *standing, left to right:* Johnny Cuviello (drummer), Louis Tierney (fiddle), Jimmie Widener (tenor banjo), Joe Galbraith (bus driver), Joe Holley (fiddle), Billy Jack Wills (bass), and Harley Huggins; *right, on horse:* Bob Wills (*Kings Camera Center, Fresno, CA; Courtesy Rosetta Wills*).

Bob Wills and His Texas Playboys in Oklahoma City in 1949. *Left to right:* Eldon Shamblin (guitar), Lucky Moeller (agent), Bob White (fiddle), Tiny Moore (mandolin), Carl Gadd (radio announcer), Jimmy Widener (tenor banjo), Bob Wills, Billy Jack Wills (drums), Johnny Gimble (mandolin), Vern Harris (bus driver), Keith Coleman (fiddle), Luke Wills (bass), Mancel Tierney (piano), Herb Remington (steel), John Wills (fiddle) (*Courtesy Lorene Wills*).

Above: Bob Wills and His Texas Playboys performing on stage at Cain's Academy of Dancing, Tulsa, Oklahoma, in 1940. *Left to right:* Gene Tomlin (drums), Al Stricklin (piano), Darrell Jones (bass), Don Harlan (saxophone), and Bob Wills at the microphone *(Bob McCormack Studio, Tulsa).*

Right: Louis Tierney and Bob Wills performing at Cain's in 1940 *(Bob McCormack Studio, Tulsa).*

Bob Wills conducting the band at Cain's in 1940 *(Bob McCormack Studio, Tulsa).*

Bob Wills at Cain's Academy of Dancing, Tulsa, in 1940 *(The Howards, Tulsa; Courtesy Rosetta Wills).*

Bob Wills on horse in 1940 *(Courtesy Rosetta Wills)*.

Bob Wills and Johnnie Lee Wills, Tulsa, in 1940 *(Courtesy Rosetta Wills)*.

Mary Lou Parker and Bob Wills during courtship days in Pawhuska, Oklahoma, in 1939 *(Courtesy Rosetta Wills).*

Mary Lou Parker in
Pawhuska, in 1939
(Courtesy Rosetta Wills).

Bob Wills in 1939 *(Miller Photos, Tulsa; Courtesy Rosetta Wills)*.

1940 Bob Wills Stampede ticket
(Courtesy Johnnie Burnett).

Left to right: Eldon Shamblin, Bob Wills, and Tommy Duncan
in 1940 in front of Cain's, Tulsa *(Courtesy Lorene Wills).*

Left to right: Tommy Duncan, Bob Wills, and Eldon Shamblin performing in Pawhuska in 1940 *(Courtesy Rosetta Wills).*

Bob Wills on horse in 1940 *(Courtesy Rosetta Wills).*

Bob Wills, Ponca City,
Oklahoma, in 1940
*(Glass Negatives,
Courtesy Velma
Falconer).*

Bob and Mary Lou Wills, Tulsa home, in 1940
(Courtesy Rosetta Wills).

Bob Wills with his horse Punkin in front of the Big House, Tulsa, in 1940
(Courtesy Rosetta Wills).

Bob Wills and Punkin, 1940 *(Courtesy Rosetta Wills).*

Bob Wills in the early 1940s *(Courtesy Lorene Wills)*.

Bob Wills, 1940 *(Miller Photos, Tulsa; Courtesy Rosetta Wills).*

Dear friend:

Bob Wills showed us the greeting you sent
him in Hollywood. We offered to answer it
so that he could spend all his time appearing with Tex Ritter in "Oklahoma Bound," or
seeing Hollywood.

Thanks from both of us for your interest in
Bob's movie debut. We hope you'll have as
much fun watching him in "Oklahoma Bound"
as we did having him in it.

Sincerely yours,

W. Ray Johnston

President
Monogram Pictures

Postcard sent to Mary Lou Wills from Monogram Pictures in 1940 *(Courtesy Rosetta Wills)*.

Robbie Jo Wills and unidentified girl, 1940 *(Courtesy Rosetta Wills)*.

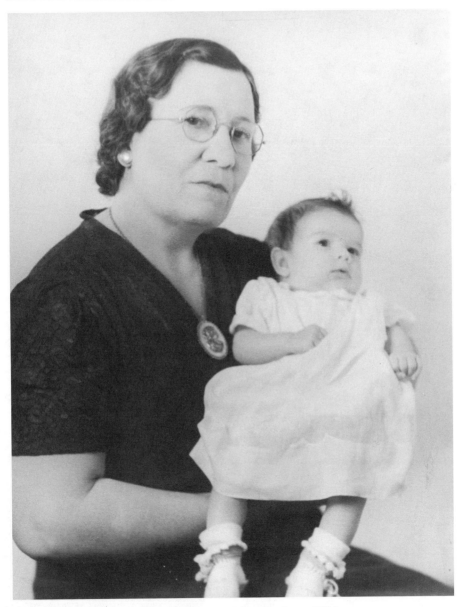

Grandma Grace Parker and Rosetta Wills, August 1940 *(Courtesy Rosetta Wills)*.

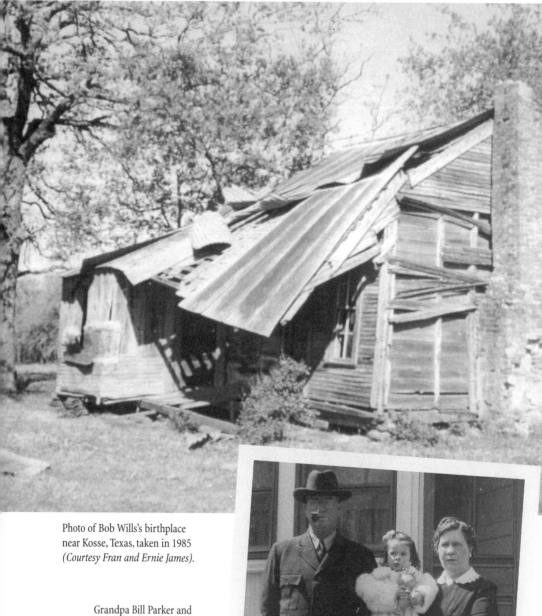

Photo of Bob Wills's birthplace
near Kosse, Texas, taken in 1985
(*Courtesy Fran and Ernie James*).

Grandpa Bill Parker and
Grandma Grace Parker
holding Rosetta Wills, 1942
(*Courtesy Rosetta Wills*).

Mary Lou Parker Wills and Rosetta Wills, 1943 *(Courtesy Rosetta Wills)*.

John Wills and Bob Wills, Turkey, Texas, in 1926 *(Courtesy Lorene Wills)*.

Opposite page: Fort Worth Doughboys, 1932. *Standing, left to right:* Bob Wills and Milton Brown; *sitting, left to right;* Sleepy Johnson and Durwood Brown *(Courtesy D. B. Johnson and Benny A. Johnson)*.

Johnnie Lee Wills and Bob Wills, Fort Worth, Texas, 1933 *(Courtesy Lorene Wills)*.

Bob Wills at the Melody Club, Carlsbad, New Mexico, in 1965
(Courtesy Harvey Tedford).

Bob Wills at the Moose Club, Carlsbad, in 1969
(Courtesy Harvey Tedford).

Bob Wills and His Playboys, Waco, Texas,
1933. *Left to right:* June Whalin, Kermit
Whalin, Bob Wills, Johnnie Lee Wills,
Tommy Duncan, and Everett Stover *(Stuats'*
Studio, Waco; Courtesy Lorene Wills).

The Bob Wills show at the Showboat in Las Vegas in June 1959.
Left to right: Laura Lee Owens McBride (vocals), Gene Crownover (steel), Glenn Rhees (saxophone), Rufus Thibodeaux (fiddle), Wanda Jackson (vocals), Wade Peeler (drums), Dickey McBride, Bob Wills, Luke Wills (bass), Johnnie Lee Wills (tenor banjo), Leon Rausch (guitar), and Darla Daret (vocals) *(Jimmie L. Garrett Day and Night Photo Service, Las Vegas; Courtesy Lorene Wills).*

Chapter 5

The Cain's Apocalypse

*Grandson and son of champion fiddlers, he quickly
established himself King of Western Swing. His famous
trademark "Ahh ha, take it away, Leon." Entered radio with
the Light Crust Doughboys in '29. Formed Texas Playboys in
the 30's. Wrote and recorded "San Antonio Rose." Appeared
in 26 Hollywood pictures. A living legend whose road map
has charted new pathways into the world of American stage,
radio, television, records, and movies.*

—Bob Wills's plaque in Nashville's
Country Music Hall of Fame

The early sixties heralded bouffant hairstyles and short skirts as well as the British Invasion of the Rolling Stones and the Beatles. Influenced by them all, my hair got bigger and my skirts got shorter. During many dances at Cain's, I stood near the stage and witnessed Bob's profound impact. A showman must possess a flair for dramatic effectiveness, and my father, the eternal showman, wielded power comparable to a cult leader. Other gifted musicians couldn't convert the masses into disciples. If he had surrendered to his preaching urge, he would have rivaled Billy Graham.

Smoky, raucous Cain's on a Saturday night. Sparks from my charged emotions ignited my mood. In my heart I felt I could be his favorite child if only he knew me better. I loved music the way he did and everyone said I looked like him. All I needed was time—some of his precious time. I wandered closer to the stage swaying to the melodic "Waltz You Saved for Me." I grew impatient for him to notice me while I peered at the large portraits of Ernest Tubb, Hank Williams, Gene Autry, Hank Thompson, and the many others that surrounded the dance floor. As soon as he saw me near the stage, he sang "Rosetta."

Then he pointed his bow at me, flashed a radiant smile, and motioned for me to come nearer. As I moved closer, he nodded to someone else. He then bent down, grasping both my hands as usual, and turned to a handsome young man with liquid brown eyes standing next to me. "James, I want you to meet your sister Rosetta."

My introduction to my brother James shocked me. But the revelation rocked James even more. My father proceeded to go on with the show, leaving us to close the gigantic gap. Nobody had told James about me or Robbie Jo. Our rapid rapport kept us conversing until sunrise. James told me that curious occurrences had happened after his family moved to Tulsa. Learning about me and Robbie Jo, as well as Bob's other marriages, finally cleared up the mysteries. When friends told him they knew his older sister, he had been confused because his sisters were younger. The more we talked, the more the subterfuge confounded us. James didn't understand how that man had so much power over us. I didn't understand it either, but I felt it.

April 18, 1964

I met my half-brother James tonight at the dance at Cain's. It was strange to meet your brother the first time when he's 18.

Meeting James led to an alliance with Betty and the other children. James's wife, Carole, and I became best friends. We four played bridge on Saturday nights, cooked meals together, and never missed a dance at Cain's.

September 25 1964:

James and I waited until the dance at Cain's was over to drive our daddy to see Bobby for the first time.

Carole had given birth to their first child, James Robert Wills III (Bobby), two weeks earlier. A warm glow engulfed me while riding in the car next to my mythical father as we drove to James's small apartment. After Carole brought the baby to Bob, I watched him gently rock the tiny bundle in the rocking chair. My mother had often told me he played with me on the bed when I was an infant. If only I could remember those times.

A few weeks later Carole and I took Bobby to visit Emmaline Foley Wills, his great-grandmother and my paternal grandmother (known as Aunt Emma to many and Big Ma to her grandchildren). She related incidents she remembered about me, and her aura of wisdom made me sad that I had not known her better during my childhood. A blurry memory of John Tompkins Wills, my paternal grandfather (Daddy Papa), hovered in my mind. I was twelve years old when my mother took me with her to visit him in the hospital a few days before he died at age seventy-two. Emma Wills died in 1971 at age eighty-six.

Fiery Carole, incensed that I was on the outside, introduced me to my stepmother as soon as possible. Betty's fragile demeanor did not mask her mighty devotion to Bob and her children. They had married when she was nineteen and he was thirty-seven and now, at age forty-one, she had been married to him for twenty-two years—an accomplishment no other wife could claim.

November 10, 1964

Carole and Betty brought Carolyn and Diane (my two half-sisters) to my home to meet me. They are sweet girls.

November 14, 1964

Went over to James and Carole's apartment and met Cindy (my other half-sister).

The disclosures disturbed shy, sensitive Carolyn, who was barely eighteen. Diane, the gregarious ninth grader, seemed to accept the news, while Cindy, then only nine years old, seemed to ignore it. Nobody ever addressed the secretiveness that had previously surrounded my existence.

I sensed an undercurrent of resentment when Betty talked about the Wills family. Perhaps she thought Bob had spent too much money helping his relatives. She never said what bothered her, but she didn't seem to want a close connection with them. I suppose he spent so little time at home, she simply didn't want to share him. Since I never had enough time with him either, I understood.

Betty suffered from ulcers that eventually caused her to have the majority of her stomach removed. Scar tissue developed, requiring several surgical procedures. A gusty Oklahoma wind could easily blow away her diminutive, ninety-pound frame. When I visited her after a surgery, she acted agitated and on the verge of tears. Her large brown eyes stared at the phone with a fierceness that could almost make it ring on command. "Bob calls me every day when he's on the road, but I haven't heard from him for two days. And he knows I'm in the hospital. You can't help wonderin' if it matters when you do so much for someone." She began to cry, but when the phone rang, her sobs stopped and her eyes lit up. It was him, the center of her life. But I wondered if she hadn't paid a grievous price for her show business marriage. He was home for only seventeen days the first year they moved to California. She often said restless Bob could not stay put anywhere for long. Nothing interested him more than playing music—it was his life.

I also wondered if their children knew him any better than I did. Despite the divorce, I had a stable childhood. The same house, neighbors, teachers, and friends had provided me permanence, while they had moved fourteen times between 1945 and 1965, forcing a continual adjustment to new surroundings and new friends. When I read Tad Richard's interview with Pam Tillis in *The New Country Music Encyclopedia,* I thought they could relate to the constant travel:

> People have a lot of preconceived notions about having a star like Mel Tillis for a father. . . . The truth of it is that country music of the fifties and sixties was about being on the road three hundred days a year, and that makes it real hard to get to know your kid—not to sound like a sob story, but it took a big toll on our family. My dad and I have an understanding, but we don't really know each other.

In 1964 Bob's second heart attack forced him to slow down and turn the band's management over to someone else. Carl Johnson, a zealous fan, had offered Bob $10,000 as a gift just to move his base from Tulsa to the Fort Worth area. After their move, Betty said Bob felt morally bound to repay Johnson so he offered to sell him the band for $10,000. Even though supposedly no money exchanged hands with this arrangement, Johnson took over and put Bob on a flat salary. Bob fronted only house bands after that.

Johnson contacted Bob's former vocalist Leon Rausch to lead the Texas Playboys, who became the house band for Fort Worth's Panther Hall. On Saturday nights they backed various performers and began a television show on Channel 11. Bob didn't actually work with the band until the next fall. In October they played to a packed house at the annual Country Music Awards banquet in Nashville. They played some dates in Carson City and on the West Coast, but Bob left the next November to go back out on the road with Tag Lambert, about whom he spoke fondly. "He's a son who didn't like the name Wills and changed it to Lambert. But I raised him. He does a beautiful little job singin' with me and playin' his guitar. Yeah, I think I done a good job on him, mighty fine boy."

Bob recorded often in the sixties, but his Nashville sessions, especially those for Kapp between 1965 and 1969, disappointed him. The too-smooth, polished version of Pee Wee King's "Slow Poke" simply does not sound like Bob Wills. As quoted by John E. Perkins in *Leon Rausch: The Voice of the Texas Playboys,"* Rausch recalled a 1965 Kapp session when Bob recorded with the Texas Playboys band he had turned over to Carl Johnson:

> In 1965 we cut some records in Nashville, using some of the boys in the band and some of the Nashville boys. The rhythm section was used in all

the recordings. We had Tommy Jackson on fiddle, added to Bob and our two fiddle players, so we had four fiddles on those particular albums.

In 1966 Joe Andrews was singing with us, and he did a couple of cuts, so we had a good session. The album *From the Heart of Texas* sold quite a few; fact of the matter is, that record now is hard to find.

Mel Tillis and Tag Lambert sang on the second Kapp album recorded in Nashville. Tillis said when he was seven years old, his mother took him to a canning plant in Plant City, Florida, to shell peas for fifteen cents a hamper. The loud speakers in the building where the families worked blared Bob Wills music all day. "Needless to say, Bob Wills was the favorite of all us pea-shellers," Tillis said.

But Music City's sidemen simply couldn't play Bob's music with the right beat and rhythm he liked, making all the albums mediocre. On *Here's That Man Again, Bob Wills,* he used twenty-one performers, similar to the big band he had before World War II. The response to his feelings about that album summed it up. "That damn bunch in Nashville just 'bout ruined my music."

Envy plagued me when Carole visited Bob and Betty in Fort Worth for days at a time. I hung on Carole's every word and asked for details about their life together. Betty devoured every word of every murder mystery she found in the bookstores when he traveled. But when he was home, they acted as if they were still on their honeymoon. Carole thought it was amazing how affectionate they were. She told me Bob usually stayed home when off the road. He didn't want to go anywhere or see anyone.

I frantically searched for the perfect outfit to wear to my father's sixtieth birthday bash and settled on a dress with a black A-line skirt and a creme-colored top with ruffles cascading from the neck and the cuffs of the short, boxy jacket. I even bought black leather pointed-toe shoes with three-inch, dime-sized high heels. Bob's friend Dewey Groom hosted the gala at his Dallas Longhorn Ranch (formerly the ill-fated Bob Wills Ranch House). Dewey said, "Bob never kept tabs on what he gave out because he never looked to get it back."

The marvelous Texas-size ballroom, as long as a football field, still entertained over four thousand dancers, but sadly the thirty-foot bar inlaid with seventeen hundred silver dollars was gone. Also missing was the unusual stall that Bob had erected for his prize stallion Punkin. Bob had had special rubber shoes molded for Punkin that allowed him to ride the horse around the dance floor. Punkin was a natural actor who played at scores of theaters and arenas throughout the country. According to a 1945 Music Corporation of America (MCA) press release, Punkin would always stand sedately in the wings until he heard the name "Bob Wills" announced. Then one ear went down as he braced himself for his run, and *wham*—he would make a speedy, dramatic dash for the center of the stage.

Phil and I sat with all the family (including six-month-old Bobby) at a table close to the stage, listening to the thunderous cheering and stomping when Bob appeared onstage, smiling and nodding his head with his customary cigar clenched between his teeth. As the listeners settled down, he said, "First of all, I want you to know it's a privilege to be here with all you wonderful folks tonight."

My grandmother Emma smiled when Bob said, "Two of my brothers are here with me, Johnnie Lee and Luke, and just to keep peace in the family, we're gonna let Luke sing. You know, ole Luke's fallen away to only half a ton! Yessiree, here's brother Luther J. startin' us off singin' about T-Town. Yes, yes, 'Take Me Back to Tulsa.'" At the end of that stirring evening, my broad smile beamed when my father bid all his children onstage as he introduced us to the audience. I stood next to the others smiling right along with them. I later learned that Robbie Jo was there, but perhaps nobody knew.

After the Dallas festivity, we drove out to their Fort Worth home, a three-bedroom, ranch-style house. At last—my chance to visit with him in his home. But disappointment soon enveloped me like a dark thundercloud when a longtime fan and his wife also arrived at the house. Time alone with my father once again escaped me. Why were there always so many others around? I examined all the details in each room, not knowing what I expected, but feeling something inescapably amiss, similar to remembering places in your childhood as larger than they actually were. I had constructed a father bigger than life. Things were too ordinary.

When our son Philip Chad Arnett was born on January 6, 1967, Phil rushed to the hospital phone to call my mother in Pawhuska. After hearing the news, my sister Donna asked, "But how did you get this number?" Phil told her he had dialed her home number. "But I'm not at home. I'm babysittin' for the Staubs down the street." We never understood how that happened.

Bob and Betty sent baby outfits from "The Texas Grandparents." Chad was three months old the next time Bob played Cain's, but his hasty disappearance after the dance without commenting on his new grandson angered Phil. Did he forget about Chad? Stories about Bob's drinking flourished, but were they truth or fiction? Was he drinking that night? Perhaps his energy level was too low to be communicative. Perhaps he needed to be alone after smiling at the crowd for hours.

The next time Bob was booked at Cain's, Carole and I dressed up Bobby and Chad in their Sunday best and took them to the motel where Bob and Tag were staying. Carole and I decided we were expected to take the children to him; he wasn't expected to visit the children. I suppose it goes with the whole music scene—long hours on the road and unspoken rules. Bob was sleeping when we arrived, but he awoke from his nap and acted the proud grandfather, lavishing attention on Bobby and Chad. He told us he wasn't able to sleep for several hours at a time so he took short catnaps. Since he had worked and traveled at night for years, he could only rest in the daytime. His exhausting lifestyle had worn him down, and the twinkle in his eyes had dimmed. "You know, you take forty years in the business, I tend to get a little nervous these days just like an old race horse," he admitted. "If you put him at the gate, he's gonna run even if he don't win nothin'. I may not win nothin' but I'm gonna run. I've helped myself a lot but I tend to be a little nervous these days."

During idle conversation at the dance later, he said, "Well, we've got a wonderful crowd here tonight. After forty years, I'm still playin' and you're still dancin'. Just think, a four-hour dance is 'bout as bad as ten hours choppin' cotton. The only thing I could do before I started playin' the fiddle was pick cotton. They got those cotton pickin' machines now. That job's gone! The first thirty years of choppin' cotton wasn't so bad either. I liked it. I liked those mules, but I don't guess I could ever go back to farmin' now. Even my dad got a tractor. He said, 'You'd begin to like that tractor that never gets tired.' So, maybe I would."

I grew restless after reading Betty Frieden's *The Feminine Mystique*, which confronted the belief that a woman's place was in the home. Women's issues, civil rights, and the cultural changes advanced by college students awakened me. Protest ballads expanded my perception of the Vietnam War. Buffy Saint Marie's heartbreaking "Now That the Buffalo Is Gone" challenged what I had learned in my history classes. Did we really trade small-pox-infected blankets for their land when their children were freezing?

I questioned the values of our friends who made rude comments after Martin Luther King's murder. "Why is the flag at half mast for him?" Phil and I attended a black church, hoping to soothe the prejudiced feelings that were tearing our society apart. In 1968 Robert Kennedy's assassination devastated me, making it impossible to enjoy my sister Donna's wedding on the same day. What was happening in the United States? Dissension had rocked the country since President John Kennedy's assassination five years earlier.

Halfway through law school, Phil had an opportunity to manage a Missouri insurance claims office so he quit school and we moved to St. Joseph. We met like-minded couples there who shared our sixties' idealism and helped begin a Head Start program at a local church. Every day Chad watched *Sesame Street,* Jim Henson's creative children's television program. In 1973 his kindergarten peers, the first children who had been exposed to the show since its inception, proved its worth with their advanced skills.

In October Carole called with the exciting news that Bob had been inducted into the Country Music Hall of Fame! "Be sure to watch him on 'Kraft Music Hall' this Thursday night." In those days the awards shows were not televised live the way they are now.

I wasn't surprised when Oklahoma City had installed him in the National Cowboy Hall of Fame a few months earlier, but Nashville came as an unexpected honor. I had never linked him with the Grand Ole Opry and, in fact, he often said, "It makes me plumb mad when I hear people callin' us hillbilly 'cause my music's not hillbilly."

I phoned my neighbor to cancel my Thursday night bridge game. "I can't make the game 'cause my father's gonna accept an award on TV."

"What! Who in the world is your father? What kind of an award?" Learning that my father was Bob Wills thrilled her. Some folks merely asked, "Who's Bob Wills?"

Even though Bob had been nominated previously for the Hall of Fame, he did not think he would ever win. He was even booked at Cain's that night, but Sam Gibbs cancelled it and encouraged Bob to attend the October 18, 1968, show. The Association had also asked him to help present an award.

They introduced Jimmie Davis, then governor of Louisiana and the composer of "You Are My Sunshine," along with Bob as presenters for the Song of the Year award. As they walked out on the stage, strains of "You Are My Sunshine" gave way to "San Antonio Rose" in the background. The large audience gave them a thunderous standing ovation. After Jimmie Davis read the nominees' names, he said, "All right now, Bob, I'm gonna open the envelope." Bob leaned into the microphone and said, "Mighty fine. Mighty fine." After the assembly responded with laughter, Bob removed his Stetson, exposing his baldness, and waved to the crowd. "I don't usually take my hat off to nobody, but I sure do to you folks." They cheered enthusiastically and stomped their feet, obviously loving him. Soon after Bobby Russell accepted the award for the single "Honey," Bob disappeared to a room backstage with Ferlin Husky. Several people anxiously searched for him. "Bob, quick! They want you back onstage!"

Our attention stayed riveted on our television set until they introduced Tex Ritter and Roy Acuff as the presenters for the final award. Tex congratulated the five finalists before he said, "Our star came from humble beginnings and grew to become a sort of folk hero, but a reachable hero who gave the people in the audience something to live up to and look up to. The music of this Hall of Fame nominee reflects a broad knowledge of the American scene, the musical scene that is, from Negro country blues to more sophisticated urban communities."

After a slight pause, he continued, "That music was first recorded for the old Okeh label by recording pioneer, Mr. Art Satherley, and each new record quickly had the label 'hit' tagged to it. To get more specific, this man always dressed conservatively, even though the boots and the cowboy hats were $100 items. His theme song went something like this, 'Howdy, everybody from near and far, you want to know just who we are, we're the Texas Playboys from the Lone Star! Ah . . . Ha!'"

As the orchestra broke into "San Antonio Rose," Tex added, "Well, he's a fellow Texan, the innovator of western swing, ladies and gentlemen, I am pleased to announce the newest member of the Country Music Hall of Fame—BOB WILLS!"

"Aw, yes!" Bob exclaimed before he let out a long holler harmonizing with the "San Antonio Rose" melody in the background. He received his second standing ovation for the evening. "Friends, I don't believe this. No wonder Mr. Johnson has been insisting for eight months I come down here with him, not that I didn't want to, but I just wasn't able. Thank you, thank you so much. Words can't express how I feel. Domino!"

Bob told interviewer Ken Hightower, "I sent my first fiddle down there to that, uh, uh, thing in Nashville."

"Oh, you mean the Country Music Hall of Fame," Hightower prompted. Typically humble, my father was not being disrespectful because he couldn't remember what to call it. His induction had not made him feel more important than the next person. When I visited with him shortly after this exciting homage, he said, "You know, they asked me for a fiddle so I sent my first fiddle down there. I didn't have to send that particular fiddle. They just asked for a fiddle. You know, when you pin a thing down like that, I wouldn't feel right if I didn't send that old fiddle. I hope people know it's the real thing." Years later when Bob Pinson gave Chad and me a guided tour in Nashville, we proudly viewed that old fiddle along with a recently unveiled Willie Nelson exhibit. I brought a copy of Ruth Thomason's 1940 KVOO radio diary for the Library and Media Center.

Back in 1945 *Time* had described Bob's music as folk in a certain sense: "Bob Wills' music is called 'folk' in the trade for want of a better name, but Wills is more a backwoods Guy Lombardo than a Burl Ives-like balladeer. His trick is to bring ranch-house music nearer to the city."

But Bob's response to their analogy was, "Please don't nobody confuse us with none of those hillbilly outfits."

In an article titled "Twenty Things You Never Knew About the Grand Ole Opry," three attracted my attention:

A woman became so excited when Bob Wills and His Texas Playboys played the Opry in 1945 that she fell out of the balcony. She wasn't hurt.
In the Opry's salad days, no drums, horns or amplified instruments were

permitted. Bob Wills was the first musician allowed to use drums.

In 1945, the average pay for performers was $10 a show.

Bob Wills and His Texas Playboys' 1945 visit to the Grand Ole Opry defied Nashville's parochial proprieties. First, they arrived in a bus. They wore white, tailored western suits, white hats, and boots. The typical Opry musician drove an old car and dressed in overalls. Minnie Pearl, who personally witnessed the phenomenon, said, "He was way ahead of his time. People were awestruck. But as soon as he left town, every hillbilly act got a bus and western outfits."

People were also awestruck over his musical instrument display, which included electric guitars, amps, and a set of white pearl Slingerland drums. Drums and horns were unwelcome because Opry founder George Hay had vowed to keep the show "down to earth." Opry perennial Dave Macon cursed and grumbled about the imposing drums, but Eddie Arnold was impressed. The Texas Playboys were the first to use drums even though all country music performers use them today. Ernest Tubb said, "Bob Wills is important because he put the beat in country music."

However, drums on the Opry's sacred stage in the forties were taboo. Various stories about the actual drums' location during their performance have circulated ever since then. When the staff informed Bob the drummer couldn't play, Bob's temper blazed. He told them he would not leave a band member out—if the drummer didn't play, the band didn't play. However, he agreed to set up the drums behind the curtains. Bob watched his drummer Monte Mountjoy set them up. Immediately after Roy Acuff introduced the band, Bob shouted, "Move those things out on stage!" And they did. Right in front of the curtains.

Chapter 6

Best Damn Fiddle Player in the World

Columbia has just released a tangy, flavorful "Remembering the Greatest Hits of Bob Wills." Hearing such of them as "Corinne, Corinna" and "Mexicali Rose" is a reminder that this lovingly remembered of country bands—with its floating vocals and subtly grooving, witty playing—was a harbinger of modern mixed country. Wills laced his West Texas roots with jazz and thereby gained rather than lost individuality.

—NAT HENTOFF, COSMOPOLITAN, 1976

My father struggled through the mob to get from Cain's front door to the stage, shaking hands along the way. Those stalking him swarmed the bandstand around his gigantic, three-tiered birthday cake, decorated with "Happy 64th Birthday." A lively cowboy in a black hat shouted, "Happy birthday, Bob!" It was 1969.

"I'm on a diet, so all you folks just come up and help yourselves to a piece of cake." He smiled as he puffed on a cigar.

Another guy yelled, "Hey, Bob, didn't you stop smokin'?"

"Well, funny thing you should ask that. I did quit cigars, but I've started smokin' them again, 'cause the doctor said if I was gonna sneak around and smoke cigarettes, I might as well smoke cigars. You know, I used to smoke a pipe, but I had to constantly relight it, though I think that was half the fun."

He arched his eyebrows, raised his bow, and began a high-spirited version of "South" shouting, "Are you ready, folks? We're not here to stay, we're here to play."

After the dance he patted his solid, beefy chest and said, "You know, honey, I feel good. I've lost sixteen pounds and feel better than I've felt in years." But two months later he suffered a severe stroke.

Governor Preston Smith had named him, along with Ernest Tubb and Tex Ritter, "Country Music Ambassadors of Goodwill from Texas." Bob attended the joint Texas legislative session in Austin to accept the award presented by Senator Jack Hightower. The next day he became extremely ill and Betty drove him straight to Tulsa's Hillcrest Hospital. After the doctor examined him, he discovered Bob had suffered a stroke. He spent weeks in the hospital and months recovering at home.

Eldon Shamblin grew concerned after he learned that Bob could no longer earn a living playing his fiddle. Every time I see Eldon, he invariably asks, "Remember that time I tuned your piano?" In the early sixties I had called a number from the Tulsa Yellow Pages searching for a piano tuner. After the man finished tuning my piano, he asked, "Aren't you Rosetta, Bob's daughter?"

"Why, yes, I am," I answered.

"Well, I'm Eldon Shamblin, and I used to play guitar with your daddy."

In 1970 Eldon contacted Ernest Tubb, who helped him organize a benefit performance for Bob. They scheduled a large array of entertainers to appear at the Tulsa Fairgrounds Pavilion. Tulsa mayor J. W. Hewgley, Jr., proclaimed the week of January 12–18, 1970, Bob Wills week. Oklahoma House Resolution No. 1057, passed on January 14, 1970, honored him on the eve of the Tulsa benefit.

Phil's last promotion had taken us from St. Joseph to his company's home office in Fort Scott, Kansas. We met other "fun lovin' dancin' fools" in the small Kansas town who savored Elvis's "Poke Salad Annie." We formed the Poke Salad Annie Club that gathered on Saturday nights for dinner, music, and late night reveling. A proper job title guaranteed membership in the local country club.

The severe winter weather prevented us from attending the Tulsa benefit, over two hundred miles away. That morning the six-degree temperature chilled the frosty air as a blanket of snow cloaked the frozen ground. Thin sheets of ice covered the slippery streets. Hank Thompson flew in on a private plane that touched down on a precariously slick runway. Stonewall Jackson literally slid in by car for the second performance. Thompson told an interviewer, "It was 'bout eight above zero, eight above zero, and it took me 'bout thirty minutes to get the car warmed up enough to get the ice off so I could even drive. So we finally got out there 'bout seven o'clock and found out they were gonna have two shows which meant they had filled the auditorium up with twelve thousand. Now this is a real tribute when people will come over ice in eight above zero weather in Tulsa, Oklahoma. I could only drive ten miles an hour to get into places. I realized that thousands and thousands of people had turned out to pay tribute to Bob Wills." Also among the more than forty acts at the benefit were Roy Acuff, Tex Ritter, Roy Clark, Minnie Pearl, Mollie Bee, Pee Wee King, Jimmy Wakely, Chill Wills (no relation), and Hoyle Nix.

The newspapers reported that one thousand were standing in line by noon for the four o'clock show. The lines continued until three o'clock in the afternoon before the show sold out, with seven thousand filling the seats. The second show that ran until midnight drew another four thousand despite the hazardous weather conditions. Roy Acuff informed the packed arena, "If Bob Wills's name wasn't on this show, we wouldn't have drawn worth a darn." Chill Wills said, "It's a good testimonial for Bob. I think it's a great thing. We came and gave away what we have to sell." Eldon said it would have cost over $500,000 if they had hired all those stars. He proudly took the show's audiotape to Bob in Fort Worth, along with a $25,000 check.

Two months later we buried Grandpa Parker in Pawhuska's cemetery. I remembered those tears in my tough Grandpa's eyes on my wedding day. He died at age eighty-six after spending his last two years in a nursing home. When Phil and I visited him, he cried and kissed Chad's picture over and over again. He often asked us to find him a job and take him from that dismal place. But then the senility shifted his conversation back to the old days that were now his reality. How disheartening to watch a vital man wasting away, his body still strong, but his mind living in the days when he worked in the Oklahoma oil fields with teams of horses. Even in his seventies he got the best of a younger man who jumped him from an alley.

Stoic Grandma broke down as they closed the casket. "Bill. Oh, Bill," she cried. Their tempestuous marriage had lasted over sixty years, but I wondered what would have happened if Joe hadn't died. Joe was a man who worked for Grandpa. After losing her four-year-old son David, Grandma had lost interest in life and in Grandpa. She worked from sunup to sunset, cooking for the hired help on a wood stove in a cabin with a dirt floor. Then her affection for Joe grew until she decided to leave Grandpa. But before she told Grandpa about her plans, Joe was killed in an oil field accident. Joe had given her chocolate-covered mints for Christmas. Every December a box appeared under our tree in Joe's remembrance.

That summer James called to tell us that Betty had taken Bob back to Hillcrest Hospital in Tulsa. My second child was due any day, but we drove to Tulsa anyway. Once again, Bob's expressive eyes communicated the same urgency I had experienced when I visited him after his first stroke. He held on to my hands tightly and stroked my fingers. I desperately wanted to share my feelings with him, but it seemed impossible since I couldn't even interpret his slurred speech. Even casual conversation was demanding.

Two weeks later on July 29, 1970, my beautiful daughter Reneé Leigh was born. Three-year-old Chad gawked at the tiny infant in the bassinet. "That's Mama's fat tummy in the basket." James came to see Reneé when she was three months old, but he came without Carole. The responsibility for Bobby and two more toddlers (Stephanie and Doug), combined with their own youth, brought problems into their marriage. After their divorce, I lost my advocate with Betty. James and I kept in touch through phone calls, but he remarried someone I didn't know, and Carole's new husband adopted the children. When Carole turned her back on the Wills family, a chapter in my life ended.

Phil's big break arrived—a new position with a Chicago insurance company and a large pay increase. I felt relieved since the Kansas country club's poker games had become too prominent in his life. We were now living the American dream in suburbia—two children, a dog, and a new Ford station wagon. Weekday mornings at seven o'clock sharp, housewives drove their husbands to the train depot for the hour-long downtown commute, returning each evening at six o'clock. Years later I finally understood why our neighbor, a Harvard graduate, quit his executive position with Quaker Oats and moved to a Wisconsin dairy farm.

Living near Chicago heightened my awareness about life in the big city and the dangers lurking in public housing. Even the enormous daily newspaper intimidated me. On a Saturday morning I bundled up my two little ones and took the train into the city for a shopping excursion. In the heart of Chicago, hundreds of policemen and thousands of spectators blocked the sidewalks to watch a mile-long Puerto Rican holiday parade down State Street. I slipped into a Woolworth's store, clinging to my children, and waited almost an hour for the crushing mob to thin out. I had never seen so many folks who didn't look like they were from Oklahoma in one place before.

We kept in contact with Bob and Betty through cards and letters and received Christmas gifts from "The Texas Grandparents." After my father's speech improved, I talked with him on the phone often. Betty sent photos taken at Merle Haggard's Bakersfield home when he hosted a recording session for former Texas Playboys Eldon Shamblin, Al Stricklin, Leon McAuliffe, Smoky Dacus, Joe Holley, Alex Brashear, Johnny Gimble, Tiny Moore, Glynn Duncan (Tommy Duncan's brother), Johnnie Lee, and Luke Wills. Several had not seen each other for thirty years. They recorded fifteen songs that are still in Merle's possession. Rumors about the reason why they haven't been released range from "They're not commercial quality due to the high winds and outside noise during the recording" to "The boys got into the whiskey too much."

Since Merle's father died when he was nine years old, he identified with Bob as a father figure. "I respected Bob as a father and talked to him a lot about personal things in my life." Bob attended the session confined to a wheelchair, unable to play with them. Joe Holley noticed Bob's frown so he stopped the music, leaned down close to the wheelchair, and asked, "What's wrong?" In a whisper Bob pointed out they were not playing it as they once did and explained what they were doing wrong.

After the session Merle asked, "Bob, how did it sound?"

"It lacked only one thing," Bob said.

"What's that?"

"Me."

Al Stricklin became inspired to write a book revealing the inside stories of the Texas Playboys' glory years from 1934 to 1942. When I read his book *My Years with Bob Wills,* I understood Al's feelings:

> So there we all sat together, working just like old times, and swapping stories during breaks. But there was something missing. That was the old master. The man who started it all; the man who could get 110 percent effort out of his musicians like a good football coach; the man who was feared and loved by his men; the man who could sell his product like nobody else, as testified to by the thousands of people who turned out to listen, even during blizzard-like conditions sometimes; the man—Bob Wills.

Bob never overlooked any requests people asked him to play on the radio show. He put Al in charge of the tiny scraps of paper they collected at their dances on the road. Demands on Bob's personal time poured in daily along with the fan mail. Citizens trusted this country boy who had experienced hard times. Many times he honored pleas to sing at funerals, sometimes taking the whole band along. He played for a woman's 110th birthday at a county poor farm and played tunes for over an hour at an elderly man's bedside. He responded to thousands over the years.

Al appreciated his generosity toward him and the other musicians, and his musicians loved him. When Al's first wife died of cancer, he asked Bob for a $600 loan for the funeral expenses, but when he tried to repay the loan, Bob said, "I didn't loan you $600, kid. I gave you $600. I don't want to hear any more about it."

Phil's next step up the corporate ladder took us to Fountain Valley, a West Coast suburb forty miles south of "Lost Angel Land." He now faced a daily hour-long commute into Los Angeles on the complex freeway system that enslaved southern Californians—no trains for them. Chad started kindergarten in a progressive Fountain Valley school. His high scores on the Stanford Binet IQ test placed him in an exceptionally gifted class that took field trips to the ocean to study tide pools. As soon as he entered first grade, my ambitious husband had landed an even more lucrative position with a San Francisco insurance company—our fifth major move in seven years.

Sunnyvale, another bedroom community forty miles south of "Hippie Harbor," became our new home. In the spirit of Scarlet, I vowed to the heavens, "With God as my witness, I'll never move again!" For the next three years Phil rode the train to downtown San Francisco. At least northern Californians didn't have such love affairs with their cars, allowing them to build good transit systems.

San Francisco's trolley cars enticed us into the city often, where we tarried with the tourists in China Town, spent hours at the zoo, and uncovered choice provincial spots the natives kept secret. Browsing in the revered City Lights Bookstore, we still searched for "beatnik emeritus" Ferlinghetti. Dobie Gray's "Drift Away" lyrics freed his soul to get lost in the beat of rock and roll in the Mark Hopkins Hotel lounge. His splendid performance persuaded us to stay for his second show (after I refused to leave). Our out-of-town treks often took us to the spectacular state parks, as well as the vast, breathtaking Yosemite.

Melodic memories of "Mam'selle" danced in my head during Frank Sinatra's exclusive Lake Tahoe appearance. Tahoe trips unfortunately rekindled Phil's gambling interest. Phil commanded confidently, "Double down," to the attractive blackjack dealer. Her table was one of scores in the expansive casino. With a coached nonexpression, she slapped down a nine and a queen on Phil's twin down cards and flipped a five onto her six-count up card.

Phil snuffed out his cigarette and swigged down the iced remains of his scotch. She then flipped her down card over—a one-eyed Jack. Her well-rehearsed sweep with the clear plastic bill stuffer put Phil's greenery, as well as that of three other players, down the currency slot. I wondered what kind of job-related stress he had endured to lose those two fifty-dollar bills. Couldn't she have at least empathized with a "Sorry, better luck next hand"?

Phil's twelve-hour days and rapid ascension up the proverbial ladder had chipped away at his emotional stamina. Gambling had become his escape. And the compulsion spiraled when California card clubs provided easy access to a twenty-four-hour poker game. My father's early recording "Mean Ole Gamblin' Polka Dot Blues" became Phil's truth. The deck was set. An ace was drawn. When the gold watch was bet he called it. Lost his money like a man.

I took a job as Scheduling Coordinator for Student Activities at San Jose State University. Ron Barrett, the amiable Student Union Director, had assembled a qualified staff who functioned like a family. We no longer wore dresses to work, only faded bell-bottom jeans and brightly colored tie-dyed T-shirts with turquoise and silver jewelry. The Santa Cruz hippies descended upon the Student Union selling their wares daily. The visible student government stayed involved in staff decisions until the apathetic, narcissistic eighties set in.

During the early seventies provocative incidents awakened the California campus. Anti-Vietnam, anti-Dow Chemical, anti-Union Carbide, and anti-big business rallies became commonplace. Bomb threats occurred when Jane Fonda commanded a vast antiwar demonstration in the Student Union Amphitheater. Campus police arrested Iranian students who led protest marches against the Shah on a weekly basis. Gay Pride Week, Black Pride Week, Cinco de Mayo, and other ethnic festivities expanded my cultural awareness as San Francisco street mimes, acoustic guitarists, and rock bands entertained the students daily. The Student Activities Committee brought Rod Stewart to the stadium and Taj Mahal (arriving three hours late) to the Student Union Ballroom.

Many suburban neighbors were graduates of EST (Erhard Seminar Training) who communicated through their newly concocted vernacular. I never succumbed to their relentless pressure to sign up for a seminar, but I did (as a curiosity seeker) accompany his devout followers to hear the guru speak at San Francisco's Cow Palace. But Werner Erhard never illuminated baffling Zen for me. His brilliant and profitable scheme to make esoteric Eastern philosophy palatable to the Western upper middle class occured during these power years. His family later divulged his deviant behavior on national television.

All my California friends were in therapy—personal, group, marriage, or family. Phil's gambling mania magnified our marriage problems and sent me rushing to my own therapist, who delved into my childhood.

"Are you illegitimate?" the therapist asked.

"No," I replied.

"Then why do you act like you are?"

"I guess I feel like I am."

"Tell me more about your father."

"Well, part of my problem is that I don't know much about him. Well, no, actually, I know things about him, like facts, but I don't know him as a person. I've talked to others who know him personally and I've read things about him, but that's not the same as really knowing him. Everyone loves him so much. When I was young, I was embarrassed because everyone knew who he was and asked me questions about him. Then when I got older and tried so hard to get to know him, he had a stroke. The last time I saw him I couldn't understand what he was saying to me. I feel we've finally broken down some barriers, but now his stroke keeps us from truly talking to each other."

"How do you feel about him?"

"Sometimes I feel hurt and rejected, but it's always exciting to be around him. He's kind and pays attention to me. He's very handsome with dark eyes and he always wears a cowboy hat. The crazy women chase after him—I've watched them at his dances."

"Why don't you write him a letter expressing your feelings about him?"

Several counseling sessions later my letter shrieked accusations. *Why did you let me grow up without getting to know me? Why didn't you tell your other children about me? You should have acknowledged me.* I listed the "shoulds," one by one. But writing down the unspeakable things freed me to express my love. After I finished blaming him for my painful experiences, I realized it didn't matter because I loved him. With tears streaming down my cheeks, I read it aloud to the therapist.

"You don't have to mail it. That's up to you."

I put it away.

Merle Haggard dedicated the album *To the Best Damn Fiddle Player in the World* to Bob in the early seventies. Personnel included six former Texas Playboys along with Merle's band the Strangers (Joe Holley, Eldon Shamblin, Tiny Moore, Johnny Gimble, Alex Brashear, and Johnnie Lee Wills). In the wake of Merle's successful tribute album, Columbia and United Artists released more of Bob's original material by 1973. Merle's re-creation of "Cherokee Maiden," a Cindy Walker composition Bob originally recorded in 1941, yielded another hit for Merle.

When I learned that Merle was scheduled to play in San Carlos, I called my father, hoping he could arrange an introduction. Merle announced my presence in the audience before he began his Bob Wills set. He had learned to play the fiddle, imitating Bob's style and mannerisms, in less than three months. His remarkable performance conveyed not only the same music, but the same feeling Bob had captured during the swing era. Unfortunately Merle's eagerness to leave equaled my eagerness to meet him. By the time security let us backstage, the bus was gone.

In 1938 Ruth Sheldon, a reporter for the *Tulsa Tribune,* wrote *Hubbin' It: The Life of Bob Wills,* a biography based exclusively on interviews with my father. The *Tulsa Tribune* editor had told Ruth, "There's a guy here that plays the fiddle and has a band that gets a thousand fan letters a week. You'd better go over and see what he's got." After interviewing him, she felt Bob Wills possessed the same rare traits that produce an Abraham Lincoln or a Will Rogers. Many have commented about "that certain something" he had. His long-time attorney David Milsten said, "We had a wonderful relationship. Never had an argument. I really honestly . . . well, didn't like him, I loved him. He had 'that something' that could have led him to the Oklahoma governor's mansion if he had the formal education to go with it, simply because he had a personality that a politician would love to have had." When Ruth commented on Bob's remarkable memory, he said, "Well, I don't have no education so I have to use my mind somehow." He told her when his friends and relatives asked him to visit, they always reminded him to bring his fiddle. She responded, "But it's not the fiddle they want—it's you, Bob!"

In the prelude to *Hubbin' It*, Ruth wrote:

> The frightened mules bolted around the corner. The hub of the wagon wheel struck a huge rock and the buckboard careened madly back and forth. The frantic driver, slipping precariously from side to side, jerked the lines and pleaded and bellowed. He and the wagon were "Hubbin' It."
>
> The life of Bob Wills has been like that . . . meeting adversity at every corner. . . . Bob Wills is not a great man, but he has accomplished a great thing. . . . Those who can make others joyous and carefree for even a little while today are giving as great a service to mankind as the scientists of many professions who fight to rid the world of disease, ignorance, crazy economic structures, and war. Bob Wills brings gaiety and forgetfulness to thousands of men and women with his music. . . . There is the bond of "hubbin' it" between them.

Even though Bob came from west Texas fiddle roots, he had an affinity for the black jazz orchestras. Musicians who traveled with him recalled that he always searched for the latest Count Basie records in the big city record stores. Bob hired fiddlers skilled at jazzy improvisations akin to the Count Basie sidemen that he admired. That prompted some to label Bob's music "hillbilly jazz." In *Singing Cowboys and All That Jazz*, William Savage wrote:

> Once, an inebriated Bob Wills hired a black trumpet player in Tulsa. The black Texas Playboy survived for one performance. A sober Bob Wills decided that Oklahomans were unprepared to accept a black man playing black music in a white orchestra.

Despite cheap talk about racial tolerance in the forties to demonstrate "U.S. supremacy" over Hitler's racist Germany, our armed forces were segregated, and volatile racial tensions exploded in Harlem, Detroit, and Chicago. Whites bought the records of black bands, but even bandleader Cab Calloway was unwelcome in Kansas City's PlaMor Ballroom. According to the white manager's dubious story, a drunk Calloway pushed him, resulting in Calloway's arrest for public intoxication.

Bob always gravitated toward the blues and once rode fifty miles on horseback to see the Empress of the Blues, Bessie Smith. "She was the greatest thing I ever heard." The blues in his music came from the days he played with black children and worked alongside black adults in the cotton fields. His outstanding versions of several old blues numbers speak of the black influence on his early Dixieland style. He was one of the first bandleaders to play old-time fiddle tunes with a horn section and drums like a jazz band. Saxophonist Ray DeGeer, who later played with

Gene Krupa and Charlie Barnet, remembered, "Bob Wills was the first man I ever heard who made a breakdown swing. His music was not country music because it did swing, like a New Orleans Dixie beat. He had an uncanny sense of time and tempo."

Bob recorded "Brain Cloudy Blues" in 1946, a spin-off of Kokomo Arnold's celebrated 1935 "Milk Cow Blues" that Johnnie Lee had put to wax in 1941. Elvis's smash "Milk Cow Blues" in the early Sun Studio days combined parts of "Brain Cloudy Blues" with "Milk Cow Blues." I cringed at age twelve when I read scandalous titles on those stacks of my mother's 78 rpm records, titles such as "Everybody Does It in Hawaii," "Bring It on Down to My House, Honey," and "Empty Bed Blues." The flip side of "Rosetta" sounded risqué for the thirties—"Ding Dong Daddy from Dumas Town—Ought'a See Me Do My Stuff." Later when I listened closely to the lyrics—which made reference to dealing drugs more potent than moonshine—I was surprised the Playboys recorded this in 1937.

Emmett Miller, a white Southerner who recorded on the Okeh label in the early twenties, notably swayed my father's style. Bob patterned his persona after Miller, especially his jivey expressions. Bob's 1935 recording of "I Ain't Got Nobody" is similar to Miller's earlier rendition. Miller sang in the bluesy yodeling style later identified with Jimmie Rodgers. (When I was a teenager I listened to Grandma Parker's old Jimmie Rodgers's 78 rpm records for hours.) Bob, partial to the blues, recorded several Rodgers's blues numbers rather than his ballads: "Drunkard Blues," "Gamblin' Polka Dot Blues," "Mean Mama Blues," "Mississippi Delta Blues," and "Never No More Blues." In 1932 Bob met the celebrated Rodgers when the Light Crust Doughboys recorded "Sunbonnet Sue" and "Nancy Jane" for Victor in Dallas. It's been reported that then-newcomer Jimmie Davis also recorded in that session.

That same year, after Bob lost Milton Brown as his vocalist, he drove around the state auditioning many singers, but the right one remained illusive. Then one day a man called him. "I hear you're lookin' for a singer. Can I sing for you?"

"Come on out. We'll see."

When he arrived, Bob immediately asked, "You know, I love Emmett Miller's 'I Ain't Got Nobody.' Can you sing that?"

"That's my favorite."

"Let's hear you get after it."

"You're hired, Tommy. You know, you're the sixty-eighth guy to sing for me."

O'Daniel fired Bob soon after Thomas Elmer Duncan replaced Milton Brown, so Tommy followed Bob to Oklahoma. "You hired me, O'Daniel didn't. Anywhere you go, I'm gonna go. And I'm not leavin' you until you fire me."

Fifteen years later Bob did fire Tommy. The band, then located at Wills Point in

Sacramento, was in a predicament. Disappointed fans resented Tommy, who fronted the band during Bob's absences on cross-country tours or excessive drinking bouts. The mounting tension between Bob and Tommy peaked one night in Sacramento when Bob overheard Tommy ask, "Wonder if Bob will even show up tonight?" Angrily he ordered Eldon, acting band manager, to fire Tommy at once. Tommy had been a member of Bob's band longer than anyone.

Many musicians who played with Bob felt that he never understood his own drinking. Bob frequently asked, "Boys, can we have a little drink to celebrate?" He loved to imbibe because he loved a good time. But sometimes he identified with the reelin', rockin', drunk again gin drinker in "Drunkard's Blues." Bob told Casey Dickens, "I'm the only Wills who can't drink and get away with it. Luke, Johnnie Lee, and Billy Jack can take a drink or two, get up the next day, and go on 'bout their business. But if I do that, I'll end up gone for a week. I think the Lord is punishin' me 'cause I was called to preach and didn't do it."

Snuffy Smith told me about a night in Huntsville when Bob left the bandstand because of a severe headache. "Bob hadn't been drinkin' but after 'bout two numbers he had to go out to the car. After the dance some guys started the dernest fight I ever saw. Old Louis Tierney and Luke both took a guy to the ground. It was all 'cause Bob left. If Bob wasn't there, it wasn't right. They all came to see Bob."

In 1949 The Texas Playboys recorded their first session without Tommy, replacing him with Jack Loyd. (The others at the time were Johnny Gimble, Herb Remington, Eldon Shamblin, Tiny Moore, Alex Brashear, Doc Lewis, and Luke and Billy Jack Wills.) Missing the chemistry between Bob and Tommy, the album lacked vitality. Tommy formed his own band called Tommy Duncan and His Western All Stars (including Joe Holley, Millard Kelso, and Ocie Stockard; Buck Owens later replaced Ferlin Husky on guitar in Tommy's band) but he was never able to duplicate the success he and Bob had had together. In an early performance Tommy told a radio audience, "Right after I announced the tune we just done, Noel Boggs just jumped all over me 'cause I didn't tell the people out on the air who it was playin' and singin' for them. This is Tommy Duncan and the Western Swing Band comin' to you from the 97th Street Corral, 97th and Main Street, in Los Angeles, the Workin' Man's Fun Spot. What am I sayin'? Well, we'll just use that. From now on this is the Workin' Man's Fun Spot."

Casey Dickens said, "Whenever you heard Bob yell, 'Come here, Thomas Elmer Duncan,' you knew he was mad at Tommy. That was his way of lettin' Tommy know he was in the dog house." Snuffy Smith added, "Tommy loved Bob. Bob once told me, 'You know I love that guy, but he'll get up before I do and go down to the hotel lobby and sit for two or three hours until I come down there and eat breakfast with him so I'll pay for it. But I love him.'"

After a decade apart, Bob and Tommy reunited and recorded three albums for Liberty: *Together Again, Mr. Words and Mr. Music,* and *A Living Legend.* Session personnel included Joe Holley, Gene Crownover, Leon Rausch, Luke Wills, Wade Peeler, Glenn Rhees, Jack Lloyd, Tag Lambert, Frankie McWhorter, and George Clayborn. The single "Heart to Heart Talk" quickly rose to the top of the charts. During 1961 Bob and Tommy even worked a few more road tours together. Sadly Tommy died of a heart attack in 1967 at age fifty-seven.

Chapter 7

Faded Love of San Antonio Rose

When their 1940 recording of "San Antonio Rose" went gold,
Wills and his band were firmly entrenched as the most
famous western band in America, and consequently, the most
famous dance band in American musical history.

—LARRY WILLOUGHBY,
TEXAS RHYTHM, TEXAS RHYME

My father's love affair with his audience as well as his band members remained faithful throughout his entire career. His intent to keep the people in motion depended on a solid beat, but his striking success also came from his mixture of music and mingling. He never accepted a tip from his fans—not a dollar or a hundred dollars. Eldon said Bob vowed, "If someone asks us to play a request, we'll play it. They don't have to give us money. If they give us any money, it's gonna make me mad. That takes away makin' everyone equal."

Even though there is more leverage in playing a stage show, Bob relaxed when he played a dance. He preferred to begin a tempo and stay right in the rhythm as people whirled around the floor. "We didn't pull any punches. We played anythin' we figured the people could dance to. And if a pop tune come along, and we could do it justice, why we'd do it. We didn't cull anythin' we thought they could pat their foot to—kind of a duke's mixture. I'm not able to do nothin' else, 'cept play it simple. Just simple."

In an interview Bob said, "Back in the early days, Jimmie Davis was very popular on some old tunes like 'Ida Red.' The Skillet Lickers, even farther back than Jimmie Davis, played a lot of the same stuff. I bought all their records when I was growin' up in Hall County although I can't think of the names of any tunes now. They would sing tunes real fast with no dance tempo so me and Milton slowed them down a bit so people could do the 'Rag' or 'Two-step' to them. We was tryin' to learn enough tunes to keep 'em dancin' without repeatin' so much."

Davis's reputation as a singer-songwriter grew after he began singing on a Shreveport radio show in 1928. His style influenced Bob in the early thirties. Davis later served two terms (1944 and 1960) as governor of Louisiana. In 1972 he was elected to the Country Music Hall of Fame, four years after Bob' induction. The Skillet Lickers recorded "Ida Red," "Down Yonder," "Sally Gooden," and other ditties during the mid-twenties. Gid Tanner, chicken farmer and wild fiddler, wailed cat calls analogous to what later became known as a Wills trademark.

"When me, Herman Arnspiger, and Milton Brown got started," Bob said, "we came to western swing, accidentally, in a round about way." Although many Texans today consider Bob a traditionalist, the creator of a genre we now call western swing, he was truly a trendsetter blazing new trails in the thirties. According to journalist Don McLeese in the *Austin American-Statesman* in 1991, today's traditionalism was yesterday's trendiness:

> Though this hybrid of country music and big-band swing has since solidified into a fixed, static style, it was forged by Wills as a vibrant response to the musical trends of his times, a musical melting pot where sophistication mixed fluidly with down-home sentiments.

In 1996 the Nashville network (TNN) aired "The Life and Times of Bob Wills" featuring interviews with Merle Haggard, Ray Benson, Luke Wills, Eldon Shamblin, Leon Rausch, Johnny Gimble, Cindy Wills, Dr. Townsend, Mark Rowland (editor of *Musician* magazine), and many others. People listened more to the comments Bob interjected than to the song's lyrics. Johnny Gimble recalled that some guy kept asking them to play "Never, Never," but the band didn't know a song called "Never, Never." When Tommy was singing "Right or Wrong," Bob whispered into the mike, "Never, Never." The guy yelled, "That's it! That's it! I knew you guys could play "Never, Never."

Initially, Gimble didn't like Bob's hollering, until he realized the real art of it. Bob often spoke about his younger days when he worked the west Texas cotton rows and listened to old black men hum tunes and cry the blues. Johnny specifically remarked about the hypnotic effect of Bob's hollering on "Bob Wills Special," a 1940 instrumental. ("Blues in A" on the 1963 Liberty album *Bob Wills Sings and Plays* is a remake of this instrumental.) "Bob's perfect pitch 'blues lick,'" said Johnny, "sounded like somethin' straight out of a cotton field."

Eldon told Mark Rowland, "I've talked to people who've listened to records but never seen the Ole Man—and hell, they say the feelings came across to them, too!

And you wonder—how come? But somehow it all comes across, the kind of person he was."

"Everything we ever attempted to play, we played by feel and to hell with execution or technique," Smoky said. "That's what we learned from Bob." Bob took liberty with all the musical rules by breaking meter or whatever when it felt right to him. For example, since "Rosetta" was a big swing band song, another bandleader who recorded it rebuked Bob for breaking meter, but Bob reminded him that he knew what he was doing. "If it feels good, I hold on to it, and my record is outsellin' yours."

O. W. Mayo recalled, "Bob recorded that song I wrote, 'Blues for Dixie,' in Hollywood in the late forties. He always gave everybody in his band a break. He'd call out their names on his radio program and give them credit for their musical ability. He was always complimentary when they did a good job. That's somethin' a lot of band leaders didn't do." When interviewers asked Bob who was the best steel guitar player he ever had, his consistent reply revealed his understanding of human nature. "The man I have with me now is always the best one."

Even though I was too young to remember the glory years of the early Tulsa Band, I am grateful that I saw my father perform many times during the early sixties. When I watched a segment of Billy Gray's TV show "Music Country Style," I noticed that Bob thanked Billy Gray profusely for having him on the show. Then, as usual, he called out each performer's name, personally recognizing each one. "Now, friends, let's hear from my boy Joe Andrews." Toward the end he stated how wonderful the entire crew was and asked to introduce the drummer since he had not yet mentioned his name. He then closed with a warm handshake and more plentiful thanks to Billy Gray. My father probably never read Dale Carnegie's *How to Win Friends and Influence People,* but he probably could have written it.

Tulsa's John Wooley wrote the narrative for a videotape, *Still Swingin': A History of Bob Wills and Western Swing,* containing additional interviews with Eldon, Joe Frank, Johnny Gimble, Leon Rausch, and others, along with old film clips and new footage of Asleep at the Wheel and Stonehorse performing at Cain's. Tracy Byrd performed Red Steagall's hit "Lone Star Beer and Bob Wills Music," and Steagall himself hosted the show that closed with "Bob's Got a Swing Band in Heaven."

In 1985 the State of Oklahoma officially recognized Bob Wills Day because of the impact Bob Wills and the Texas Playboys had on the American music scene for half a century. I met Ray Bingham, Steagall's booking agent, at a 1988 Bob Wills Day celebration in Oklahoma City. "Faded Love" permeated the Oklahoma Senate chamber and fourth-floor rotunda as we talked. Ray recalled accompanying his late father, who sold bootleg whiskey to parking lot clients, to Bob's dances in Claremore. The half-pints for $1.25 were the best-sellers because they were easier to hide in belts or pockets. Young Ray could not legally enter so Bob let him carry his fiddle into the Claremore armory. "If I walked in with Bob Wills, I'd get to stay inside."

Jack Frank, station manager for PBS Channel 11 in Tulsa, conducted interviews with Eldon and Smoky at Cain's for a show called "Oklahoma Magazine." The interview segment received such a positive response that the station repeated it. After more phone calls from viewers, they added movie clips from *Take Me Back to Oklahoma, Riders of the Northwest Mounted,* and *Vigilante Riders,* supplied by Guy Logsdon and Glenn White, and they aired the entire production again.

Smoky said, "Bob had a big heart, as big as this ballroom. If I saw it happen once, I saw it happen a hundred times. After our noon broadcast some guy in overalls would walk up to Bob and whisper in his ear. Bob would reach in his pocket and give the guy a hundred-dollar bill. The story was always the same—the guy had a sick mother who was always in California and he always needed money for a bus ticket. After the guy was out of earshot, Bob would say, 'You know, that guy's probably lyin' but I can't take the chance.'"

Eldon added, "I remember when he would see an old woman in the crowd dressed in shabby clothes. He would find out her name and then tell Ada [his secretary] to take the woman downtown and buy her a new outfit, coat, dress, shoes, the whole thing."

Smoky's dark eyes lit up as he continued, "We had fun, lots of fun. Bob had a real sense of humor. One night I climbed up on top of the bus to fasten the tarp over the instruments and before I could get down, the bus took off, leavin' me hangin' on the back. A policeman pulled us over, took me up to the front of the bus, and asked Bob if he knew someone was hangin' on the back. Bob and every guy on that bus said they didn't even know who I was, so I got thrown in jail. A few hours later Bob said, 'Well, boys, guess we had better go get Dacus out of jail.' We had a good time in those days."

In the Tulsa Band, Bob used two front lines, one of horns and the other of fiddles. Duke Ellington, Cab Calloway, Charlie Christian, and Earl Hines inspired the men who joined him. They did not consider themselves country musicians. When Charlie Christian changed the guitar's role in Benny Goodman's sextet by making the rhythm guitar a lead instrument, Eldon was doing the same thing in Tulsa. Leon, former pupil of Milton Brown's steel player Bob Dunn, added speed and richness to "Steel Guitar Rag," the tune that did more to make steel stylish than any other single record. He and Eldon, who was also unmatched on rhythm guitar, cut the first twin guitar record, "Twin Guitar Boogie." At one time the Tulsa Band included four saxophones, three trumpets, and two trombones.

In 1941 big band dance music dominated Bob's Hollywood recording sessions for

Columbia. Many musicians noticed the similarity between Bob's band and Bob Crosby's Bobcats. Trumpeter Danny Alguire often spoke about their Bob Crosby influence. Alguire became interested in playing with Bob after he learned that Benny Strickler, another hot trumpet player strictly associated with jazz, had joined the band. After drummer Bob Fitzgerald started playing with them, he was compared favorably with Ray Baduc, drummer for the Bobcats. "Ten Years," written by Johnny Bond, became a favorite for many. Leon Huff's vocals and the big horn Dixieland sound appealed to jazz enthusiasts. Bond said, "Art Satherly asked me to write a song or two for Bob. Later on he told me, 'Bob's done some of your songs and he's playin' down at the Santa Monica Pier, so why don't we go down and listen to him?'"

Bond continued, "Would you believe it? It would never happen this way again, but as we walked into this ballroom full of thousands of people dancin' to Bob Wills's music that you could hear three blocks away—guess what they were playin'? 'Ten Years!' You've heard that old sayin' 'bout the thrill that comes once in a lifetime—well, that was my reaction."

Bob eagerly anticipated Satherley's approval of his big band sound. After finishing the first swing tune "sans fiddle" in the 1941 session, Bob waited for Uncle Art's praise. Art agreed the band sounded like Tommy Dorsey's, but he also emphatically reminded Bob that if he had wanted Tommy Dorsey, he would have hired Tommy Dorsey. "Get your fiddle, Bob!"

High regard for the band continued to grow until World War II stopped the music. Tommy, Leon, and Eldon enlisted in the army and Al Stricklin took a defense industry job. Until the end of 1942, Bob did the Cain's broadcasts, played dances, made records, and starred in western movies. Shortly before he broke up the band to join the army he played the Los Angeles County Barn Dance at Venice Pier for three nights, attracting attendance beyond 15,000. The police made them quit selling tickets at eleven o'clock because they feared the dance floor would collapse. At that time the line outside was ten deep and lined up all the way into Venice.

On December 26, 1942, Bob Wills and His Texas Playboys did their final KVOO broadcast. After his army enlistment, Grandma Parker saved newspaper clippings that contained such attention-getting headlines as "Bob Wills Almost AWOL Even Before He's in Army," "Bob Wills on KP Duty at Fort Sill," and "Bob Wills Quits Music Career, Enlists in Army Under Deadline."

One article referred to him as "Bob Wills, a Tulsa musician, crooner, composer, actor, and rancher." When reporters asked him about his career and his four marriages, he said, "Wives just don't understand men in public life. Regardless of bands, movies, music, and wives, horses are my real weakness. Especially Palominos. I've got about 16 more horses than I've had wives." (I wondered how my mother felt about that.)

Missing the early bus taking the inductees to Fort Sill got him off to a bad start, but after several army personnel conferences, they extended his reporting time until midnight. Arriving in his Cadillac instead of by bus did not impress his superior officers. Only three months away from his thirty-eighth birthday, he joined the army before voluntary enlistments ended for men between the ages of eighteen and thirty-eight. It was rumored that a draft board member had sworn Wills would serve in the army. Based at Camp Howze near Gainesville, Texas, his discharge came six months later, in July 1943.

His child support payments fell behind during his army days, causing my mother to write to Mayo and Bob's commanding officer. I found the following letters in her cedar chest:

April 26th, 1943

Dear Mary Lou,

I am in receipt of your letter of April 16th and upon receipt of same I wrote to Bob about the baby not having as yet received the government allowance as benificiary [sic].

Then, I saw him Saturday and talked with him further about it and he said that his immediate superior or whoever he had discussed the matter with, said the payments should have already been made. However, he said that he would go into the matter with them again and advise me concerning same as definitely as possible by letter this week.

As stated in my previous letter, Bob is only getting $21.00 per month himself. Therefore, they are holding out of his salary the amount that is supposed to be held out in order to make these payments. I readily appreciate your position in regards to the matter and will do all I can to get the matter straightened out and the payments coming.

Yours truly,
O. W. Mayo

June 8, 1943

Dear Madam:

I have just had a talk with Pvt. Wills concerning his responsibility to you and his child. He informs me that he never completed the necessary papers for your allotment because he is under consideration for discharge in the near future. However, he promised me that he would take care of the back payments regardless of whether or not he executes the necessary papers for the Government Allotment.

I expect him to fulfill his obligation to you and his child regardless of whether he remains in the army or is discharged. Let me know whether or not he fulfills his promise he has made to me.

Very truly yours,
Cecil R. Searcy, 1st Lt. 335th Infantry

Yarns spread about his difficulties in the army, mostly made up from sketchy details. However, his "Private" role didn't agree with him the way his "Band Leader" role had. Like other entertainers during World War II, he sold war bonds and recorded patriotic melodies such as "White Cross on Okinawa" and "Empty Chair at the Christmas Table." On his first Oklahoma tour after his stint in the army, officials stated that he was largely responsible for the state's going a million and a half over its quota.

When he moved to California he continued his patriotic work. At the Alcazar Theater in Bell, California, a single night's performance grossed $158,000 in war bonds sold in place of admission tickets. He soon assembled an orchestra comprising premier musicians who played mostly big band swing music. His acceptance in the west drew capacity crowds wherever he played. Folks who had migrated from the Southwest to California during the Depression years, especially Oklahomans fleeing the Dustbowl, created a vast audience for western swing and honky-tonk music. Spade Cooley (Bob's biggest rival) and Hank Penny ("Won't You Ride in My Little Red Wagon?") also attracted western swing zealots to dance halls at Venice Pier and Redondo Beach. As quoted by Nick Tosches in *Country: The Biggest Music in America,* Hank Thompson said, "I remember seeing Wills and Cooley perform at Redondo Beach when I was stationed in San Pedro during the war. It was not uncommon to see ten thousand out at that pier." Snuffy Smith also recalled a Battle of the Bands between Bob and Spade Cooley at Santa Monica Beach when they called out the highway patrol because there were so many cars on the pier they feared it could collapse. Vocalist Laura Lee Owens recalled the huge crowds in California. "Bob had six bodyguards 'cause people were wantin' to pull his clothes off him. He was a master showman."

In order to get the fans to accept a female vocalist in 1943, Bob had to do a grand selling job. "Bob called me up and told me that after he heard me sing my daddy's song 'Cattle Call,' he wanted a Texas Playgirl," Laura Lee remembered. "Bob knew what we could do and knew it better than we did. Even if we were sick, we couldn't let him down. He told me to sell him and he would sell me to the people. He was right—-it worked."

These California western swing bands depended on large orchestrations playing mostly pop swing music. Cooley's slicker sound used a harp and accordion that appealed to ballroom audiences. He cut his biggest release, "Shame on You," during his first Columbia session in 1945. Cliffie Stone's Saturday night radio show "Hometown Jamboree" featuring Tennessee Ernie Ford gained popularity on the West Coast during this time. Irving Berlin published three Bob Wills's song books containing band photographs in the immediate postwar years. Jimmie Widener, who played with Bob in California said, "Bob Wills was like Elvis back in those days."

Bob signed a contract with Music Corporation of America (MCA) to handle his bookings, the same agency booking such big bands as Harry James, Bob Crosby, and Kay Kyser. In 1944 the agency reported, "Bob Wills recently broke all records in Oakland . . . his appearance out-grossed even Tommy Dorsey and Benny Goodman's outfits."

His California band with twenty-two members who played horns, reeds, electric guitar, and drums duplicated the Dorsey or Goodman sound. The large band lasted through only one Pacific Northwest tour before he downsized again. His profitable cross-country tours frequently took him back to Oklahoma and Texas. Even though he agreed to play a fraternity dance on the University of Oklahoma campus, he was afraid the college students wouldn't like his music. None of the two thousand students were dancing after they had played two big band songs. Then a shy young man approached the stage and asked Bob to please play his fiddle, which, by the way, was still in the case. "Well, friends, before too much has been said, let's all dance to that old tune called 'Ida Red!'" As soon as those kids heard that first note, they were on their feet.

Bob bought a sixty-acre ranch in the San Joaquin Valley near Fresno, planning to establish a following in the area. While negotiating a contract with a Los Angeles radio station to sell Zoom, an instant cereal, the McKinney Sisters (Dean and Evelyn) auditioned for him in Birmingham, Alabama. As soon as he landed the show, he sent them a telegram asking them to join the band.

"We were only 'bout twenty then," Dean said. "We had never traveled even though we had been on the radio since we were 'bout twelve. We had finally made the big time—Bob was it! We packed our suitcases and took the train to Fresno. A man met us at the railroad station and took us to a roomin' house where some of the other musicians were stayin'. That night someone picked us up and took us out to Bob's ranch. That was when we first met Eldon. We sang for 'bout an hour while Bob sat and did his 'mental cataloging.'" The radio show failed because Bob was constantly on the road. Or perhaps, as Bob said, "Nobody could eat that cereal." But the show's announcer, Jack Webb, later went on to become Sergeant Friday in the TV series "Dragnet."

The McKinney Sisters, decked out in their cowhide uniforms with maroon and navy blue cowboy boots, soon struck out on the road with the band. Dean, impressed with Bob's total protectiveness of her and Evelyn, said, "He was such a dear man. He was absolutely death to those guys if they said a bad word in front of us or made any passes at us. They all treated us like their sisters 'cause of Bob." Despite Bob's paternal watch, Cupid ended their singing careers when Evelyn became Mrs. Billy Jack Wills and Dean became Mrs. Tiny Moore. Bob refused to let them continue as band members after they married. Dean speculated, "Perhaps he thought the other musicians wouldn't be happy if their wives couldn't come along on the road, too."

Due to misguided counsel, Bob severed his association with Columbia Records in 1947 to sign with MGM (an extension of the Metro-Goldwyn-Mayer film domain.) But he never received MGM's promised movie role or bonus money. In a couple of weeks the band cut twenty-six sides heavy on the blues. For the first time since Bob began using drums in 1935, he featured Johnny Cuviello on "Texas Drummer Boy." Cindy Walker's "Bubbles in My Beer," another song from that session, quickly climbed up the charts. Tommy Duncan inspired her when he envisioned a man sitting at a bar alone, not talking to anyone—just watching the bubbles in his beer. Walker said, "You can bet I didn't wait for the water to get hot before I put that one on paper."

Later Bob bought the Aragon Ballroom near Sacramento and renamed it Wills Point. The property also had a large swimming pool, an amusement park, and some apartments. In 1950 he recorded "Faded Love" in another MGM Hollywood session. According to Pat Rolfe of the American Society of Composers, Authors and Publishers (ASCAP), "The song is a genuine standard in the same class with any of the great Hank Williams's songs such as 'Your Cheatin' Heart.'" Billy Jack added lyrics to the old song, which had originally been recorded as an instrumental in the forties. It hit number one on Billboard's C&W charts in September 1950—only a few weeks after Grandma took me to visit my father in Fairfax.

My grandfather John Wills had originally learned the "Faded Love" melody from my great-grandfather Tom Wills and often played it at ranch dances in West Texas. Aunt Lorene said, "If Papa couldn't sleep at night, he'd go out on the back porch and play the fiddle, usually 'Faded Love.' I can still hear that beautiful, lonesome song playin' in the still of the night. No one could play it like he could."

Excerpts from attorney David R. Milsten's eulogy for John Tompkins Wills in 1952 spoke about my grandfather's fiddling days:

John Tompkins Wills, better known as "Uncle John," spent his youth in Limestone County, East Texas, near the town of Grosebeck. His great-grandfather was the community doctor who prescribed for the sick folk and delivered hundreds of pioneer Texans into the Lone Star state. It was from such a background John inherited his stamina as well as his kind and understanding nature. . . .

He was blessed with that rare talent of grasping and bringing to life the music of the western cowboy, better known as western folk music. In his teens he learned to play the fiddle and soon became known as one of the best fiddlers of his community. . . .

John never lost his love for the people he met or his respect for the Golden Rule. If someone became ill and a doctor was needed, it was John who would get up in the early hours of the morning or late at night and ride into town to bring help to the distressed. If a neighbor was in trouble, they would turn to John, who had fiddled his way into their hearts with his talented bow and kindly smile.

Aunt Lorene recalled one night at Cain's when Billy Jack wanted to dance. "Billy wasn't too good a dancer, but I don't think any musician really is. When Bob started playin' a jitterbug number, Billy said, 'Come on, let's just really turn loose here.' We got right in front of the bandstand where Bob couldn't miss us. Then Billy slung me out real fast and I fell down. We got so tickled we couldn't stop laughin' until we noticed Bob frownin' at us as he leaned back with that cigar in his mouth. We were so embarrassed we could hardly get off the floor fast enough."

Billy Jack formed his own band to play at Wills Point after Bob moved to Amarillo in 1953. Billy Jack Wills and His Western Swing Band consisted of Billy Jack, Tiny Moore, Vance Terry, and Tommy Perkins. Their style focused on a "Jump Blues" sound, the forerunner of R&B and rock 'n' roll using a four-four beat rather than Bob's two-four time. While at Wills Point, Billy Jack backed up major names such as Lefty Frizzell and Hank Williams. Drummer Tommy Dee told Leon Rausch, "From Odessa I went to Big Spring with Lefty. We then started playing at Gail's End up on the hill in Big Spring. Lefty put five fiddles together. He loved Bob and Bob Wills's music."

A great photo of Lefty and Bob taken at Wills Point appears in Daniel Cooper's biography *Lefty Frizell.* Cooper described Lefty's early days in El Dorado, Texas, when he listened to Roy Acuff on Nashville's WSM and Bob Wills on Tulsa's KVOO. "Lefty heard it all, but mostly had ears for the Playboys' smooth-voiced singer, Tommy Duncan. Sliding along through 'Trouble in Mind,' Duncan's casual phrasing made perfect control sound lazy. Lefty would not forget that lesson."

Billy Jack often told others about an experience with Hank Williams at Wills Point. "Hank had finished his show and was out in the audience when I did a song of his called 'May You Never Be Alone Like Me.' After I got done, I got to talkin' to him, and he said, 'If you don't have a recordin' contract, I'll get you one right now. Everybody else tries to sound like me when they do my songs, but you don't. You don't sound like anybody else.'" Billy Jack was signed to Four Star Records at the time so he couldn't accept Hank's offer.

The live Sacramento KFBK radio show soon lost the battle to burgeoning television, but Vance Terry saved some radio transcriptions that have recently been rereleased on Jeff Richardson's Joaquin label in San Francisco. Bob insisted that Billy Jack's cover of Bill Haley's "Crazy, Man, Crazy" was better than Haley's own version. Bob told him, "Billy Jack, you've gotta stay with what you got 'cause you're drawin' a younger crowd. They'll grow up with you, just like the ones that come to see me did." Surely Billy Jack was ahead of his time.

The next year Bob once again moved back to California and reorganized Wills Point, putting the ballroom under one management and the swimming pool and amusement park under another. Bob's tours took him as far east as Newark, New Jersey. He received a rousing welcome from a huge Terrace Ballroom gathering when he appeared at a jamboree sponsored by Don Larkin and Lyle Reed, two of New Jersey's favorite disc jockeys. But he spent most of his time in Los Angeles taping a television show and recording for his new label, Decca. His first session included eighteen selections with an emphasis on the older blues and jazz sounds associated with the twenties' so-called race music.

After a fire destroyed the Wills Point ballroom in 1956, Billy Jack dissolved his band and joined Bob on the road again. Johnny Gimble said he felt Billy Jack was one of Bob's best drummers because he played the way Bob wanted a drummer to play. According to Bob, "You can play anything up front, but the beat is what they dance to."

When Bob played in Fresno at The Barn, Billy Jack, Joe Holley, and Alex Brashear joined the Playboys onstage. Billy Jack asked drummer Casey Dickens to let him sit in on a few tunes. "Well, my gosh, it was Billy Jack Wills, the guy who had introduced me to Bob back in 1949. So, I said, 'Well, sure, Bill.'"

"Case, got any brushes?"

"Bill, are you sure you want brushes?"

"Yeah, Tommy has been playin' drums for me, and I haven't been playin' much lately so I need to start off on brushes."

Bob called "Beaumont Rag," a tune strongly dependent on a potent rhythm section. Suddenly the bottom fell completely out! The Playboys cringed when they saw the back of Bob's neck start turning pink. The worse the music sounded to

Bob, the redder his neck got, and by the time they finished the tune, Bob's neck was as red as a beet. Bob spun around to discover Billy Jack on drums.

"Bill, you know the only thing brushes are good for?"

"What do you mean, Jim Rob?"

"Brushes are for paintin' houses, not playin' a Bob Wills dance."

Billy Jack immediately threw the brushes aside and grabbed Casey's sticks. "Yes, sir, whatever you say."

Billy Jack, known for his outstanding sense of humor, loved to play for fun. "It just got to where I didn't want to do it for a livin'. You know, if you're just playin' for yourself, it don't make no difference if you forget the words." He and Evelyn had two children, Jacqueline and Johnny. Billy Jack died at age sixty-five in 1991.

Later in California, string instruments again became dominant, mainly due to economics. They still used horns but with less significance. The front line or fiddle ensemble consisting of Bob on fiddle with one or two other fiddlers founded another "Wills Trademark." Bob spoke fondly about his fiddle. "You know, the fiddle is my life. It tickles me when someone comes up and asks for one of the old fiddle tunes like 'Gone Indian,' one of my daddy's favorites. We do a world of singin', practically everything, but I love to play in Texas 'cause they do know what fiddlin' is. Unfortunately, I didn't record even one-tenth of my own daddy's and granddaddy's tunes."

In a taped interview with Hugh Cherry, Professor Charles K. Wolfe of Middle Tennessee State University stated:

> When Wills started recording in 1935 and 1936, country music had kind of reached a dead-end of sorts. The traditional Southeastern style had gone about as far as it could go. Wills was able to draw upon sources such as black blues, the mariachi music of the Mexican border, and the swing band music and to fuse this into something new and different. As a result, you've got the development of the western component of country and western music and Bob Wills.
>
> One of the things, I think, in spite of all his changes and additions to the music, is that he was an innovator who was still very much aware of his own traditional roots. He didn't turn his back on them. Bob always came back to the fiddle. His father was one of the best fiddlers in Texas.

The 1965 session for Dewey Groom's Longhorn label accented old fiddle tunes, interspersed with bits of conversation. A small, informal group composed of Sleepy Johnson, Marvin Montgomery, and Luke Wills backed up Bob's fiddle on guitar, banjo, and bass. "Many may think this album won't be recognized, but I want to do this for the old timers who request these old tunes at my dances. We don't play them at dances 'cause they don't fit, but this way, they can sit back at home and listen to them. This next tune, 'Faded Love,' is familiar to all, but I want to play it just like my granddad did years ago. You know, my baby brother Billy Jack put the words to it."

Artists ranging from Willie Nelson to the Boston Pops have recorded over three hundred versions of "Faded Love." Felix Slatkin's sweeping orchestration showcases the splendid melody in an album called *Hoedown* (which also re-creates a beautiful "Maiden's Prayer"). Other arrangements by Elvis Presley (fast, upbeat), Ray Price, Mickey Gilley, George Jones, and Patsy Cline offer a variety of interpretations. Bob expressed appreciation for Patsy's rendition when he said, "Boy, she did that up right. Didn't she do that right!" Delaney and Bonnie's (Bramlett) intriguing recording on their *Motel Shot* album (1973) keys the melody primarily from the piano with no fiddle included. Appropriately, Tulsa talent Leon Russell is at the keyboard and can probably be credited with the unique gospel arrangement.

In 1988, thanks to State Senator John Dahl's efforts, "Faded Love" became Oklahoma's official western song, as proclaimed by the Oklahoma Congress on February 1, 1988. This is not to be confused with the official state song, "Oklahoma," or the official state waltz, "Oklahoma Wind." Naturally, the official state musical instrument is a fiddle.

"San Antonio Rose" had the biggest commercial impact for Bob; in his words, "It was the song that took me from hamburgers to steaks." The fashionable big band sound combined with Bob's distinct western swing style strongly appealed to the average American at that time. Without this crossover, Bob probably would have remained unknown beyond the Southwest. After its success, a featured article in Metronome described the band as "some of the finest jazzmen you've ever heard."

Bob often told an amusing story about his first instrumental recording of "San Antonio Rose." He had composed "Spanish Two Step" while living in Roy, New Mexico, in 1927, but he didn't record it until the 1935 session. By the 1938 session Bob had added Joe Frank Ferguson on bass and Ray DeGeer on saxophone. Uncle Art asked, "Bob, does the band have another 'Spanish Two Step'?"

Bob startled the musicians when he answered, "Oh, yeah, we sure do. Okay, boys, let's just play 'Spanish Two Step' backwards." He continued, "What I actually meant was, I usually start in A and then Leon goes to D, so I wanted to start in D and let Leon go to A."

Satherley named this perfect example of quick innovation "San Antonio Rose." Bob said, "How silly to call somethin' more or less close to a breakdown 'San Antonio Rose.' Do you know how much time was spent on the music part of 'San Antonio Rose'? Only 'bout five minutes. And even though it became our most well known song, another one just as popular was 'Trouble in Mind.' People thought we done it first, but we didn't. It had already been recorded, but ours caught on."

After the first "San Antonio Rose," composer Irving Berlin's imposing firm expressed interest in publishing it, if Bob added words. Fred Kramer flew to Tulsa and offered Bob a $300 advance if Bob agreed to write some lyrics (contingent upon company approval) and sign a publishing contract with the Berlin organization. Everett Stover helped Bob write the lyrics, but Berlin's company chose to substitute their own.

Bob's attorney David R. Milsten wrote several letters to Saul Bornstein, Berlin's treasurer and general manager, expressing Bob's dissatisfaction with the changes. Bornstein wrote, "I don't know whether it would be better in its original form, but I'm inclined to believe, having had 25 years' experience in this business, that it would be more acceptable in the corrected form." Milsten reminded Bornstein that he had originally told Bob the song had "that certain something that would stand out." Milsten explained that Bob Wills was not trained in the elements of music, but he had a following that was beyond comprehension, exactly because he had that "certain something." As quoted by Charles Townsend in *San Antonio Rose,* Milsten wrote:

> This entire situation might be likened to the late, beloved Will Rogers. If someone had taken Will and endeavored to school him in the art of public speaking, causing him to lose those treasured eccentricities of speech and mannerisms which he possessed, he would have been just another speaker without appeal, rather than a character whose memory is revered throughout the country.

Finally, after months of legal wrangling, Bob's words were reinstated.

The 1940 version, named "New San Antonio Rose," was the last selection the band recorded for Columbia in Dallas with eighteen musicians. Bob had added Tiny Mott, Louis Tierney, and Don Harlan on saxophones; Everett Stover and Tubby Lewis on trumpet; and Wayne Johnson on clarinet. Even though the earlier instrumental rendition had a beginning fiddle lead and a steel guitar lead in the middle, this rendering with lyrics did not use a fiddle or any other stringed instrument except a guitar. It sounded like any other "popular song of the day," but it was known as western music since it was associated with Bob Wills. Not only was it Bob's most prominent record, it was also one of the few versions he ever recorded without his fiddle. (Most standard selections do feature the fiddle.)

The song's popularity brought Bing Crosby and Bob together in 1942 at Tulsa's Southern Hills Country Club. Mayo said, "Bing came in from the course where he had been playin' golf. And Bob came down with his fiddle in his hand. He had been in California makin' pictures, but he was between pictures. Mr. Way of KVOO was the guy that promoted that thing. They had a lot of people out there 'cause Bing was quite an attraction. When they got ready to do the number, Bing couldn't remember the words! So I had to go off to one side and write the words down for Bing to read so he could sing it."

They recorded a record (an acetate disc) during this live KVOO broadcast and offered it to the person buying the most war bonds. An article in the *Tulsa World* on September 19, 1942, reported that Joseph Bowes, president of Oklahoma Natural Gas Company, set the pace by purchasing a $50,000 bond and Bing gave the record to him. However, several collectors have checked out this story and discovered that Bowes never received the record. It is also alleged that a wealthy oilman paid $250,000 for the limited edition, but this story has not been confirmed.

Since "San Antonio Rose" was in the national spotlight during World War II, many war stories evolved. San Antonio reporter George Carmack wrote:

> I'll never forget one night on the island of Leyte in the Philippines late in World War II. Special Services got a movie. There must have been 500 soldiers sitting on the ground in this little tropical clearing. Tall coconut palms were at the sides and behind the screen. The moon was almost full and not more than 50 yards behind us the white surf was pounding in on a long white beach.
>
> After the movie 'Pygmalion' finished, a short subject came on the screen—Bob Wills and His Texas Playboys singing 'Deep within my heart lies a melody...' Soldiers started hollering, shouting, standing up, and pounding each other on the back. You would have sworn the Japanese would have heard it back in Tokyo.

From the serenade by astronauts Charles Conrad and Alan Bean during Apollo 12 mission in outer space to background music in American shopping malls, "San Antonio Rose" lives on.

Chapter 8

Take Me Back to Tulsa for the Last Time

Died. Bob Wills, 70. Western bandleader and fiddler. . . .
Composer of "San Antonio Rose" and other songs. . . . Wills
developed the Western Swing that featured drums, horns and
electric instruments, besides incorporating elements of jazz
and the blues. Such sounds in the 1930's helped pave the way
for today's blend of country and western music.

—*NEWSWEEK*, MAY 26, 1975

In late 1973 my gut-level feeling knew time was running out for my father. The letter I wrote in therapy, declaring my pain and my love, lay tucked away in a bottom drawer. I agonized for days before mustering the courage to put it in an envelope. I finally mailed my fateful letter that he never read. My stepmother's power surfaced again when James phoned to tell me she felt Bob was too ill to read my letter.

"I love you, honey," my father said at the end of our next phone conversation before I uttered my perfunctory, "I love you, too," and hung up. The impact of his words struck me as I stared at my harvest gold phone anchored to my avocado green kitchen wall. I hoped he didn't think he was talking to one of his other daughters. But then my inner voice asserted, "No, Wait! Don't question it. Just cherish the moment."

A few weeks later Tex Ritter told seven thousand people attending a Fort Worth benefit, "When the Nashville Sound was born, Bob Wills was there." Soon after that, a Nashville audience rose to their feet when my father appeared in his wheelchair to accept a special citation from ASCAP. The award read, "For his long, productive, and creative association with country music—and his unequaled leader-

130

ship as a musician and man." While in Nashville, Bob asked Tommy Allsup to help him fulfill a longtime dream by setting up a recording session with some of his former Texas Playboys. Tommy told me, "I was thrilled when Bob asked me to produce the album. He liked me 'cause I had grown up with a western swing background. I used to work for Johnnie Lee back in '52 and '53."

Tommy's path to producing Bob's albums began after he eluded fate on February 3, 1959. Tommy on guitar, Waylon Jennings on bass, and Carl "Goose" Bunch on drums had replaced twenty-two-year-old Buddy Holly's Crickets (bassist Joe B. Maudlin, guitarist Niki Sullivan, and drummer Jerry Allison). Oklahoman Tommy had joined the group for recording sessions at Norman Petty's studio in Clovis, New Mexico, after Niki Sullivan left the band. A few years earlier Buddy had befriended Waylon, a local Lubbock disc jockey, and even produced Waylon's first single. Buddy and Waylon had grown up in the west Texas plains with their parents listening to native son Bob Wills. The Cotton Club, Lubbock's only real nightclub, had booked everyone from Duke Ellington to Bob Wills to Elvis Presley.

Rockers Ritchie Valens, Dion DiMucci, and J. P. "Big Bopper" Richardson were also on the shabbily conducted tour through minor midwestern cities, rolling from town to town on board an aging bus that suffered from a chronic heater malfunction. Following the Iowa Dance Party at the Surf Ballroom in Clear Lake, Buddy booked a small private plane locally to shuttle him and two passengers to Minnesota, mainly so he would have time to catch up on his laundry before their next gig at the local Moorhead Armory.

Initially, Tommy and Waylon planned to join Buddy on the flight. However, the Big Bopper, suffering from a nasty cold on the frigid sojourn, begged Waylon to let him fly and avoid the chilly bus. Ritchie's win of a coin toss with Tommy allowed him to accompany the other two airborne singers. Dion simply preferred to save his $35 for rent. The three legends—Buddy Holly, Ritchie Valens, and the "Big Bopper"—flew into immortality on that frozen morning when the plane went down. Twelve years later Don McLean's "American Pie" perfectly symbolized the sorrow of "the day the music died."

On December 3, 1973, several former Texas Playboys gathered at the Dallas Sumet-Burnet Studio with my father attending in a wheelchair. (Leon McAuliffe, Eldon Shamblin, Smoky Dacus, and Al Stricklin from the late thirties band; Johnny Gimble, Keith Coleman, and Leon Rausch from later bands; and Hoyle Nix and his son Jody along with other musicians and good friends sat in on the session.) Although the reunion brought many Texas Playboys back together again playing the same songs, Bob's leadership magic was missing. The band faltered but carried on without direction from him—the one who had always made it happen. He contributed one weak "Ah Ha" during "What Makes Bob Holler?" Smiling people yelled, "Hey, ole Bob can still holler!" But after five hours, weakness overcame him and he asked Betty to take him home. That night he suffered a massive stroke.

Merle Haggard arrived in Dallas the second day, missing his chance to record with Bob. Merle said, "Calling Bob's music 'country and western' is as narrowly misleading as saying Louis Armstrong was a trumpet player, period." The two-day session spawned twenty-seven tunes exhibiting the basic blues, jazz, and fiddle breakdowns that define western swing, including three new songs written by Cindy Walker ("Going Away Party," "What Makes Bob Holler?," and "When You Leave Amarillo, Turn out the Lights"). The *Homecoming* album was appropriately renamed *For the Last Time*.

Dr. Charles R. Townsend won a Grammy for Best Album Notes, and the Library of Congress recognized *For the Last Time* as a historical document, establishing my father's contribution to American popular music in general and country and western in particular. The reunion session that produced *For the Last Time* ended my father's forty-four-year recording career that began in 1929 and manifested more than 550 recordings with over a hundred recorded at his career's end between 1963 and 1969.

James phoned the morning after Bob's stroke to tell me they feared he would not live through the weekend. I knew then my children, Chad (age six) and Reneé (age three) would never know him as their grandfather. I called Grandma to tell her the sad news. "Don't you worry, Rosie. Your daddy was saved. He's gonna go to Heaven." Ironically she died within two months and my father lingered in a coma for over seventeen months.

In 1974 Dr. Townsend and his wife, Mary, visited our Sunnyvale home to talk about my recollections of my father. Dr. Townsend's biography *San Antonio Rose*, a definitive book about the etiology of Bob's music, also includes a comprehensive discography and filmusicography compiled by Bob Pinson of the Country Music Foundation. While researching the book, Dr. Townsend interviewed Bob along with former Texas Playboys, collectors, fans, and family members. Dr. Townsend believed that my father's humility did not allow him to feel worthy of a biographical study and felt that the only reason Bob granted interviews was to talk about music. "I was struck with several of Bob's personal characteristics, but most of all by his unbelievable humility."

Grandma Parker called with the news that Pawhuska police had arrested my nineteen-year-old brother Billy for possession of marijuana, a felony during the 1974 reign of Governor David Hall. I sat helpless in California while my weeping Grandma walked the floor, wrung her hands, and stared at the hilltop Osage County jail from her front porch. She didn't believe her guileless grandson was in possession of anything evil or understand why they locked him away in a cell. The officer asked her to leave her purse with him during her visit. After she returned home, she phoned me. "Rosie, the bakin' soda I carry with me for my heartburn was missin' from my purse after I got home from the jail." I wonder how the officer who confiscated the suspicious white powder in the plastic baggie felt after the laboratory analysis.

Grandma, then eighty-three years old, would not discuss leaving her home of thirty-three years. When she experienced a bad fall, she dragged herself to the phone and called her neighbor Mildred for help. No broken bones, but a broken spirit. Four days later she suffered a fatal heart attack. I phoned her every Sunday evening—except that one.

"If I Have Wounded Any Soul Today, God Forgive" played softly during Grandma's service. Remembering her words, "Rosie, be sure they play this at my funeral," I had unearthed the old, ragged sheet music from the piano bench. We also honored her request to be buried in a lovely white shawl she had received for Christmas. My sister Donna and I chuckled when we recalled the time she had asked Grandma if she could borrow the shawl. Grandma's retort, "No, I'm gonna be buried in that," convinced Donna never to ask her if she could borrow anything again. And Grandma's prophecy, "All my people die in February," came true. We buried her next to Grandpa and little David on February 16, 1974.

Even when I was a grown woman with my own children, Grandma called me "Rosie, my baby." Sorting through her belongings after the funeral, I found her note on the back of a 1940 calendar: "This is the year Rosetta was borned [sic], July 25, 1940 at 11:30 am Thursday, This I am keeping for you honey always, Remember me when you see this, will you, and be a good girl. Honey I love you so much too much. Granny Grace."

Billy's dignity kept him from attending Grandma's service in handcuffs escorted by an officer (his only option). When I visited him in jail, he didn't grasp the major crisis facing him. Missing a Dallas concert was his biggest perceived problem. He moaned, "This is Dylan's first tour in eight years and I've got tickets." Misguided youth. However, due to an acclaimed, expensive lawyer's skill and the first offense charge, he escaped the prison sentence Grandma had feared and received five years' probation instead.

On May 13, 1975, James phoned again. "Daddy died today." Although his recovery from his last stroke had seemed impossible, I held on to a faint hope that somehow it wouldn't end this way. Sadness over the death of my dream overwhelmed me. I wondered if it would have made a difference if he had read my letter. But it was over. My father was gone. I drove around the neighborhood trying to sort out my feelings, but as soon as I turned on the car radio, I heard his music playing in the background during the newscaster's report of his death. I heard the report on another radio station and then again on the ten o'clock TV news after I returned home. How bizarre to hear something so personal through the impersonal media.

Phil planned to take a flight the day after my departure and return to California soon after the funeral while I stayed in Oklahoma for a few weeks. My stress level skyrocketed as I drove around the airport frantically searching for a parking place. I had recently broken my right arm when my skates collided with the broken sidewalk jutting up in front of our house. (Chad had warned me not to borrow Kenny's skates, but it looked like so much fun.) After lifting children and loading luggage on the shuttle bus with my arm in a cast, my physical exhaustion intensified the scary take-off. My irrational fear of flying consumed me. Surely trains commuted to and from California, I thought.

The Wills family, the graying Texas Playboys, and close friends gathered at Johnnie Lee's Tulsa home. The somber mood with muffled conversations among minute clusters penetrated the large living room. Most people, including relatives, were strangers to me. Attractive Aunt Ruby looked younger than her age. When introduced to my half-sister Robbie Jo, I didn't know what to say. "Is your mother here?" When she answered, "No, of course not," I wished I hadn't asked. Betty stayed in the back bedroom with her children while Robbie Jo stayed in the front part of the house with the Wills family. After Betty asked me to ride with her in the family car, I wondered about Robbie Jo. I knew hard feelings between them had never been resolved, but I didn't know the whole story.

Years later Robbie Jo told me, "If I hadn't shown up at the funeral, I don't think I'd have been mentioned in the service as one of his children. Betty and I didn't get along. Did you know I slapped her one time?" Apparently Bob visited Robbie Jo and her mother quite often, even between wives, and cried on their shoulders about his current troubles. "He came over one day and told us that Betty was tryin' to trap him and he didn't know what to do. He said he wanted to get out of it. A few minutes after he left our house, Mother said, 'Robbie Jo, let's go for a ride.' I don't know why Mother did this. I guess she just knew him too well."

Betty was eighteen then, only five years older than Robbie Jo. Edna knew where Betty's parents lived so she drove over to their house. As soon as they turned the corner, they spied Bob's car parked at the side. Edna sent Robbie Jo inside to get her father. When she walked through the open front door, she was shocked to find Betty in Bob's arms. When Robbie Jo demanded he leave with her, he refused. She walked over to Betty and slapped her. "I thought I was defendin' my father."

After that scene, Robbie Jo refused to talk to Bob for the next six months. That Christmas her cousin Bobbie Nell arrived in a taxi to take her to visit Bob. Robbie

Jo said, "As soon as Bobbie Nell showed me this big ring she said her sweet Uncle Bob had given her, I knew she had been bribed." The taxi took them to a western wear store near Cain's where Bob and the boys bought their clothes. He was sitting in the back of the store with his back to the front door. After Robbie Jo walked in, he stood up and turned toward her. He held out his arms. "I ran to him and hugged him. We never talked 'bout it. Nothin' more was ever said."

I sat in the front row of the Eastwood Baptist Church with the Wills family. Johnny Gimble, Keith Coleman, and Curley Lewis gently played the fiddles while Eldon moved the pick lightly across his guitar strings. As the familiar "Faded Love" melody played quietly in the background, Clem McSpadden, former U.S. Congressman from Oklahoma, read the eulogy, recalling the Depression years when Bob's daily broadcast added cheer to the gloomy times.

Betty broke down when the pallbearers rolled the casket to the back of the church after the fiddles began "San Antonio Rose." Long lines slowly passed by the casket to view his body. Months of lying in a coma had made him almost unrecognizable. In an appalling lack of privacy, the television cameras focused on Betty's tear-stained face as she left the church.

They buried Bob under the elm trees in Memorial Park Cemetery, where he rests beneath a headstone bearing the epitaph "Deep Within My Heart Lies A Melody."

We sat together in silence on the ride back to Johnnie Lee's house. Even though the last seventeen months had been a tremendous burden, I knew Betty was devastated. She had stayed devoted to the end. Family and friends came back to the house to reminisce about the old days. James and his wife, Eva, left with Phil and me since it was our first opportunity to spend some time together since the early seventies. It was good to see James again. I had missed him.

I rode the train to Houston to visit Donna and her husband, Don, before returning to California. That weekend I had a heart-rending experience when we met some San Antonio friends in a small piano bar on the River Walk. After the pianist learned I was in the audience, he played "San Antonio Rose" in tribute to my father. Everyone in the bar stood up.

The ten-hour rail trip with two restless children temporarily cured my fear of flying. The next week I boarded a California-bound plane and ordered a double scotch phobia-buster. My children ran rampant up and down the aisle as I listened to soothing music on the headphones until we touched down in San Francisco. When we arrived home, the overflowing mailbox and pile of newspapers on the dry, scorched grass broadcast Phil's absence while I was gone. Hours turned into days when "Deal again" dominated his life.

Friends sent me clippings and articles about my father's death from numerous newspapers and magazines all over the country (*New York Times, National Observer, Houston Chronicle, Tulsa Tribune, Tulsa Daily World, Dallas Morning News, Amarillo Daily News, Rolling Stone, Kansas City Star*).

The *Dallas Morning News* of May 16, 1975, reported:

> Wills died the other day at 70 after years of retirement from the business at which he succeeded so admirably—the business of making Americans happy. . . . His style is a musical genre that is of the people, by the people, and for the people: The people Bob Wills moved so regularly, so joyously. And who will surely miss him.

The May 26, 1975, issue of *Time* read:

> Died. Bob Wills, 70. Western Swing bandleader-composer. Wills turned out dance tunes that are now called country rock introducing such C&W classics as "Take Me Back To Tulsa" and "New San Antonio Rose."

Ironically, I noticed dancer Ann Miller's photo appeared on the opposite page of the *Newsweek* obituary. I recalled she had starred as a dance hall girl in Bob's 1940 movie, *Go West Young Lady*, when she was only eighteen years old. (Her mother sat on the set during the entire filming.) Yousuf Karsh's photo for an *Esquire* interview had captured her coveted image. The caption read: "All my life I have tried to be an eight-by-ten glossy."

I soon received a phone call from a troubled Robbie Jo concerning our father's will. Her letter with a copy of the will and an estate inventory arrived the next day:

> *May 17, 1975*
>
> *Dear Rosetta,*
> *Here is a copy of the will and inventory—I really question separate property because any records, etc. before they were married is separate. Oh, well, I guess since all royalties are left to Betty, it makes no difference. It's late. It was nice talking to you.*
>
> *Sincerely,*
> *Robbie Jo*

My heart pounded as I unfolded the Last Will and Testament of James Robert Wills, scanning the written words quickly, and settling on the major points of interest to me:

... I hereby declare that I am married, that my wife's name is BETTY LOU ANDERSON WILLS, and that of my marriage to Betty Lou Wills four (4) children have been born, to-wit: JAMES ROBERT WILLS, a son, and CAROLYN WILLS, DIANE WILLS, and CINDY WILLS, daughters.

I further declare that I have two children by former marriages, to-wit: ROBBIE JOE [sic] CALHOUN, formerly Robbie Joe [sic] Wills, a daughter; and ROSETTA ARNETT, formerly Rosetta Wills, a daughter. I declare no other children have been born to or adopted by me.

(1) I hereby give, devise, and bequeath unto my daughter, ROBBIE JOE CALHOUN, formerly Robbie Joe Wills, the sum of One Dollar ($1.00) and my love and affection.

(2) I hereby give, devise, and bequeath unto my daughter, ROSETTA ARNETT, formerly Rosetta Wills, the sum of One Dollar ($1.00) and my love and affection. . . .

The last phrase attacked me like a sharp dart striking my heart. The sum of One Dollar ($1.00) and my love and affection? I had never expected to receive anything, but those words offended me, even if it represented legalese written to keep heirs from contesting a will. At least my name was spelled correctly. I understood Robbie Jo's concern as she and her mother, Edna, had preserved an alliance with Bob and the Wills family for years. Robbie Jo had stayed close to her father, who had paid her college expenses at Southern Methodist University. But Betty alone received the sizeable estate, including all existing royalties, without sharing it with the Wills family or his two older children. I visualized my Aunt Lorene's flaming black eyes when Betty told her that Robbie Jo and I had been left out of the will and imagined her angry response, "Well, that sure doesn't sound like Jim Bob to me!"

My analytical mind refused to let anger destroy my family relationship with Betty. Many events had taken place since this will was written twelve years earlier following Bob's first heart attack. In 1963 Betty did not have a friendly connection with Robbie Jo, and she had never met me. Bob knew Robbie Jo and I were both married, but if anything happened to him, Betty would be left alone with no skills to support four children. Since he lost his royalties to "San Antonio Rose" and other valuable property during the early fifties, he probably assumed there wouldn't be a considerable estate. He didn't know that years later entertainers would rally together and play benefits in Tulsa, Fort Worth, and San Antonio that raised large sums. Or he may not have even read what he signed. Surely he would have noticed Robbie Jo's name was spelled wrong. My acceptance of the will was crucial to my future relationship with Betty and my peace of mind. Let it be.

"Look out, friends, here's Leon! Take it away, my boy, take it away!" Hearing my father's voice startled me. Then Leon McAuliffe's time-honored "Steel Guitar Rag" played through the P.A. system in the SJSU Student Union. Definitely not Barbara Mandrell's version. I soon learned that KFAT radio had gained favor with the students by featuring old C&W music daily. Western swing had achieved momentum again with groups like Pure Prairie League (with lead singer Vince Gill), Cornell Hurd, Dan Hicks & His Hot Licks, Asleep at the Wheel, and Commander Cody and His Lost Planet Airmen performing in the San Francisco scene. Commander Cody played Austin's Armadillo World Headquarters and Tulsa's Cain's in 1975.

"Why don't you call a KFAT deejay, tell 'em who you are, and get us some free tickets to Willie's upcoming concert?" my friend Judy suggested.

"Gosh, Judy, I don't know. I never thought about doin' anything like that. Willie's pretty big, you know."

In 1963 Bob had written the liner notes for a Liberty album by an unknown artist titled *Here's Willie Nelson*. Ten years later Willie's Outlaw Music rose to stardom. He often played "Stay a Little Longer," "Milk Cow Blues," "Bubbles in my Beer," and other Wills's standards. I had become a genuine Willie fan after listening to his *Phases and Stages* album. In 1974 Willie wrote an exceptional article about my father for *Country Music* magazine that was reprinted in a 1984 issue.

When Willie was thirteen, his brother-in-law Bud Fletcher (married to his sister Bobbie) booked Bob to play a dance in Whitney, Texas. Willie managed to get onstage and play along on a couple of songs. He grew up in Texas playing small clubs where folks easily recognized a Bob Wills tune. "Until Hank Williams came along, it was just Bob Wills. He was it. I have been an admirer of Bob Wills all my life."

"Is that Willie Nelson?" I didn't recognize him the first time I saw him backstage wearing a wandering troubadour's cap and dirty tennis shoes. I expected a Waylon Jennings look-alike wearing a white hat and cowboy boots. The KFAT deejay had put me in touch with Mark Rothbaum, Willie's business manager, who arranged for free tickets and backstage passes. Loose backstage security in the mid-seventies allowed folks to help themselves to the beer in the iced-down barrel sitting next to the stage or relish the joints being passed around.

Willie got carried away with hats. He walked over near the stage's edge, took off his hat, and threw it to the onlookers, enjoying the wild struggle to catch it. Then when someone tossed another hat to Willie, he wore it until he threw it back. He continued this game throughout the concert. One night Phil caught Willie's dark brown felt cowboy hat with tiny Lone Star Beer and State of Texas replicas on it!

"Bob's daughter is in the audience tonight. Stand up, wherever you are." Unaccustomed to public acknowledgment, I froze in my seat when the spotlight swept over the Oakland concert audience. Then Willie launched into an upbeat "Stay a Little Longer." At another outdoor concert in Oakland, hundreds of Hell's Angels came roaring backstage on mammoth, bellowing Harley-Davidsons. The backstage pass stuck onto the right thigh of my jeans let me move freely backstage, but I didn't see their passes. I asked the security guard if they had passes, too. He asked me, "Sweetheart, have you ever tried to keep a Hell's Angel from goin' backstage?"

In 1976 Waylon Jennings introduced "Bob Wills Is Still the King" (an Austin anthem) during an Austin Opry House concert. He later recalled his days on the road that inspired that song (as quoted in *Waylon: An Autobiography*): "I played San Antonio twice a month—the Stallion Club, the Mustang Club, or somethin' like that. They all had those big Bob Wills' dance floors. I'd get up on the long bandstand, built for a twelve-piece cowboy orchestra, and I'd be tellin' my four guys to start spreadin' out. . . . The people liked our songs, but they couldn't dance to them."

Crossing that Red River scored the difference between the formal Nashville concert scene and the informal Austin roadhouse scene. Waylon's proclamation about Bob Wills still being the king regardless of who lives in Austin caused the folks to scream with surprise because they assumed Waylon was putting Willie down on his own turf. But the truth is, it was just a little jab because Waylon knew Willie agreed: "By now country music is mixed up in everything. But it was Bob Wills who put it all together for me, and it was our old Philco radio that taught it to me. As Waylon says, Bob Wills *is* still the king."

During an Outlaw concert in San Jose featuring Willie, Waylon, Jessie Colter (Waylon's wife), and Tompall Glaser, security escorted us back to the dressing rooms where I watched Jesse meticulously apply her make-up while Waylon wrote a note to my children: "To Chad and Reneé, Your grandpa was the greatest and so are your mom and dad. Love, Waylon Jennings."

Intrigued by the story of my first meeting with my father, an aspiring young songwriter helped me compose a ballad. I excitedly called James to tell him about the song, but he sounded uninterested and said it was about time I just let Bob's memory die.

GOD BLESS YOU, HONEY
By Dave Younger and Rosetta Wills

Ahh-Ha, it's Saturday night, Take it away, boys . . . take it away.
He arrives in his yellow, convertible car.
He's known by his white hat, fiddle and cigar, He's the King of the
  Country,

This Western Swing star.
To them his life is pure delight, He's loved by all.
His work is light.
He's their king
Western Swinging, singing star.

The crowd came to see him
From factory and farm, They're hungry for music and his special charm.
How can the child who's seen him so rarely
Remind him she's been left behind?
She approaches him shyly, Her lips start to tremble,
"My name is Rosetta" is all that came to her mind.
She is so young to have lost her first man.
He hasn't seen her so long, what can he say to this ten-year-old child?

His life is his music, and the words come from a song:
God bless you, Honey.
God bless you, Honey.

They sit in a coffee shop, Hero and fan,
The ten-year-old daughter
And her Western Swing man.
But the crowd's cheering louder,
Now what can he say?
So he says, "God bless you, Honey;
God bless you, Honey,"
and they take him away.

Grandparents John and Emma Wills, Tulsa, Oklahoma in the 1950s *(Courtesy Rosetta Wills).*

The Wills Girls. *Standing, left to right:* Ruby, Olga, and Eloise; *seated, left to right:* Helen and Lorene *(Courtesy Lorene Wills).*

The Wills boys with their parents. *Standing, left to right:* Luke and Billy Jack;
Seated, left to right: Johnnie Lee, John, Emma, and Bob *(Courtesy Lorene Wills).*

Bob Wills at his sixtieth birthday bash at Dewey Groom's Longhorn Ranch, Dallas,
March 6, 1965 *(Courtesy Rosetta Wills)*.

The sixtieth birthday bash. *Left to right,* Johnnie Lee, Emma, Bob, and Luke
(Courtesy Rosetta Wills).

The sixtieth birthday bash. *Seated, left to right:* Phil Arnett, Rosetta Wills Arnett, Carole Wills, Bobby Wills, Carolyn Wills, Cindy Wills, and Betty Wills; *standing, left to right:* Diane Wills and James Wills *(Courtesy Rosetta Wills).*

The sixtieth birthday bash. *Standing, left to right:* Dorothy Wills, Helen Wills McKee, Emma Wills, Johnnie Wills, Eloise Wills House, Jim McKee; *seated, left to right:* Carolyn Wills, Betty Wills, and Bobby Wills *(Courtesy Lorene Wills).*

Left to right: Betty Wills, Bob Wills, unidentified man, and Merle Haggard at Haggard's Bakersfield, California, home in September, 1971 *(Courtesy Rosetta Wills).*

Bob Wills and unidentified girl in 1948 *(Courtesy Lorene Wills).*

Left to right: Luke Wills, Johnnie Lee Wills, Bob Wills, and Billy Jack Wills, early 1950s *(Courtesy Lorene Wills).*

Bob Wills in the early 1950s *(Courtesy Lorene Wills).*

Above: Buck Wayne Johnston and Bob Wills, KROD-TV on-the-air interview, El Paso, Texas, in 1952 *(Courtesy Buck Wayne Johnston).*

Left: Bob Wills and Tommy Duncan in the early 1960s *(Courtesy Lorene Wills).*

Bob Wills and His Texas Playboys in the forties. *Left to right:* Junior Barnard (guitar), Johnnie Lee Wills (guitar), Bob Wills (fiddle), Cotton Thompson (fiddle), Luke Wills (bass), Jesse Ashlock (fiddle), Harley Huggins (guitar), and Millard Kelso (piano) *(Courtesy Rosetta Wills).*

Overleaf: Bob Wills and His Texas Playboys at the Casa Mana in California, 1943. *Left to right:* Noel Boggs (steel guitar), Jack McElroy, Joe Holley (fiddle), Joe Galbraith, Louis Tierney (fiddle), Billy Jack Wills (drums), Rip Ramsey (bass), Bob Wills (fiddle), Millard Kelso (piano), Jimmy Wyble (guitar), Laura Lee Owens (vocals), Cameron Hill (guitar), and Tommy Duncan (vocals) *(Courtesy Rosetta Wills).*

Above: Tommy Duncan and Bob Wills in the 1940s *(Courtesy Harvey Tedford).*

Right: Bob Wills and Billy Jack Wills in the 1940s *(Courtesy Lorene Wills).*

Chapter 9

Urban Cowboys to Aging Playboys

*Wills' music has not dated. The combination of jazz, blues,
bar stories and hot strings reaches so freely and resonantly
into what Wills called "human feeling" that it retains its
immediacy. And its utterly relaxing, flowing ease.*

—NAT HENTOFF,
"THE TIMELESS FIDDLER," *WALL STREET JOURNAL*

Sunday morning my friend Judy suspiciously eyed my turquoise-beaded leather
choker with the bright red feather in the center. "Some things never change. I put
on my white gloves to go to church. Rosetta puts on a feather to go see Willie
Nelson." Her gaze then swept past my skimpy baby blue halter top and bell-bottom
jeans, and rested on my earth-tone sandals. "Proper attire for Willie's Fourth of July
Picnic, I suppose?" My friends just nodded and snickered as we checked out of
Pawhuska's sole motel, headed home (or to a picnic) with fond memories of our
twentieth high school class reunion in 1978. A few days before the reunion I had
asked a stranger in a Tulsa bar wearing a familiar orange-and-black sweatshirt
boasting a large "P" on the front (Huskies' colors) if he was also from Pawhuska, but
he curtly informed me his "P" stood for Princeton.

Five hours later the Dallas Cotton Bowl attendant said, "Rosetta Wills already
picked up her tickets and backstage passes." I flashed my driver's license in his face
again, insisting loudly, "I'm Rosetta Wills. I haven't picked up anything!" We pleaded and begged until he finally gave the six of us passes. We socialized backstage as
we sipped complimentary drinks from a frozen margarita machine.

Fellow revelers rushed the immense stage for the choice seats quickly filling up
in the wings. Phil and my brother Billy won the shoving match with a security
guard who refused to let us up there. Sitting a few feet from the performers, we
surveyed the same sea of humanity stretching for miles in front of the stage. What

a vantage point. In the free-spirited atmosphere, the unbearable heat spurred young girls sitting on boys' shoulders to shed their tops.

The strong, sweet aroma swirling around in the outdoor air got you high just breathing. My brother-in-law Don's Camel cigarettes crushed in his back pocket required effort to roll and repair before lighting. A security guard frowned as he watched him light up. He quickly approached him from behind, tapping him on the shoulder. "Hey, man, can I have a hit?" Don calmly handed over the cigarette. After inhaling deeply the guard said, "Oh, man, that's good stuff." Don grinned at the power of suggestion. "Sure, man, have some more."

As the sun went down the gala spectacle kept me spellbound. Thousands screamed loudly when Waylon belted out, "Once you're down in Texas, Bob Wills is still the King." My spirit soared higher when Willie began a medley with "Will the Circle Be Unbroken" and closed with "Amazing Grace," bringing back special memories of my Grandma Grace. The grand finale "Whiskey River" once again took my mind and whisked the audience into jubilant hysteria.

Rita Coolidge "watched closely now" when gorgeous Kris Kristofferson swept me up in a big hug as he kissed my forehead. His deep, sexy voice whispered in my ear, "Your daddy was a hero." Donna tried to capture the moment on film, but my curly hair blocked out Kris's handsome face. Then I spotted native Tulsan Gary Busey standing nearby. I wanted his autograph for eleven-year-old Chad, who had built his first drum set out of cardboard boxes and played *The Buddy Holly Story* soundtrack constantly. Gary scrawled "To Chad, Bob Wills Is *Still* the King. Yours—Gary Busey" on the back of a blank deposit slip I hastily extracted from my purse.

Fifteen years later, I again spotted Gary Busey backstage, this time at Willie Nelson's sixtieth birthday party at Antone's. Busey had arrived in Austin from Dallas, where he had unveiled bronze memorial busts of Texans Buddy Holly, Blind Lemon Jefferson, and Bob Wills for the Texas Music Alley exhibit. (In 1929 Blind Lemon Jefferson had recorded "Corrine, Corrina," eleven years prior to Bob's first recording. But Bob's vocal version became a bluesy western swing standard. Even Bob Dylan and Eric Clapton have recorded the old tune.)

Busey's gaze scrutinized Chad's girlfriend Cindy, an attractive twenty-two-year-old U.T. student with long, straight black hair. After overhearing several flirtatious remarks, Chad whispered in Cindy's ear, "Hey, did you tell him you were only seven years old when he did *The Buddy Holly Story*? Huh! Did you tell him?"

Chad's friend Mike, unduly animated after meeting Gary Busey in the flesh, kept jabbering, "Mr. Busey, Mr. Busey, this is such a thrill! I loved you in *Under Siege*. Gosh, Mr. Busey." Busey admonished Mike to calm down or everyone would think he was wired. Mike assured Busey he was clean. "Oh, no, sir, I don't have any drugs. But if I had any good drugs, I'd give them to you." Busey emphatically denied any interest in illegal drugs but cautioned Mike about the possible presence of "narcs" backstage.

During that 1978 class reunion, Phillip Fortune's camera had clicked at me constantly. I soon learned he had collected my father's records and other memorabilia ever since high school, but I didn't even know he was a fan. The next year Ralph Emery interviewed Phillip on *Nashville Now*. Phillip had been a longtime Jack and Woody Guthrie fan and was elated when Arlo Guthrie appeared on the same show. I appreciated his concern when he said, "All of us collectors feel Bob's biggest fault was not spendin' enough time with you. I know in the music business an entertainer rarely has any free time at all."

Phillip helped organize the first annual "Legends of Western Swing" music festival held at the Pawhuska Fairgrounds in 1988. Luke Wills, Johnny Gimble, Frankie McWhorter, Glynn Duncan, and Speedy West played for the first event. West had served as a pedal steel player on more than six thousand jazz, pop, and C&W records during the forties in California.

I nervously climbed the wobbly steps leading to the stage microphone where Dr. Charles R. Townsend introduced me. A strange sensation fell over me as I spoke to the strangers about my father, recognizing that many had traveled long distances from other states. After the show, folks asked me to sign scraps of paper as their memories harked back to Bob's dances. The steadfast supporters who attended those dances have never forgotten my father, and I wondered how large the Pawhuska crowd would be if he were still performing. Aunt Lorene and Uncle Luke were the only other family members there. I was pleased to learn that some of Luke's recordings on Victor had recently been reissued by the Bear Family, a West German record company.

Aunt Lorene said, "I was about fifteen years old when Bob married your mother. I remember Mother and I were sittin' at the table with Bob that day. With a very solemn expression he said, 'I'm gonna go get Mary Lou and we're gonna go get married tonight.' I said, 'Well, Jim Bob, you're gonna go get married tonight and you're eatin' onions!' You know, he loved onions. When he used to come in off the road to the house, we'd all be so proud to see him. Mother would get in the kitchen and fix him a big breakfast. One time he said, "Oh, Mama, this is everythin'. It's just so good but there's one little thing missin'." She said, 'Oh, Robbie, I know, but we're out of 'em.' Of course, it was onions they were talkin' about."

Aunt Lorene and Bobbie Nell (Aunt Ruby's daughter) began attending Cain's dances when they turned sixteen. "As I've always said, Bob had eyes in the back of his head. He didn't miss a thing. He told us, 'If you hear anybody talkin' about us or sayin' anything, you ignore it. Act like you didn't hear it or you don't know who they're talkin' about.' We were brought up to never open our mouths about anything. If we wanted to go anywhere after the dance, we had to check with him. We were as leery of him as we were of Daddy."

Uncle Luke joined Bob's band after Johnnie Lee disbanded his Ryhthmaires in 1938. He played the banjo until his chance to learn the bass fiddle came along. "You know, Bob always played a tune twice. He would finish and then start over again. That came from the days when he played ranch dances with Papa. They had to play to the dancers in one room of the house and then turn and play it again to the dancers in another room of the house."

Uncle Luke smiled as he pondered, "I got started with Bob when the band was still in the stagin' process, what I mean, it was growin'. Biggest thrill of my life was gettin' to play the bass. I got into likin' the bass pretty good and didn't even dread the next job if it was two hundred miles away." We reminisced about the times he played the old Pawhuska Whiting Hall. "We used to haul them instruments up three flight of steep steps. Kinda like climbin' a slanted ladder. Now they have an elevator. I ought to really be mad about that. They used to have a big old mine fan. I don't know if you're familiar with that, but it's big and round. Used them in mines to blow gas or somethin' out. Them people that danced by it nearly lost their step every time."

Our 1978 return to Oklahoma did not save our marriage even though I thought going back to our roots just might heal our wounds. Twice I had tried to file for divorce in California, only to leave the lawyer's office in a physical panic. We had too much history. But we also had too much pain. For years my idealizations had kept me from acting. My parents' divorce when I was less than a year old adversely affected me. Divorce is never easy for children; there are just different problems with different ages. Chad (age thirteen) and Reneé (age ten) were crushed. After our 1980 breakup, I drank too much wine when I listened to Jackson Browne's morose lyrics from his *Late for the Sky* album written after his wife's suicide. And Willie's "Till I Gain Control Again" became my theme song.

Michael Jackson's "Beat It" blared from Reneé's bedroom when she practiced her junior high cheerleading routine over and over. At the other end of the hall upstairs, Chad's drums, Eric's bass, and Richard's guitar blasted "Purple Haze" throughout the house, making my eclectic taste in music a blessing. I had lost control over my teenagers after they passed their driving tests. Their obsession with propelling themselves through space began innocently when we pulled them around in wagons. Then tricycles pedaled independently led to small pedal-type cars, skates, skateboards, bicycles, mopeds, and motorcycles—culminating with the almighty car. At age fourteen Chad legally rode his moped on his paper route and progressed to a real motorcycle by the next year. With his arm held out, he rode it past a pole and smashed his right hand; he rode it into a pond and buried it in deep mud; he rode it off a steep hill and broke his collarbone and his right arm. I sold the motorcycle.

In 1984 David Stallings of Delta Records rallied as many as possible of the six-hundred-plus musicians who had played with Bob for a reunion show in Tulsa. Bob always said, "Any ole boy was an original Texas Playboy if he played one night with me—and got paid." Tiny Moore once told his wife, Dean, "You won't believe this, but I actually met a musician tonight that never played with Bob!" The fiftieth Anniversary Texas Playboy Reunion (fifty years since the first KVOO broadcast) had its share of drama. On the night before the concert, in a jam session at the hotel across the street from the Convention Center, drummer Bill Mounce, age sixty-seven, died of a heart attack.

Many attendees loaded down with cameras and tape recorders came from California's Bay Area. I even ran into "Stompin'" Steve Hathaway, a collector and publisher of the *Western Swing Newsletter,* whose premiere issue came out in early 1985 and which still serves as a clearinghouse of information for western swing aficionados to present preliminary discographies and articles on the subject. In the seventies when I took Chad and Reneé to his Sunnyvale apartment to view 16mm films of Bob's movies, I had a better appreciation than I did in the fifth grade, but Bob's grandchildren laughed. "He's corny." C'est la vie.

After Bob's death, I lost contact with Betty even though I had talked with James a few times. Since she wasn't aware that I had returned to Tulsa, my attendance at the Tulsa show surprised her. She had remarried in 1976 but sadly informed me that her husband Jimmie Sheets had died of a heart attack three months earlier. She asked David to send me complimentary tickets the next year. Diane and Cindy attended with her, but Carolyn was living in Seattle. I have never seen James at any celebrations for our father.

KVOO's Billy Parker (Academy of Country Music Disc Jockey of the Year Award winner twice in the seventies and again in 1984) and Leon McAuliffe hosted the 1985 event, which drew over four thousand. The Original Texas Playboys opened the show with "Brother" Al Stricklin, now seventy-eight, still pounding that piano, and Eldon Shamblin carrying it all with his rhythm guitar. After the show the cameras clicked steadily as I visited with the musicians. Brother Al, who wandered around hugging everyone and shaking hands, told me, "Our 1937 recording of 'Rosetta' was the best one among that bunch. Your daddy did a beautiful job of singin' it." The reunion, more of an event than a concert, once again played the music that made you feel warm inside.

I spotted Michael Gerald in the packed auditorium. A few weeks earlier at a party in my home, my friend Janell had whispered, "Three guys are hangin' out in the kitchen who nobody knows." I took a look and decided I had found the man I was looking for. "Don't worry, Janell. I don't think they'll steal the silver." My friend Barbara had invited her friend Carmenita, who had invited her friend Murl, who had invited his friend Howard, who had invited his friend Michael, who kept a persistent gaze on me as I rocked to Bob Seeger's "Old Time Rock and Roll." Toward the end, the hard-core partygoers played Bob's old records as they poured another drink. Parties at my house ended with the late-nighters dancing to Wills classics and "stayin' all night," even if they didn't throw their coats in the corner.

Meeting Michael introduced positive changes in my life, but 1985 also brought tragedy. Puzzling fatigue and swollen joints confirmed eighteen-year-old Chad's diagnosis of Systemic Lupus Erythematosus (SLE). Lupus, a chronic sickness, affected his body's immune system by producing too many antibodies (the opposite of AIDS). They attacked his healthy organs, targeting his blood and kidneys. No cure existed and remission was his only hope. He battled the illness and subsequent drug addition in cold, sterile hospital rooms, turning his days into nightmares. His sudden malady touched the whole family. During his earlier hospital stays, we all took balloons, candy, cards, and special gifts to the room. Eight years later we were promising to visit him if we weren't too tired at the end of the working day.

Our focus on Chad thrust fifteen-year-old Reneé into the background. Sensitive, caring Reneé kept a journal, and the Tulsa Junior League magazine published one of her poems.

UNDERSTANDING

Hanging on for quiet desperation,
Looking for alleviation,
Tired of living in this constant
hibernation.

I'm needing, needing to find
the one to end my search,
to tell me exactly what it is
I am looking for.

I need someone to finish
what all the others just started.
I watch the world through saddened eyes,
understanding so much that I seldom
wish to belong.

The games are just too involved.
All reality is gone.
I say too much that no one understands,
unless they read between my lines,
or see through the vail of vagueness
that I often hide behind.

Collective concern over Chad's cruel illness thawed the cold war between Phil and me. Chad's torment forced us all to examine what was important in life. Our love for our children had kept a bond between us, and we gradually became friends again, releasing our anger over our failed marriage. Control over his gambling addiction had brought peace back into Phil's life. A commitment to Michael tempted me, but the end of his five-year marriage the previous year made him skeptical about relationships. At my stubborn insistence, he patiently listened to Pink Floyd's double album *The Wall,* but our common admiration for Cat Stevens's 1973 *Foreigner* gave me whimsical hope. If he could live with my insatiable appetite for music, he could surely live with my teenagers.

Important things took place in Tulsa after Larry Shaeffer bought Cain's Dancing Academy located at 423 North Main Street, perhaps the most famous address in the Southwest. He revived the old-fashioned dance hall by booking many new, rising groups (mostly not country) throughout the eighties, including the Pretenders, the Sex Pistols, U2, Annie Lennox, R.E.M., Van Halen, Pat Benatar, Bon Jovi, INXS, Elvis Costello, the Police, Huey Lewis, and Eric Clapton, as well as Muddy Waters, Ernest Tubb, and Arlo Guthrie. Cain's, now designated a historical site and dubbed the "Carnegie Hall of Country Music," is the one place in Oklahoma all bands want to play at least once. Uncle Luke told me, "Everything centered around Cain's. It seemed like we were raised right there. That's where it all happened."

Endless stories about Cain's performances abound by word of mouth and printed material. Even Hank Williams (whose photo hangs on the wall) allegedly passed out on Cain's red couch and slept through his second show. Hank was so embarrassed about missing the set that he asked then Cain's Manager Mayo to just buy him a ticket back to Nashville for his pay. In 1979 Jerry Lee Lewis reportedly consumed twelve Coney Islander hot dogs and two quarts of whiskey before he entertained a full house for three hours. Arlo Guthrie made a film there for the Smithsonian Institute and Francis Ford Coppola used Cain's as a setting in his 1983 film *Rumblefish.* In 1994 when Hal Ketchum filmed a C&W music video there, he said, "It's a real shrine to the Wills boys and all the great artists of the western swing era."

Larry has expanded Bob Wills's birthday tributes into annual two-day festivals. (Luke Wills, Truitt Cunningham, Eldon Shamblin, Bobby Koefer, Clarence Cagle, Curly Lewis, Bob Boatright, and Tommy Perkins played the 1995 event.) Larry told a Tulsa reporter:

> Bob Wills was charismatic. Everyone in the crowd felt he was Bob's personal friend.
>
> One of the most important things in musical history happened right here at 423 North Main Street. I've been here for 18 years, and in that time, I've heard a lot of things about just how popular Bob Wills was.
>
> I've been told, for instance—and this may be electronically impossible, I don't know—that some of the boys in World War II were able to pick up portions of the live broadcasts from Cain's in the Philippine Islands.

My father's legacy has allowed me to meet superb entertainers such as Alvin Crow, David Allan Coe, Bonnie Raitt, Melissa Etheridge, and others who have performed at Cain's. Alvin Crow played his fiddle with the same feel as Bob evidenced by his rare form on "Gone Indian," the old breakdown Bob learned from his father. Alvin and his Pleasant Valley Boys performed their classic hit "Nyquil Blues" during their Cain's show. Alvin told me my father had a tremendous influence on his music, and that he, too, had grown up in a family of fiddlers.

David Allan Coe looked as if he might melt from the heat generated by his heavy black leather outfit during his electrifying act. After the show Larry took Billy and me out back to David's bus. Sitting in the driver's seat still dripping from his shower with a towel casually thrown across his lap, the informal Coe invited us in. We spent the next half hour discussing music and filmmaking.

As an early Bonnie Raitt fan ever since I saw her perform on California's Stanford campus in 1974, her Cain's show thrilled me. It took another decade for the music world to acknowledge her brilliance. In the nineties my younger friends refused to believe *Nick of Time* was not her first album. After her Cain's gig she unexpectedly showed up at the Paradise, an after-hours club, where she jammed with Jimmy Byfield and Debbie Campbell. She astonished me when she told the band, "Hey guys, this is Bob Wills's daughter! Isn't that great!"

At another Cain's show an unknown performer, billed as an acoustic folk singer, dazed us with her driving rhythm after she hit her first lick on her twelve-string guitar. Six years later we caught Melissa Etheridge's Austin show at Bass Concert Hall, a year prior to her opening for the Eagles' *Till Hell Freezes Over* tour in the imposing San Antonio Alamodome. But her commanding performance in the more intimate Cain's setting was easily the most memorable (with her Kansas parents in the audience).

Memories of listening to Bob's late-night radio broadcasts, attending my first Cain's dance in the fifties, and watching him perform there in the sixties tug nostalgically on my senses. No matter whom I watch on that stage, his framed three-foot by four-foot likeness watches me. I treasure a drawing of me next to his Cain's portrait, sketched by Tulsa artist Jack Miller. In my mind, Cain's and my father are one.

In 1996 I once again sat under his watchful eye when I attended a play performance at Cain's. *Take Me Back to Tulsa,* written by Northeastern State University professors Carl Farinelli and James Walker, told about Bob's flight from the stifling "Pappy" Lee O'Daniel. The realistic re-creation of Light Crust Flour commercials confused an elderly gentleman near the stage who said, "I wish they would quit advertisin' that flour 'cause you can't get it around here no more." Tim Gilliam, the young actor who portrayed Bob, captured Bob's mannerisms as he pointed his fiddle bow at the authentic Playboys who joined him onstage at the end for a heart-rending conclusion. Carl said, "It was a dream of ours to actually perform on the same stage where it all started over sixty years ago."

"Brother, Can You Spare a Dime?" In retrospect, that song is a theme for the thirties, the Great Depression years. When times were hard, jobs were scarce, and nobody had any money, the luxury of entertainment was unimaginable unless the prices were low. Back then a dime paid a child's way into any movie theater in the country. But most folks got free entertainment from the radio—the theater of the mind that required the listener to become an integral part of its presentation. Most radio shows came from the networks, but the Tulsa radio scene was Bob Wills and His Texas Playboys, who enticed hundreds to their Cain's broadcasts. Thousands of radios were tuned in at noon each day, an Oklahoma ritual for farmers and ranchers who came in from the fields to listen to his music during lunchtime. In the fifties when I came home from school each day for lunch, Grandma's little round white radio sitting on top of our round white refrigerator played Johnnie Lee's interpretation of "Silver Bells."

In 1984 Merle Haggard, a timeless Bob Wills fan, re-created a typical noon KVOO broadcast. In front of fifteen hundred people, Mayo introduced them through a microphone that hung in front of the stage with an ON THE AIR light suspended above the dance floor. Those giant pictures next to the stage looked down upon Merle's band the Strangers, also featuring former Playboys Eldon Shamblin and Tiny Moore. Merle's uncanny impersonation of Bob from the opening "Texas Playboy Theme" until the closing "Goodnight, Little Sweetheart" worked perfectly. He played only Wills's music that day, taking the audience back in time. Ten years later he took his place alongside Bob Wills as a member of the Country Music Hall of Fame, the year after Willie Nelson was inducted.

At Merle's broadcast I noticed that sitting a few seats away from me was my uncle Johnnie Lee, a handsome man with snappy brown eyes. I wondered if he always felt that he was in my father's shadow. Why wasn't he on the stage with them? He performed the noon broadcast for sixteen years after Bob moved to California. Why weren't they talking about him, too? I waved at him as I thought about what my mother had told me. "You were crazy about your Uncle Johnnie Lee when you were little. I remember takin' you to see him play and you danced on the stage for him when you were about three years old. A few weeks later I met a woman on a bus who started talkin' to me about Johnnie Lee. She said, 'Do you know he has a mistress? They even have a little girl. I talked to the little girl and she told me he was her daddy.' I asked her, 'Did she have long, dark curls? Was she wearin' a pink organdy dress?' 'Why, yes, I think so.' I had to explain to this woman that you were my little girl, he was your uncle, and you only told everybody he was your daddy because you liked him so much."

When I moved back to Tulsa I visited Johnnie Lee's western wear store to get reacquainted with him, his wife, Irene, and other Wills relatives. Aunt Lorene, also genuinely personable, had recently returned to Tulsa and now worked there too. (The Wills sisters agreed their parents spoiled Lorene because she was the last daughter.) Aunt Irene told me, "Soon after Bob and your mother got married, Bob asked me, 'Irene, would you and Johnnie Lee move in with us and teach Mary Lou how to cook and clean?' Well, we stayed as long as we thought we could help, but your mother really wanted a maid. She didn't want to do dishes or anything except stay in the bedroom with Bob. That's the way it was. So we decided it was time for us to leave and let him get her a maid. And he got her a German lady to come in."

Uncle Johnnie Lee occasionally played at the Caravan Ballroom on 11th Street. His friendly nature made sure I met all the guys in his band. My father used to remark, "Oh, I can't say John's a fiddle player. Breaks his heart. He won't hardly play a program if he knows I'm in the country. But he's the greatest rhythm banjo man I ever heard." Johnnie Lee died at age seventy-two, only six months after Merle's broadcast and a month after Aunt Ruby died. Mayo commented, "I never met a man whose honesty and integrity I respected more than Johnnie Lee's. He came as near to countin' his friends by the number of people he knew as anyone I've known. Johnnie Lee and Bob always respected the public."

In September 1996 Tulsa named a stretch of 17th Street running from Louisville Avenue to the Expo Square Pavilion "Johnnie Lee Wills Lane." Clem McSpadden, who gave the eulogy at my father's funeral, attended the dedication ceremony. Turning around the renowned quote of his well-known relative Will Rogers, he said, "I never heard of a man or woman who didn't like Johnnie Lee Wills." His widow, Irene, and their son Johnnie Lee, Jr., still live in Tulsa, and their daughter Millie Ann resides in Tennessee. The Tulsa Historical Society Museum later put together an exhibit called *The Tulsa Sound* that devoted a whole room to the Wills Brothers, clearly demonstrating the influence that Wills's music has had on the musicians who followed them.

While in Tulsa I checked out the sizeable collection of my father's posters and pictures in Bill's Barbershop on North Sheridan, profiled in the *Tulsa World*. My mother and I also cruised out to the Tulsa Bounty Lounge to have our photo taken with Bud Stefanoff, the fan responsible for promoting the renaming of First Street running in front of Cain's to "Bob Wills Main Street." Terrell Lester, *Tulsa World* columnist, and Betty Boyd, Oklahoma state representative, had supported the idea, encouraging Mayor Rodger Randle to honor the request.

At the dedication ceremony Betty Boyd told the crowd, "We are here to celebrate not only Bob Wills, but the whole Wills family." Aunt Lorene responded, "It really makes me feel proud. I think all of this is pretty wonderful. Bob would probably say, 'Well, what's all this about? About me? I'm nobody.' I don't think Bob ever realized just what he did mean to the public. I'm still amazed at the way people feel about him after all these years."

Mayo, then ninety-one, spoke after a standing ovation. "I don't know if any of us ever expected something like this to happen at Cain's Ballroom. Bob had a sense of rhythm he just seemed to feel and could pass on to other members of the band the way nobody else could. Just came natural to him. He wasn't just a bandleader, he was an artist and a professional. When he was in his prime, nobody would get more out of that fiddle than he could. He had a touch when he was fingerin' that fiddle and pullin' that bow." O. W. Mayo died in 1994 at age ninety-three.

The Heritage Place auction barn in Oklahoma City hosted the Texas Playboys' sixtieth anniversary of their first KVOO broadcast. Leon Rausch and Johnny Gimble emceed as thirty-four former band members performed. The reunion fell on the same weekend that thousands assembled in New York to commemorate Woodstock's thirtieth anniversary. Johnny Gimble shouted, "The kids have their Woodstock. This is Livestock!" Jimmy Young, who played fiddle with Tommy Allsup, did a Bob Wills impersonation that astounded the folks. He simply transformed into Bob Wills. He tipped his hat, greeted people, and pointed his bow the same way Bob did, causing hundreds to rush to the stage in amazement. Uncle Luke said it gave him an eerie feeling. Over 4,000 cheered loudly when thirty-eight former Texas Playboys and Playgirls filled the stage to sing "Faded Love." Aunt Lorene said, "There wasn't a dry eye in the house once they started playin' 'San Antonio Rose.'"

Country music came into vogue after John Travolta became the Urban Cowboy of the early eighties. When the sun went down, lawyers, doctors, and computer nerds donned cowboy hats, levis, and boots and headed out to the Tulsa clubs to line dance. After becoming acquainted with the security guard (another fan) at Duke's, a gargantuan club on Tulsa's far east side, my single girlfriends and I were able to meet almost everyone who played there—except for Hank Williams, Jr., whose backstage doors were locked tight.

George Strait's "Marina del Rey" and other recordings didn't connect me with western swing until I heard him sing with his Ace in the Hole band at Duke's. Standards like "Big Balls in Cow Town," "Milk Cow Blues," "Take Me Back to Tulsa," "Right or Wrong," and "Cherokee Maiden" expressed the band's expert feel for western swing. Band member Gene Elders's rapturous fiddle solo on "Cherokee Maiden" revealed his classical violinist training.

Richard Casanova, who once met my father, took my friend Sharon and me backstage to meet George and his family. They both autographed a poster depicting a tall glass of beer with *100% Strait Country* written across it to advertise George's album of the same name. "To Chad and Reneé, Hope to see you soon. Best Always, George Strait." Richard wrote, "To a very special lady, Rosetta. Thank you and your family."

How thrilling to sit on the couch next to the young, handsome George as he talked about what a big Bob Wills fan he had always been! "Bob Wills and His Texas Playboys are simply the best band that ever was and my band is modeled after them." I stood next to his wife a few feet behind him in the wings gaping at the many women who hurled roses at the stage.

Emmylou Harris autographed a color photo, "To Chad and Reneé. Happy Trails, Emmylou Harris." In the seventies her harmonious duets with former Flying Burrito Brother Gram Parsons soared with operalike innuendos. Gram's aim in life was to get the rock fans and truck drivers talking to each other—way before Outlaw music actually did. This paradoxical long-haired country boy performed at Austin's Armadillo World Headquarters in his Nudie suit adorned with marijuana leaves and illustrations of nude women before Willie Nelson became the local hero. Gram even performed on the Grand Ole Opry stage during his four-month stint with the Byrds in 1968. His records didn't sell when he was alive, but his vision of a rock-country fusion profoundly influenced other entertainers such as Tom Petty and Elvis Costello. As Emmylou once told Chris Hillman, "Gram existed on another plane."

My friend Sharon and I were convinced we were finally going to meet Merle Haggard after his show, but he had boarded the bus before we got there. Someone on the bus yelled, "We're stayin' at the Sheraton," as it pulled away, but we weren't bold enough to follow them.

I clipped a magazine article with interesting comments made by Clint Eastwood after he and Merle Haggard recorded "Barroom Buddies." An interviewer asked Eastwood, "Did you have any background in country music?"

I was never terribly knowledgeable about country music. The first real taste of it I got was when I was 18 or 19, working in a pulp mill in Springfield, Oregon. . . . I saw Bob Wills and His Texas Playboys. They were good. It surprised me a little bit, how good they were. Also, there were a lot of girls there, which didn't surprise me at all. So I guess you could say that lust expanded my musical horizons.

Eastwood's *Honkytonk Man* (1982) cast Johnny Gimble as Bob Wills and his 1993 film *Perfect World* starring Kevin Costner used a sound track that moved back and forth between pop and country to define Texas music in 1963. Bob's "Ida Red" and Perry Como's "Catch a Falling Star" coexisted on the same airwaves during that time.

The early eighties' obligatory mechanical bulls bucked off pseudo-cowboys in Tulsa clubs where I learned to two-step. The bands played "Cotton-Eyed Joe," the model *schottische* dance number Bob had played years ago at ranch dances and first recorded in 1946. John Anderson sang his hit "Swingin" (or rather "Swangin'") from a local "Willie's" stage many a night. Since no backstage area existed, we hung out in their bus. Fiddler Tom Morley pointed his fiddle bow at me when they played Bob's classics. After five years on the road, Tom quit to spend time with his wife in Nashville. His Opryland connection provided us with free tickets when Chad and I journeyed to Nashville via Memphis, where we Presley fanatics paid homage to the King of Graceland.

Chad, who was now playing drums for the Flag Burners (a garage band), brought one of the group's tapes for Tom, who commented, "Hey, you guys are good. You sound like R.E.M." A highlight of Chad's drumming days came when he sat in with Alvin Crow on the historical Cain's stage during one of Bob's birthday tributes. "Playing on that stage was awesome!"

Danny Fallis, the lead singer and songwriter for the Flag Burners, spent hours in our home rehearsing with the band. One day he spotted *San Antonio Rose* in the bookcase. "Hey, Chad, did you know Bob Wills was married to my grandmother?"

"Oh, yeah, well, he was married to my grandmother, too," Chad replied, assuming Danny knew Bob was his grandfather.

Then Richard jokingly said, "Hey, ole Bob Wills was married to my Grandma," as he turned to Roselinda, Chad's girlfriend. "Wasn't he married to your Grandma?" Danny didn't know Chad was Bob's grandson. Chad didn't know Danny's grandmother Ruth McMaster was Bob's second wife.

Ruth McMaster, the educated concert violinist, and Bob, the self-taught Texas fiddler, came from radically different backgrounds. He took violin lessons from her for two years before their 1936 marriage. In awe of his accomplishments without formal training, she was not surprised that he pioneered the most sought after band in that part of the country.

Bob said, "I'm not smart enough to understand real long-haired music, but I love it. I know the touch and feel, you know. I don't know the story behind some of those songs, but I love the music. I really do." The Tulsa Musicians' Union denied membership to Bob and other band members because, in the Union's opinion, they could not read or play viable music. When asked if any of his Texas Playboys could sight-read, Bob responded, "Sure, several of them, but it don't hurt their playin' none. People don't like to see no musician with his nose buried in a sheet of music when they're dancin'."

Since the band's fame had grown without recording benefits, in 1935 they recorded twenty-four songs in their first recording session for Brunswick (bought out by Columbia in 1938). The participants were Tommy Duncan, Johnnie Lee Wills, Son Lansford, Everett Stover, Zeb McNally, Herman Arnspiger, Art Haines, Jesse Ashlock, Leon McAuliffe, Sleepy Johnson, Smoky Dacus, Al Stricklin, and Ruth McMaster. Aunt Ruby also accompanied the band to Dallas. When Ruth played violin on "Blue River" in the fiddle ensemble, Aunt Ruby remarked, "She looked like an angel with that violin in her hand."

In the spring of 1936, when Ruth hadn't seen Bob for a few months, she felt they had gone their separate ways. But when she returned to Tulsa after working in Denver, he proposed to her. Two days later they were married in nearby Sapulpa. Bob called upon Aunt Ruby to train his second wife properly in the art of housekeeping and cooking. But their diverse backgrounds compounded with Bob's moodiness and mistrust brought the marriage to an end in less than four months. Ruth told Charles Townsend, "I don't think Bob knew what he wanted out of life. Like the child looking for the star on the Christmas tree, he never could quite reach it."

Brunswick constructed a makeshift studio in the back of a Dallas stock room for that 1935 session. Recording engineers from New York brought dozens of trunks containing equipment and waxes. The original master recordings were made on inch-thick, wax-based discs that were then shipped in large barrels to an eastern processing plant. Don Law (protégé of Art Satherley) recalled, "The original waxes we recorded could not be played back without ruining them so we had to be sure we did things right the first time." Law had worked with Englishman Satherley in early recording sessions for Al Dexter (composer of the World War II hit "Pistol Packin' Mama") and blues pacesetter Robert Johnson. Traveling throughout the south with mobile recording equipment, Satherley discovered various so-called cowboy singers such as Gene Autry. He produced important records for Roy Acuff, Little Jimmy Dickens, George Morgan, and Bill Monroe. He later signed Carl Smith and Marty Robbins before he relinquished reign to fellow Britisher Don Law. In 1971 Art Satherley was inducted into the Country Music Hall of Fame. He died in 1986 at age ninety-six.

The 1935 session got off to a touchy start as proper Satherley could not envision a horn section in a fiddle band. The horns violated Brunswick's ordained "string band category" and belonged in the "race records category." Mixing the two was considered musical heresy. The future "Mr. Columbia Records" knew what he wanted, and he did not want horns. However, the future "King of Western Swing" also knew what he wanted, and he wanted horns. After Bob threatened to pack up and go home, Satherley relented.

The band recorded "Osage Stomp" first because Bob figured if they could make it through that tough one, they could play anything. Without much delay, Bob bellowed, "Take it away, Jesse!" before he threw in, "It won't be long now!" Then he christened "Zeb" McNally "Mama's Little Man!" By the time they really got with it on "Get with It," his illustrious "Ahh Ha!" burst on the scene. At this point, Satherley abruptly halted the music. The band members stared at Satherley in shocked amazement as he confronted Bob again. He complained that Bob's talking and hollering covered up the music. Nobody had ever told Bob not to holler.

"You hired Bob Wills, didn't you? You want Bob Wills, you get Bob Wills. I like horns and I like to talk and holler when I feel like it!" After a brief silence, the fidgeting Englishman once more relented, but not without reservations. "Ahh Haa, *don't* tear it down, Mr. Man, *don't* tear it down."

In a sixties interview with Bob and Tommy Duncan at Texas Tiny's Truck Stop in Long Beach, California, Bob told the deejay of his recollection of that first 1935 recording session. "Ole Art Satherley told me they wanted Tommy's singin' and my fiddlin', but they didn't want no horns. I said, 'Well, Uncle Art, I can save me and you fellas a lot of trouble. You either want what we got or you don't want to see us at all.' Bob jokingly added, "You know, I was feelin' pretty important 'cause we was pretty rich by then."

"Yeah, we already had a bus," Tommy added. "Stretched-out job we gave $150 for." More chuckles followed.

Bob continued, "Well, Uncle Art said he wanted what we got. So, I said if he wanted to see me, I wanted to see him."

More recording sessions were scheduled in early 1936 and 1937. Since they kept the windows closed to screen out the street noises, the session manager brought in six galvanized bath tubs filled with a hundred pounds of ice and set up large fans to cool the discs. But ice, fans, and beer were not enough to cool down the band in the intense Dallas heat. In his aristocratic tongue Satherley quipped, "All present were working in their underwear. It was quite the thing to do under the circumstances. I know Bob was completely comfortable working under the conditions that were provided for him in those days."

The 1938 Dallas session propagated many hits ("Ida Red," "Beaumont Rag," "Drunkard's Blues," "Gambling Polka Dot Blues," "I Wonder If You Feel the Way I Do," and "Yearning") as well as a spontaneous creation called "Lisa, Pull Down the Shades." Many winning numbers recorded to fill out the allotted studio time weren't released until years later. In a taped interview with Hank Penny, Bob discussed "Lisa, Pull Down the Shades."

"We done that just for foolishness after we was give out one night in Dallas years ago. We didn't have any name for it. Uncle Art asked, 'Well, have you got another tune, Bob?'

'Yes sir, we got one.'

"I told the boys to just start playin', kickin' it, 'cause he won't know the difference. We was just havin' a little fun out of him, but after we finished, he come out and said, 'Bob, that's a masterpiece. Have you got it named yet?'

'No.'

'We'll call it 'Lisa, Pull Down the Shades.'

Hank asked, "Bob, do you know why he named it that?"

"No, I don't."

Hank said, "I think it's because right on the end of the record, you said, 'Lisa, you can lift those shades up now.'"

"Oh, no, wait a minute! I didn't make myself clear. After we run through it for him, he named it. Then when we actually recorded the master, I added that at the end just 'cause of what he named it!"

Chapter 10

The Kings of Rhythm

"I want a Texas country band, a kickin' band, true to the Bob Wills' style."

—PAUL MCCARTNEY, 1990

For Christmas my mother gave Chad a book called *Rock Stars,* with Mick Jagger on the cover. As Chad thumbed through the pages, he unexpectedly found an article flaunting a full two-page photo spread of Bob Wills and His Texas Playboys. Rock stars? Evidently Timothy White thought so: "Pop music had never seen such an anomalous musical amalgam, but early rockers understood and were profoundly affected by Wills's iconoclastic tastes."

A seventies Bob Wills's album review by Dan Hicks of *Rolling Stone* considered Bob a rapper years before the nineties term originated:

> Bob Wills and His Texas Playboys were funky in their music and their scenes, it seems. The lyric content of their material lets you in on what they did on the side. Cocaine and groupies ain't all that new. . . . Bob Wills' charm on those old records was his constant sparse rap through most every side. He'd give everybody in the band a bad time. Taunt, jive, jibe, and joke.

And 1986's illustrated *Rock of Ages: The Rolling Stone History of Rock and Roll* even had two photographs of the Texas Playboys on the first page!

Who started rock and roll anyway? Did it begin with the so-called "race records" of the twenties? Or is Elvis the "father" as well as the indisputable "king"? For over forty years since rock's accepted emergence, the origins are still muddled. Documentation suggests that early folk, country, jazz, blues, ragtime, and pop definitely influenced the genre. In an attempt to clarify this, Jann S. Wenner's introduction to *Rock of Ages* states:

When all is said and done, the story of rock and roll is the story of a sound. It is the sound of rural blues and folk instruments and voices, disseminated through the technologies of radio and records and eventually electrified. . . . It continues to grow and evolve, hybridizing with jazz, folk, rhythm and blues, country and western, and even classical.

In 1955, when Muddy Waters introduced Chuck Berry and his demo tape of "Ida Red" to Phil and Leonard Chess, founders of Chess Records, they asked Berry to record it again, only faster and with different words. No royalties were associated with the public domain status of "Ida Red," hence the dawn of Berry's now copyrightable, newly titled "Maybellene." When legendary deejay Alan Freed reportedly agreed to promote the song if named as co-author, Berry accepted the deal. Four weeks after its release, it hit the top of the R&B charts before it broke into the pop charts and stayed in the top ten for weeks.

Who would ever have associated "Maybellene" with Bob's popularized rendering of "Ida Red"? Forty years later, when Cleveland's Rock and Roll Hall of Fame opened, newspapers carried stories about a *Mystery Train* film featuring Bob performing "Ida Red." The personnel suggested you view the film before browsing in the museum. According to Michael Corcoran in the *Austin American-Statesman*, "Folks who are quick to accuse white rockers with ripping off the blues aren't aware that Chuck Berry, 'the father of rock 'n' roll,' has credited Wills' version of 'Ida Red' for inspiring his first hit 'Maybelline.'"

As I bopped to my idol's "Shake, Rattle and Roll" and waited in a long line to see *Blackboard Jungle*, I had no idea that Bill Haley idolized my father. In 1950 while singing with the Four Aces of Western Swing, Haley cut his first record on the Cowboy label. As Peter Guralnick stated in *Lost Highway*, "The music of Bob Wills widely known as Western Swing incorporated elements of blues, big-band jazz, country music, and boogie woogie in a style that Bill Haley would adapt and fuse with rhythm and blues in the early fifties." When I turned fifteen, "Rock Around the Clock" rose to number one on the charts. Bob's "Bottle Baby Boogie" recorded in 1953 has that same Haley flavor. Cindy Walker penned "So Let's Rock" (another Haley sound) for Bob's Decca recording session. When vocalist Lee Ross asked, "Mr. Wills, do you like to rock?" Bob's enthusiastic response spoke the truth. "Ah, yes, I've been rockin' and rollin' for a very long time!"

In 1938 Bob recorded "Keep a Knockin' But You Can't Come In," years before Little Richard's big hit, and he recorded "Worried Mind" twenty years prior to Ray Charles's rendition. Ray Charles later cut Bob's 1946 classic "Roly Poly." In 1956 Fats Domino soared to stardom when he scored four singles in the top 30 (R&B category). Fats told Tommy Allsup he had patterned his rhythm section after that of Bob Wills.

So, when I was "Walkin' to New Orleans" and "Findin' my thrill on Blueberry Hill," Bob influenced Fats himself. John McEuen of the Nitty Gritty Dirt Band said:

> In putting the swing back into country music, Bob Wills not only ener-
> gized the form itself, but opened the door to the exploration of other pos-
> sibilities as well—through the mutant of rockabilly to the core of what
> became rock 'n' roll. Bob's heavy beat and swinging rhythm impacted
> both rockabilly and the emerging rock 'n' roll. Even though he has been
> credited for his influence on country and western music, his bearing on
> rock 'n' roll has almost been ignored.

In the fifties Bob explained in an interview that western music was the type that had been around for years and would always remain popular. After all, he was still playing the same music his great-grandfathers had played years ago. "So often things change. Western music may slack off for a while, but one of these days a golden voice will record some honest-to-goodness tune like 'Tennessee Waltz' and make a million. It will build again." According to biographer Charles R. Townsend, "Bob Wills was the bridge between race music of the twenties, thirties, and forties, and early rock of the fifties." Bob himself declared in 1956:

> Elvis Presley? Why, man, he's big now but I get the feelin' he's tryin' to
> change his style and go Crosby on his fans. He oughtn't to do that. The
> kids like him the way he is. Rock 'n' roll will be around forever. What I
> mean is that people don't change much. We didn't call it rock 'n' roll back
> when we introduced it as our style in 1928, and we don't call it rock 'n'
> roll the way we play it now.
>
> But it's just basic rhythm and has gone by a lot of different names in
> my time. It's the same, whether you follow just a drumbeat like in
> Africa or surround it with a lot of instruments. The rhythm is what is
> important.

Bob said, "I like rock 'n' roll, but you young deejays don't realize there are thou-sands out there who would like to have a mixture. I'm all for these youngsters who have hit on rock 'n' roll. Oh, boy, I'm for them!" Bob exclaimed. But he quickly added, "I think the radio stations are forgettin' about a lot of older people." In the deejays' defense, he told a story about discussing this issue with some Longview followers who bitterly complained about never hearing his music on the radio. "Now, wait a minute, fellas, how many of you have called a radio station and asked for a tune?" Of course, none of them had. He then asked, "How many of you have teenagers who call the stations?" Of course, they all did. "You see, the disc jockeys are gonna cater to the people they hear from."

Uncle Johnnie Lee's "Rag Mop," an early fifties top ten C&W hit written by Deacon Anderson may "actually be the first rock 'n' roll song," according to Tulsa music historian Guy Logsdon. "Critics said it was the downfall of American music." I remember singing "Rag Mop" (R-A-G-G, M-O-P-P," sort of an alphabet song). Johnnie Lee also recorded "Peter Cottontail" in 1950—what a bizarre year for him.

Sam Phillips suggested that even Elvis record "Rag Mop." In author Nick Tosches's words, "It was an easy song with impressively dumb lyrics, but Elvis' awkward rendition didn't work, prompting a disturbed Sam to ask, 'Elvis, what in the hell can you sing?'" The next year Elvis cut "Heartbreak Hotel" for RCA-Victor, making the answer well known. When RCA announced they were promoting Elvis not only as a country artist but also as pop and R&B, the industry thought this major label had lost its corporate mind. Ed Ward explained in *Rock of Ages,* "The day had finally arrived when an artist who combined elements from each field would appeal to everyone—urban and rural, black and white—-embodying a fusion that had been building since the days of Jimmie Rodgers, Bob Wills, and Nat "King" Cole."

After Elvis's breakthrough, rock 'n' roll became my musical preoccupation. My passion for music had always ruled even though I never played an instrument other than the piano when I was a youngster. Recital performances during elementary school encouraged me to become a female Chopin, but when I discovered rock 'n' roll in my teenage years, I became content just to listen occasionally to Chopin.

Another vivid memory of falling in love with a radio voice took place one hot summer day in 1956. While rocking on the front porch swing, I suddenly heard through the open windows a seductive voice moaning about a"Be-Bop-A-Lula baby doll who gives more" and more. Who was this Gene Vincent? Was he the next Elvis?

Or was Buddy Holly the next Elvis? As the sole employee (except for the owner, Mrs. Streetman) of Pawhuska's "combination sporting goods/record store" during my senior year, I sold more Buddy Holly records than any larger, metropolitan stores throughout the state, according to the sales rep. I stood behind the turntable and *demanded* that every person who came to buy a fishing pole listen to Buddy. His music blaring from the outside speakers lured other passers-by into the store. Back orders multiplied exponentially as the distributor struggled to keep our bins stocked.

Despite my absorption with Gene Vincent and Buddy Holly, Elvis was still my king. Along with ten thousand other fanatical teenagers, I saw him perform at the Tulsa Fairgrounds Pavilion for admission ticket of $1.50. I clawed my way through the horde rushing the stage and managed to get on the stairs next to the stage entrance. As he dashed past me to the microphone, my fingers briefly brushed the peak of his pompadour, quickening my rapid heart palpitations until I almost fainted.

April 19, 1956:

> *Dear Diary,*
> *I will never, never forget as long as I live what a thrilling experi-ence it was to see Elvis Presley in person!!*

We four swooning, screaming teenagers caught up in the delirium shared our deepest secret—after hearing Elvis sing "Only You," we would "go all the way" if he asked. (Maybe that's why parents worried about his influence.) The news clipping in my scrapbook branded the show indecent and bureaucratic grievances were sent ahead to Oklahoma City officials where he was scheduled to appear the next night.

Jim Downing wrote the feature story:

> Elvis Presley headed for Oklahoma City Thursday with at least two major questions unanswered:
>
> Is his rock and roll presentation of hip-wiggling bumps-and-grinds objectionable?
>
> Can the 21-year-old truck driver sing or not?"
>
> In the backstage interview with Elvis:
>
> I don't know what you'd call my voice. I'm a lead singer. Is that tenor?
>
> Sir, how can I combat this dope-pusher rumor? If I deny it, people say, "Sure, he would." If I laugh at it and tell them I use everything, they nod and laugh.
>
> Naw, sir, I don't need nothin'. Why, I don't even smoke and I've never tasted alcohol.

Thirteen thousand teenagers jammed the Oklahoma City Municipal Auditorium only to see a tame show, thanks to forty policemen and the presence of Baptist minister Rupert Naney, the chairman of the Mayor's Board of Censors. The head-line read "Elvis Pressley's [sic] Oklahoma City Show Is Tame." Elvis told reporters, "I wasn't trying to be vulgar and sexy. I just get carried away with the music."

When Elvis attended Bob's dance in Houston, he asked promoter Biff Collie to introduce him to Bob after the dance. According to Peter Guralnick's *Last Train to Memphis*, Elvis cringed when Collie confided that Bob had barked, "Bring the young punk back." But in the early sixties my father told me, "You know, I played a package show with Buck Owens and Elvis Presley. Honey, Elvis is such a nice, clean boy—doesn't smoke or drink." A young bassist for Ray Price later stole Collie's wife, Shirley, away from him. When he sang "San Antonio Rose" adorned in a rhinestone Nudie suit, Shirley fell helplessly in love with Willie Nelson.

As I recall my fascination with both Elvis Presley and James Dean in the mid-fifties, I understand why Ruth Thomason, one of my father's greatest devotees, wrote her "Guidelines for a Bob Wills Fan." Penning your emotions about someone provides a powerful release. Her intense, uncritical devotion to my father reminded me of my ardent admiration for James Dean. Forty-three years later, my emotions about the fatal car wreck are still preserved in smudged pencil on the back of my Big Chief tablet cover:

For James Dean
(Written in Study Hall, 4th Hour, 1955)

I can't stand it. I can't take it any longer. I've got to write. It keeps building up inside of me. Bigger and bigger. I think I shall die thinking of it. Perhaps you're wondering what could be the root of all this trouble. If I tell you, you will laugh and call me a foolish child. The trouble is that in my heart I have a love and desire for something that shall never, never be mine. I have a feeling of sadness. Because this person, whom I so sincerely worship, is dead. His talent, his personality, and his love will never be. He is gone. Sometimes we fail to understand God's purposes. We ask ourselves that question. Why? Only God knows why.

There is one thing we can truly thank God for. He gave us James Dean. Maybe for only a short while, but his short memory will live in the hearts of all who knew him. Knew him? Yes, I say "knew him." Because I know that everyone that watched him perform really knew him. I weep useless tears. I long for it all to be a lie. That fatal car wreck! That one car wreck destroyed in a few minutes what no actor or man will ever again excel!

They say if you love a person too much, you will lose them. Maybe people caused him to die by loving him more than God. We should never put anyone before God. God forgive us!

I would give anything to have the real talent to write what I feel and have the other person comprehend. James Dean is a subject very dear to me. It's impossible to say what he really means to all of us. He was a great actor. I know as a person, he was strong—yet kind and gentle. He was everything a girl would want in a man and more. He's not just another movie star that all the girls went mad over. He was more—much more— than that. I know, perhaps you don't believe me. He was a symbol of everything good.

He was human. He probably made a lot of mistakes. Yet I know he was everything we think he was. I know it. I can't get him out of my mind. The only way I can relieve myself is to write about him. Those eyes—so blue—his hair—so light—and that red jacket— are so vivid in my memory! His arms were so strong and brown. He was so gay and laughed at nothing all the time. He laughed for the pure joy of laughing. You say I don't know. You think he's just like all the other movie stars. Worthless. Maybe I am crazy. Maybe I don't know. But I believe it and that is all that matters.

Chapter 11

Flock to Turkey

The analysts' pitfall in trying to explain Wills' astounding appeal and unique contributions is in not recognizing his genius.

—RICHARD MARSCHALL,
THE ENCYCLOPEDIA OF COUNTRY & WESTERN MUSIC

My father sat helplessly in his wheelchair during the unveiling ceremony in his hometown, even though he was stronger than he had been since his stroke four years earlier. His impaired speech allowed him to utter a few faltering words, and he still had the use of his left hand but not his right. The citizens of Turkey, Texas, had erected an impressive thirty-foot red granite monument with etched figures of him holding his fiddle and cigar. Other panels portrayed memorable periods in his life such as his war record, his movie career, and a list of his musical hits (Spanish Two Step," "San Antonio Rose," "Faded Love," "Ida Red," "Time Changes Everything," and "Steel Guitar Rag"). Two fiddles rotating on top of the tower trumpeted his music continuously. After they commissioned sculptor Bill Willis to design the monument, he made a model of his idea and showed it to Bob. "I'll never forget the expression on Bob's face and his big grin of approval when he saw it."

That afternoon during the program in the football field, Bob's penetrating dark eyes remained fixed on brothers Johnnie Lee, Luke, and Billy Jack, along with Al Stricklin, Leon McAuliffe, Jesse Ashlock, Curley Lewis, and Sleepy Johnson as they played onstage. He nodded and winked at them like old times, but now he was an observer, not a participant. They knew he needed to play with them, point his fiddle bow at Al and holler, "Here's Al Stricklin, that ole piano pounder," or call out, "Take it away, Leon," as if it were the old days. After a couple of hours he told Sleepy he wanted to play "Faded Love." Many eyes misted over when he tucked the instrument under his chin and fingered the notes while Sleepy handled the bow.

At the twenty-fifth anniversary of Turkey's annual Bob Wills Day, Curly Lewis reminisced about that 1973 event. "Of course, Bob bein' there made such a difference. I remember that Bob and Sleepy played a tune on the fiddle that day. Bob noted it with his left hand and Sleepy bowed it with his right hand, both on the same fiddle. I think it was 'Faded Love' or one of Bob's old tunes. Yeah, Bob was notin' and Sleepy was bowin'." Three years later, Sleepy Johnson finished the show and then collapsed with a fatal heart attack. Leon Rausch said, "He just put his little banjo down and fell over." No nobler way to depart this earth exists for a Texas Playboy. Earlier that day Leon McAullife had said, "The Texas Playboys will keep comin' back to Turkey as long as we're physically able."

Eldon Shamblin and Joe Frank Ferguson, two of the remaining three members of the early Tulsa Band, attended the 1996 celebration. That Friday evening after Truitt Cunningham, San Antonio Rose Band leader, introduced me before singing "Rosetta," Eldon (eighty years old) collapsed onstage. An ambulance rushed him to the nearest hospital in Childress, forty miles away, and even though he recovered, he was unable to play Saturday. Frail Joe Frank (age eighty-two) sat quietly on the Saturday afternoon stage, smiling at the adoring followers. Smoky (age eighty-five) didn't make the trip at all. The loyal zealots who attend each year are aware they may be witnessing a Playboy's "for the last time" performance. Eldon said, "I've tried to make Turkey every year 'cause that was important to Bob. That's one of the things he used to tell us. 'Boys, if I die before you do, try to go to Turkey.' That's one of those things I've tried to do."

Don Dennis, Bob's close friend, told me he would always attend the Turkey commemoration. "Your daddy was like a second father to me. I never had a better friend or anyone I admired any more than your daddy. We had some good times way back in the old days." One time he and Luke drove Bob from the West Coast back to Tulsa. Along the way Bob bought an old car from a guy in Arizona for Luke's wife, Dorothy, and asked Luke and Don to follow him. The car overheated in the extremely hot weather, and finally even the muffler fell off. Bob kept right on cruising through a small town, but the old car just quit. Luke found a mechanic who worked for hours to get it running again, but Bob was way down the road by then.

When they arrived at Snuffy's club in Hobbs, New Mexico, the dance was over. Don helped the musicians pack up and load the bus. "I thought things were okay. I saw Luke sittin' in the car with Bob so I opened the back door and got in. Then Bob's temper flared as he yelled at Luke, 'I don't know if I can run this outfit without you or not, but I'm damn sure gonna try. You're fired.' Then Bob turned to me and said, 'Donald, you go with Luke and take that car to Dorothy. Pick up another car in Tulsa and meet me and Keith Coleman in Dallas.' I said, 'Yes, sir, anything you say, Bob.' For years I tried to tell Bob we were tellin' the truth, but he never did believe us. He was convinced we tipped a few too many and lost our way."

Playboy Flour advertisements, dance posters, photos, awards, plaques, and citations cover the walls of the Bob Wills Museum in the old Turkey High School. Another attraction, the Bob Wills Memorial Archive of Popular Music, is located in nearby Canyon's Panhandle-Plains Museum. A close friend of Bob's, Harold V. "Tex" Brown, organized the Bob Wills Foundation to commemorate Bob's contributions to western swing. Ten thousand to fifteen thousand flock to Turkey each year for this Western Swing Woodstock. People from all over the United States, even parts of Europe, descend upon the tiny town the last Saturday in April. The two-story Turkey Hotel, where Bob played in the late twenties, is reserved for the family and former Playboys. Since the closest motel is forty miles away in Childress, a sea of tents, campers, and RVs flood the parking lots.

When Michael and I made our first pilgrimage, we stopped in Estelline, the last town in a wet county twenty-five miles from Turkey in dry Hall County, to have our picture taken at the B&W Liquor store sign that reads "Bob Wills Slept Here." (Wouldn't "Bob Wills Drank Here" be more apropos?) When we arrived at the museum around noon, my nervousness dominated until Betty and my two half-sisters Diane and Carolyn greeted us with VIP buttons. My stepmother made an exceptional effort to make me feel part of the family.

Musicians armed with fiddles and guitars had already assembled on the outdoor stage before the large throng began to gather. Hoisted video cameras hovered in front as Dr. Townsend introduced the band's standard cry: "The Texas Playboys are on the air!" The swinging rhythm of "South," the familiar opening number, erupted from the stage, attracting applause and shouts from the audience. When Dr. Townsend introduced us, flattering but foreign attention floored me. Goosebumps rippled down my back during the finale when we gathered onstage to sing the immortal "San Antonio Rose." The audience rose to their feet joyfully clapping and singing along with us. After the show, the musicians graciously signed autographs, shook hands, and posed for pictures.

About a mile away from the museum in a rambling park on Turkey's southwest edge, hundreds of college-age kids were *mud-bogging*. The publicized Bob Wills Day lured them there, but they were in their own world, quite different from the older folks on the other side of town listening to western swing. The kids began mud-bogging after officials pumped two feet of water into the long depression in the park's center. They drove their large four-wheeled vehicles through the mud time after time, until it became deeper and stickier. The less powerful vehicles and more inebriated drivers soon found themselves stranded in the bog. The onlookers wildly cheered rescue attempts as Spring Flingers fell and rose covered in brown ooze. Michael and I survived the bucking bronco ride in a 4x4 truck without being rescued, thank God!

I appreciated the genuine concern Diane expressed to me about a book sold in the Turkey museum. *The Bob Wills' Family Album* contained photos only of Bob and Betty with their children. But it was another reminder. Due to the perpetuated myth of Betty being the only wife, John McEuen's liner notes on a Hall of Fame album read, "In 1926 Bob married Betty Anderson." In 1926 Betty Lou Anderson was three years old.

The next year Betty asked Michael to drive the car in the Saturday morning parade. My mouth felt glued open around my teeth after smiling and waving at the people lining the streets. How do politicians do it? We followed the flatbed truck carrying the Playboys—dressed in familiar white hats, starched white shirts, and bolo ties—through the downtown area. The previous day we had stopped at the B&W Liquor store again to chat with the owner, who quipped, "By the way, your sister, the singer from California, was just in here. She's gonna be in Turkey this year." I told him I didn't have a sister in California. He then handed me a business card bearing the name Dayna Wills underneath the drawing of a fiddle. I thought she must be an impostor because none of the Wills brothers had a daughter named Dayna.

Betty had filed an injunction against an impostor named Bob Wills, Jr., who claimed to be Bob Wills's son. His story would be more plausible if he didn't claim that Robbie Jo's mother, Edna, was his mother also. Paternity may be difficult to prove, but maternity can certainly be verified. Edna emphatically denies she delivered more than one child. When the rolling credits read "Bob Wills, Jr." in the movie *Baja, Oklahoma,* many believed he was genuine. An Austin newspaper later ran a story picked up from the *Los Angeles Daily News,* in which he described how he had slowly recovered from a 1985 stroke by planting a gigantic garden. If he had a stroke in 1985, I wonder how he managed that bit part in a 1988 movie.

Vivacious Dayna Wills was no impostor. She had taken the maiden name of her mother Helen (my father's fourth sister). Years earlier I had met my aunt Helen and Dayna's brother Jim Rob (named after Bob) at Bob's sixtieth birthday bash in Dallas. Helen was a beautiful woman whom everyone loved. She was living in Las Vegas when she died at age fifty-one. Her son Jim Rob began his musical career playing drums for Bob at Wills Point near Sacramento in 1955. In 1960 he went on the road as a Playboy, this time playing guitar. After touring in bands for years, he quit the road and settled in Stockton, where he continued to play locally. He died at age fifty-six in 1994.

Dayna and her husband Gary live in Stockton, where she sings in local clubs and energetically promotes western swing. She, as well as k.d. lang, Willie Nelson, and Janie Frickie, have recorded Cindy Walker's "Sugar Moon," a big hit for Bob in 1946. She even recorded "Rosetta" for me.

Her rendition of "Misery" on her newest release equals Merle Haggard's and Marty Stuart's former ones. Her music director Tom Morrell and producer Don Dennis did an excellent job, along with Billy Briggs, Benny Garcia, Amos Hedrick, Bobby McBay, Tommy Perkins, and Larry Pierce. When Dayna was in high school, she loved the theme song "Let's Ride with Bob" that kicked off Bob's California dances—a full horn sound with a slow B-flat blues pattern full of openings for his hollering in perfect pitch.

When our Uncle Johnnie Lee invited Dayna onstage at Cain's for her singing debut, she was in the ladies' room and didn't hear him. As soon as she returned, her mother assured her she would have a second chance. During the next set, he called her up again. She recalled that as she walked to the stage, he told the audience why she had missed the first call. "Now I can laugh about it, but when I was fifteen years old, it was pretty embarrassing."

Dayna hasn't missed a Bob Wills Day since 1989, singing onstage and jamming around late-night campfires. When the windy weather created problems for her wrap-around skirt as she belted out "My Window Faces the South," guitarist Bobby Koefer laughed loudly rather than offering help. Thank goodness for the soundman's duct tape. She's the only female Wills performer these days and should be applauded for carrying on the family tradition with aplomb. These observances resemble Wills family reunions bringing uncles, aunts, and cousins together. Aunt Olga still lives in Tulsa, but her health problems prevent her from attending.

Many musicians attend each year to reminisce about the old days, swap stories about Bob, or just jam with old friends. In addition to the three original Texas Playboys (Eldon Shamblin, Joe Frank Ferguson, and Smoky Dacus) who attend when they can, others who played with either Bob or Johnnie Lee during their careers have become Turkey regulars, including Clarence Cagle, Bobby Boatright, Benny Garcia, Tommy Perkins, Glenn Rhees. Johnny Cuviello (age eighty-two), in rare form for his perennial "Texas Drummer Boy" exhibition, told me, "Jeannie Shepard called out my name on TNN one day last year. She said I was her favorite drummer and she'd like to have me call her up. Do you believe she actually said that before thousands of people? Since then I've been gettin' lots of jobs. I've got three jobs in the San Francisco area in June."

Casey, who now leads the Casey Dickens and Former Texas Playboys band, said, "It's hard to explain your daddy. He was just such a wonderful personality. He could tell stories and go on and on about things. Why, I've seen guys like Tennessee Ernie Ford and Ernest Tubb just sittin' around on the hotel floor for hours listenin' to your daddy tell stories."

Casey's most prized possession is a saddle Bob gave him in the early sixties. "Your daddy loved horses and I loved horses. I ended up with Buddy, one of Punkin's colts." When Bob, Tag Lambert, and Jesse Ashlock stopped by Casey's house after playing a dance in Fort Worth, Casey proudly showed them the new $300 saddle he had bought for Buddy. Several months later Bob surprised him when he called. "Casey, you know, I've been thinkin' about your little saddle. It looked nice, but you know Buddy's a pretty big horse and that little saddle just don't look right on him. Snuffy Smith has my favorite saddle, but Snuf don't ride much anymore. Would you like to have it?"

Snuffy, a large man Casey described as a tough cookie, later phoned Casey. "There's not enough money in the world to buy that saddle, but as a personal favor to Bob, I'll pass it on to you. I can't turn the 'Ole Man' down, but if you ever sell it, I'll whip your ass all over Texas."

Bob's famous palomino Punkin lived to be twenty-five years old and died on Roy Parnell's ranch outside Fort Worth. Bob said, "Punkin was the smartest horse around. Most performing horses had to be trained for years, but Punkin never had any formal schooling. He just naturally knew what to do at the right time and that's more than a lot of us humans know." Roy Parnell and Bob were good friends who grew up together in West Texas. Casey recalled, "Roy was one of the few guys who ever spent the night in your daddy's home. Did you know his son Lee Roy Parnell is a big country star these days?" (Lee Roy once told a *People* magazine reporter, "If you can listen to Bob Wills' music without tapping your foot, there's something wrong with you.")

Evidently Snuffy Smith wasn't the only tough cookie who worked for Bob. Snuffy himself told me about "Ole Indian Joe." One night while cruising Hollywood Boulevard, a "drunk" Indian Joe started giving a then "sober" Bob a hard time. After a few hostile words, Indian Joe ordered Bob to stop the car on the spot so he could whip him. After they got out of the car, Joe took a swing at Bob, but two of Joe's fingers ended up caught in Bob's mouth. "You see, Bob could bite. Joe did the damnest Indian war dance on Hollywood Boulevard in history!"

Collector Johnnie Burnett of Ponca City, Oklahoma, sent me an audiotape that contains a radio interview with Jim Downing, Jr., son of Bob's ex-wife Ruth and Jim Downing, Sr. I had clipped a feature story written by Jim Downing for *The Tulsa Tribune* in 1957 titled "Wills Brothers Together Again—Bob Back with Heavy Beat" for my scrapbook. The article compared Bob's style with the current rock and roll craze. Of course, at the time I didn't know that Jim Downing had married Ruth McMaster.

In October 1947 Bob was scheduled to play in Columbus, Ohio, where Ruth and Jim lived. Jim Jr. told the deejay, "My dad wanted to meet Bob, so my mother called him at the hotel and invited him over. I think he was scared my dad might deck him so he brought Tommy Duncan along with him. Well, they all got to talkin' and drinkin' whiskey. My dad talked Bob and Tommy into playin' and sin-gin' 'San Antonio Rose.' We had an old Silvertone console radio that could record an acetate record so my dad recorded it that night." When the disc jockey played the scratchy home recording, it verified the whiskey's role in the party.

Michael and I were married on March 5, 1988, at the Little White Chapel in Las Vegas underneath the towering red and white sign "Dynasty's Joan Collins was married here." Although I had written to the Chamber of Commerce requesting a list of dignified wedding chapels, they discreetly left out any mention of the gaudy sign. As we sipped champagne from stemmed glasses, the wedding party ahead guzzled long-neck Buds. Our friends shed appropriate tears even though the min-ister pressed the Stop button about twenty seconds into "Here Comes the Bride." I suppose the ceremony's brevity allowed the preacher more quickly to attend the next expectant couple waiting in line outside.

The next day we called on Uncle Luke and Aunt Dorothy before taking in the act of their son John David Wills & the Family Tradition in the Stardust lounge. Their two other children, Joyce and Luke, Jr., also live in Las Vegas. John David said, "You know, Bob Wills is to west Texas what the queen is to England."

Uncle Luke recalled the annulment hearing in Pawhuska when Bob told his lawyers to call it off and reconciled with my mother. "I rode down from Tulsa to Pawhuska with our friend Claude Breedlove and his brother. I wasn't there as a witness or anythin'. That trial got heated up in the process. One of our friends, Bill Newport, he's dead now, well, he and your Grandpa, Mr. Parker, got into it. It was my first time to be in a courtroom. Naturally I didn't know the lingo or what was gonna happen. Would have made a good episode on a soap opera though!"

Michael's dad, Frank, told me he was introduced to my father in the early fifties in an Oklahoma City hotel. At Papa Frank's ninetieth birthday party, Mama Lucille put on Bob's records and everyone danced, including Papa Frank. After visiting their Cuero home we drove to Turkey for another Bob Wills Day, meeting Chad and his friend Eric at the Turkey Hotel. Since our previous visit Scott and Jane Johnson had completely renovated the sixty-five-year-old hotel, turning it into a cozy bed and breakfast chockful of elegant antiques.

At the Friday night dance, Betty smiled blissfully when she introduced us to Herb Voss, her new husband. "He treats me like a queen." Too many beers encour-aged Chad to become the band's new drummer. When Dr. Townsend introduced us, Chad seized the microphone and told the crowd how much he knew his grand-father appreciated his eternal fans.

Michael and I left early the next morning to attend Arlo Guthrie's first ever concert in Okemah, Oklahoma, the hometown of his renowned father, Woody. But back in Tulsa, the recorded message shouted, "Mom, it's urgent! Send bail money to get me and Eric out of jail." The whiskey that accompanied Chad and Eric to the Saturday night dance had clouded their judgment when it came time to drive the car back to the hotel. Police parked at every intersection on Main Street (which was only a few spots in this small town) stopped every swerving car or staggering drunk. Eric was the driver, and his history of upaid traffic tickets did not help his credibility. Even Chad's loud pronouncement that he was Bob Wills's grandson failed to impress the officers who promptly escorted them to the Turkey jail. Of course, Mom wired the bail money.

The Turkey jail. In 1929 the Turkey jail played a pivotal role in Bob's career. Bob and his friends spent a Sunday afternoon drinking at a Lakeview baseball game before they drove back to Turkey. When his friends went inside a Turkey drugstore to buy some cigars, Bob's loud, unruly behavior upset the young ladies in the car parked next to him. They reported his "disorderly conduct" to the police, who arrested him and locked him up in the tiny, hot, one-room jail with its single, barred window. After his friends figured out what had happened, their wrath scared the two lawmen, who decided to lay low by disappearing until the next day. The next morning, when an officer unlocked the jail, he said, "Jim Bob, you gotta lay off that booze."

"What!" Bob vented loudly. "You've probably got a hangover yourself. Everybody in this small town drinks, but I was the only one you threw in jail. I'm leavin' this town and never comin' back."

Bob angrily stomped down Main Street as people along the way stared silently. He didn't return to Turkey until his musical success stories had traveled back home. Five years later when "Jim Bob" played a dance there, everyone turned out to shake the hand of Turkey's new hero. Sixty years later the tourist brochures for Turkey, Texas, read, "The home of Bob Wills and a lot of other fine folks."

Chapter 12

Willie Outside Austin City Limits

Bob had a presence about him. He had an aura so strong it just stunned people. I doubt very seriously if Bob was aware how much that had to do with his popularity. . . . It was because of his charisma, his natural ability to take control. . . . Bob Wills is more than his music is what I'm saying. Elvis was the same way. You had to see him in person to under-stand his magnetic pull. John the Baptist had the same pull. John the Baptist could sit in one spot for several days and attract thousands of people.

—Willie Nelson,
Willie

"Hello, Rosetta? This is Willie Nelson. I got a message you called." Mmmm . . . what a sexy, mellow voice, I thought.

"Oh, yes. Yes, I did. I mean I did," I stammered before gaining my composure. "I met Billy, your son Billy. I met him at the Broken Spoke and told him I was lookin' for a job. He said I should call you. But I've found one."

Soon after we moved to Austin in 1989, Ray Benson introduced me to Billy Nelson at the Broken Spoke during an Asleep at the Wheel show. Billy and his attractive companion from San Antonio joined us at our table. We spent the evening discussing Bob, Willie, and golf. When we started to leave, Billy said, "Be sure you call my dad." He handed me a business card with Willie's phone number on it. I kept the card in my wallet for weeks until I finally dialed the number. I waited breathlessly, carefully rehearsing my written script: *Hi, this is Rosetta Wills, Bob Wills's daughter. I met your son Billy at the Broken Spoke.* . . . But the assistant who answered told me Willie was out of the country and wouldn't be back until next month.

"I'm glad you found a job," Willie continued. "What are you doin'?"

"I'm workin' for Libby Doggett at the Arc of Texas," I explained. "It's an advocacy organization for people with disabilities."

"That sounds very rewarding." What a nice man, I thought.

We discussed plans for the upcoming tribute session for the late Texas Playboy Jesse Ashlock. Evie, Jesse's widow, had told me that Willie and some other Austin musicians were going to record Jesse's songs soon. "Hope I get to visit with you sometime soon," Willie said before he hung up the phone.

We attended Music Mania's tape release party for *Doing It Jesse's Way: A Tribute to Jessie Ashlock*. Proud Evie smiled as Alvin Crow, Kimmie Rhodes, and Texas Tornadoes' Doug Sahm (former Sir Douglas Quintet leader) performed "Still Water Runs the Deepest" and "The Kind of Love I Can't Forget." Evie said, "I want to do somethin' to keep Jesse's name alive." She had recently introduced us to Kimmie at the Broken Spoke. Unfortunately, a few weeks later we missed Willie's surprise impromptu performance during Kimmie's show.

Jesse, who patterned his fiddle playing after jazzman Joe Venuti, claimed the music he and the Playboys played was not western swing, but just swing. "If you're playin' swing, you're playin' swing." Evie said, "You know, Jesse was with Milton Brown and then with Bob for years. Even though he would break up with Bob, he always went back. He sure loved him." Jesse stood on a Tulsa street corner for hours one bitterly cold winter day waiting for Bob to pick him up. He finally gave up and called a cab. When an angry Bob scolded him for being late for rehearsal, Jesse reminded Bob that he had forgotten to give him a ride. Bob walked away without saying a word. "That very next day Bob had a new car delivered to Jesse."

I didn't have an opportunity to speak with Willie again until Evie phoned. "Will you go somewhere with me tomorrow?"

"Sure, Evie, where do you wanna go?"

"Willie's daughter Lana said they're filmin' a movie or somethin' out at the ranch and needed some extras. Maybe your husband would like to go, too."

We three arrived a half hour before the scheduled Wednesday morning shoot time at the mock western town erected on Willie's ranch. As we walked up the steps into the small white-frame chapel where others gathered, Willie drove up in his golf cart. He stopped abruptly and jumped out to hug Evie. It had been almost twenty years since the first time I met him backstage in California. Evie said, "You've met Rosetta before, Bob Wills's daughter. And this is her husband, Michael." I reminded him about his phone call when I first moved to Austin and thanked him again. I wanted to express my sadness about Billy's suicide, but the timing was wrong. I will always remember Billy's thoughtfulness the night I met him at the Broken Spoke. He exhibited the same charm and humility as his father.

At least a hundred extras had shown up for this mysterious filming of Lana's creation, possibly a movie about a fictitious C&W star or a documentary about Willie's life or perhaps a music video for CMT. Pianist Floyd Domino, who had helped lay down some tracks in the studio, said, "I heard it's for CD-Rom. Oh, well, who knows? It's a Willie thing."

The camera crews set up while the stunt men rehearsed a fight scene outside the town's saloon. Cowboys circled on horses and in carriages as a lady in prim nineteenth-century apparel walked the board sidewalks. Musicians arrived and started setting up on the stage for Willie's appearance. Jimmy Day, renowned pedal steel player, gave me a hug. When silver-haired Johnny Gimble saw me near the stage, he smiled at me and drew his bow across his fiddle as he hummed a few bars of "Rosetta."

I had chatted with Johnny a few years earlier at an Austin Symphony Square show. His reputation flourished after playing on Merle Haggard's tribute album to Bob, and the Country Music Association named him Instrumentalist of the Year in 1974. Bob admired Johnny's fiddling style and asked him to play in the 1973 session that produced the album *For The Last Time.* Johnny picked up his jazz persuasion in his younger days when he played with Pete Fountain before he joined Bob's band in 1949.

Johnny's first onstage encounter with Bob came in Waco when Bob said, "There's a little fiddle player in the house tonight. The boys hired him, and they say he's good. Well, he dang well better be!" The then-twenty-three-year-old Gimble said, "I was scared to death! I was shakin' in my boots. He made you play more than you imagined you could." Twenty years later Bob told the audience, "We got a real fiddle boy up here, Johnny Gimble. Don't let anybody kid you. He's one of the greatest I ever listened to. I'm pretty good at fakin', you know. For years I played medicine shows, black face comedian, tried to be, and I know how to fake it, but he's the real thing. That's the difference between the two of us."

Johnny Bush (composer of Willie's "Whiskey River" standard) started setting up drums on the stage. He had given me his new CD *Time Changes Everything* when fiddler Howard Kalish introduced us. It includes a song written for my father titled "Bob Said It 'AW' (And Called It Western Swing)." Later when I listened to Johnny Rodriguez sing, I remembered a photo of him and my father together at the 1973 San Antonio benefit. He told me, "Meeting Bob that time in San Antonio was a big thrill for me."

Michael and I positioned ourselves in a strategic spot near the door of Pooh Bah's Backstage Cafe, not knowing Willie would make his entrance through that door. The camera caught us in the foreground as he stopped to speak to Kinky Friedman (Texas's "Singing Jewboy" turned author). Unless we end up on the cutting room floor, we will make our screen debut lounging on the cafe's porch or dancing in front of the stage.

During a break I sat under a large shade tree behind the stage and watched Johnny Gimble patiently instruct Willie's young son how to play a miniature fiddle. Johnny and Willie entertained the extras standing around the stage with jokes and jam sessions between takes. As we stood motionless, poised for the next shoot, the director counted down through his bull horn "three . . . two . . . one . . . action." Willie shouted, "Okay, everyone tense up!"

After ten hours in the hot sun, we decided to call it quits, even though the crew was still filming. A few months later the *Austin Statesman* ran an article about a film titled *Tales Out of Luck* shot on Willie's ranch. (At this writing, we're still waiting for the theater release or television debut.)

When Willie left the stage, I caught up with him. "I have a picture of you with my mother, but not with me." We posed as Michael's camera flashed. I thought about a Tulsa evening when an unusually quiet, almost deserted backstage area awaited us as we went to see Willie after the show. Our friend Jim snapped my mother with Willie, who later autographed the photo and returned it with a note: "Dear Mary Lou, Thanks for coming to see me. I was glad to meet you. Love, Willie P.S. We sure do take a pretty good picture." Jim also snapped Willie's then-wife Connie with Delbert McClinton, well-known Lubbock blues singer, who told me he also grew up listening to my father's music.

Willie's 1995 July Picnic scene at Luckenbach differed greatly from the one I had experienced seventeen years earlier backstage at the Cotton Bowl. In-vogue bottled water replaced the free, potent margaritas. Large signs warned pot smokers that drug-sniffing dogs were on the premises. Willie's long, gray-streaked hair still flowed around his shoulders, but Kris Kristofferson's short gray hair didn't even cover his ears.

Willie grinned as he glanced at Ray Price, revealing his immense enjoyment. The old familiar rush started when Ray began singing the opening lines of "San Antonio Rose." Standing in the backstage extension behind Ray and Willie during the finale electrified me. I watched bodies blend into one giant mass of waving arms and filter through the blinding spotlights flooding the stage.

After the show Ray told me, "Your father had a big influence on me and my music." Ray met Bob in Dallas when Bob owned the Ranch House, and when he was on the road, Ray often played there. He had included Bob's tunes in his dance sets for years before cutting a single of "Faded Love" in 1957. "If you were gonna play dances in the western part of the country, you had to play some Bob Wills's music. He was that famous." Ray's *San Antonio Rose* (1961) was one of the first tribute albums ever released, and it predates Haggard's tribute by ten years. Ray and Willie recorded an excellent duet album in 1980, also called *San Antonio Rose*.

On Reba McEntire's *Live* concert album (1989), she expressed her appreciation for her male influences, who included Ray Price, Merle Haggard, and Bob Wills. After performing "San Antonio Rose," she said, "People ask me all the time who are my musical influences. Well, I guess it's just kind of natural that since I was raised in Oklahoma that one of my musical influences was Bob Wills's music. When I was in college we used to sneak off down on the Oklahoma and Texas border and go to dances. It just didn't get any better than dancing to Bob Wills's music. It really upsets me that I never got to meet Bob Wills." Along with John Anderson and Leon Redbone, she was just another willing but disappointed artist who wasn't included on Ray Benson's *A Tribute to Bob Wills* (Liberty Records, 1994). Benson said, "Our only problem was that we couldn't do a four-record set. We already had a two-record set, so we had to go with what we had."

Willie Nelson, Garth Brooks, George Strait, Vince Gill, Marty Stuart, Brooks & Dunn, Merle Haggard, Dolly Parton, Lyle Lovett, Johnny Rodriguez, Chet Atkins, Suzy Bogguss, Lucky Oceans, Cindy Cashdollar, Ricky Turpin, Riders in the Sky, Jody Nix, Huey Lewis, Eldon Shamblin, Leon Rausch, Johnny Gimble, Herb Remington, and Ray Benson all performed on *A Tribute to Bob Wills*. As Mark Rowland, wrote in *Musician* magazine:

> The Liberty Records press release hailing this album as "the music event of the decade" is not an overstatement. Garth Brooks . . . along with others . . . is part of the widest-ranging lineup of country superstars on one record in memory—which is only fitting, since Bob Wills, the subject of this tribute, was the most eclectic, and arguably influential, figure in the history of country music.
>
> Members of the Texas Playboys often remarked that Bob Wills' mere presence had a powerful effect on their music. If he didn't show up for a gig, the band sounded flat, yet as soon as he walked in the door, his spirit somehow lifted everything to a higher level.

The star-studded recording project, sanctioned by maverick Jimmy Bowen, was nominated for the 1995 CMA Top Country Album of the Year, but *Common Thread: Songs of the Eagles* won. However, the tribute won three Grammy Awards: Buddy Jackson for the recording package, Eldon Shamblin for his instrumental "Red Wing," and Asleep at the Wheel and Lyle Lovett for their duo on "Blues for Dixie."

Willie's monumental *Across the Borderline* (1993) recorded shortly before his sixtieth birthday transcended anything he had done in years. The day after his celebration at Antone's, he signed autographs at Tower Records on The Drag. Chad's girlfriend Cindy waited in line to tell him we were disappointed we didn't have a chance to talk with him at Antone's. Willie snatched some paper and wrote, "Rosetta, I'm sorry I missed talking with you last night. Love, Willie." I placed the note behind another refrigerator magnet and waited for Michael to notice it.

"Oh, Willie must have stopped by and left me a note."

After carefully inspecting it, he asked, "How do I know this is Willie's handwriting?" I assured him it was, but I waited a few hours before confessing Willie hadn't been to the house.

Ever since the early seventies, music lovers nationwide knew about the Armadillo World Headquarters, home of the progressive sounds of Willie Nelson, Jerry Jeff Walker, Michael Murphy, and Doug Sahm. The Progressive Country label, however, didn't fit all the Austin musicians. Michael's niece Dayna, living in Austin during the "Outlaw" era, admitted she had never heard of Bob Wills until Waylon sang "Bob Wills Is Still the King." Her claim to fame was a meager part in the movie *The Songwriter*. "I was the girl in the bedroom scene with Kris Kristofferson."

Michael and I moved south to "The Live Music Capital of the World" to be closer to the touted music scene furnishing abundant choices for folk, country, jazz, rock, and blues. Sharing our passion for music, Reneé and Chad soon moved to Austin. I chuckled when I recalled that Chad and I had seen U2's movie *Rattle and Hum* on the big screen three times. One time we were the only people in the theater so Chad was able to sneak his beer in under his coat. Later we watched Bono begin the concert in our living room, pounding out his hell-bent "Helter Skelter" revival on videotape. "This song Charles Manson stole from the Beatles. We're stealin' it back again!"

The comfortable Cactus Cafe on the University of Texas campus has a hideaway atmosphere and features varied acoustic artists. After his Cactus performance, we spoke with Ramblin' Jack Elliott, the quintessential Brooklyn singing cowboy (born Elliott Charles Adnopoz). Ramblin' Jack had accompanied Woody Guthrie on his last cross-country trek in 1953 before Woody became hospitalized under the debilitating effects of Huntington's disease. He told us Woody had seen Bob perform at Cain's in the thirties and even owned one of his fiddles. Bob recorded Woody's classic "Oklahoma Hills" in 1946.

"Well, he's gone, but I don't worry, 'cause I'm sittin' on top of the world," exploded from an extraordinary voice on the Stacy Park stage. I had never heard anyone except my father sing "Sittin' on Top of the World." We introduced ourselves to Keri Leigh & The Blue Devils, namely Keri and Mark Lyon, who had moved here from Oklahoma City to ply their blues on the Austin scene. In turn they introduced us to another Oklahoma transplant who played solo that day,

Stillwater's Jimmy LaFave. Since that time these Austin musicians have soared with success.

Keri had been working with Stevie Ray Vaughan on his biography for three months before the tragic Wisconsin helicopter crash took Vaughan's life in 1990. Overwhelmed by his untimely death, she labored for three years to finish writing *Soul to Soul.* Country music guitar players influenced Stevie Ray and his brother Jimmie during their youth in the Dallas suburb of Oak Cliff. Bob's band members visited the Vaughan household for parties, showing the young boys how to play. On a 1985 MTV guest host spot, Stevie Ray discussed Texas musicians and related stories about Bob Wills, Buddy Holly, Willie Nelson, Janis Joplin, Johnny Winter, Lightnin' Hopkins, and T-Bone Walker. When reading her book I learned that the old Howlin' Wolf song "Sittin' on Top of the World" was one of Stevie's favorites. She autographed our SRV biography, "Yes, I'm still sittin' on top of the world."

Garydon Rhodes sent me a tape he directed titled *Fiddlin' Man* that has footage of Bob singing "Sittin' on Top of the World." He arches his heavy eyebrows, rolls his piercing eyes, and sways to the rhythm. This clip was one of seven film shorts shot by MGM in 1951, when Bob was forty-six years old, but he looks younger. A couple of other popular ones feature Joe Frank Ferguson singing "Blue Prelude" and Carolina Cotton yodeling on "Yodel Mountain." These Snader Telescriptions filled spaces between local programs on TV stations, another first, and a harbinger of MTV's musical videos.

I discovered an upbeat, vigorous interpretation of "Sittin' on Top of the World" by Bob Dylan on his first acoustical release in years. According to Richard Williams's *Dylan: A Man Called Alias,* thirty years earlier Dylan had played harmonica on Victoria Spivey's and Big Joe Williams's rendition on *Three Kings and a Queen.*

Austin City Limits featured the Original Texas Playboys on their first airing (1976), which turned out to be the most exciting piece of the series. An unedited tape exists where the camera caught Leon McAuliffe and Leon Rausch openly sipping their beers as Al Stricklin discreetly sipped his from a cup on the piano—hidden from view by his white hat. Program director Bill Arhos had asked Joe Gracey, an Austin deejay and columnist, to act as a talent consultant for their first season. Gracey tracked down former Texas Playboys and planned to line them up until he learned that Betty (who owned the Texas Playboys' name) didn't want any performance reunions after Bob's death. However, after he contacted her, she agreed and even attended the show. Clifford Endres wrote in *Austin City Limits:*

> While Gracey had 11 Playboys signed on for the show, he had money to
> pay only five. What to do? Bobby Earl Smith, manager and bass player for

Alvin Crow, headed directly to the Broken Spoke, a venerable Austin dance hall, whose manager James White happily agreed to book the Texas Playboys on short notice . . . and that's how the Playboys made expenses.

When the Original Texas Playboys opened with the stirring "Faded Love," scores cheered and shouted as if the Beatles had returned. According to Steve Millburg in a *Southpoint* magazine article, the Texas Playboys—under the leadership of Bob Wills—had been "the Beatles of the Southwest in the 1930s."

Speaking of the Beatles, Leon Rausch described a Chicago engagement where his seven-piece band played for Paul McCartney's five hundred guests at Soldier's Field. As recounted in John E. Perkins, Jr.'s biography *Leon Rausch: The Voice of the Texas Playboys*, McCartney had requested a "Texas country band, a kickin' band, true to the Bob Wills' style" for his 1990 tour Wrap Party. Paul was excited to meet Leon and also Tommy Allsup, who had worked with another of Paul's idols, Buddy Holly. After all, it's been reported the Beatles chose their "bug" name after the Crickets.

The Original Texas Playboys attended the Country Music Association awards as nominees for the 1977 Instrumental Group of the Year, but they had no expectations to win. After their announcement as the choice, they received a standing ovation as tears streamed down the cheeks of Loretta Lynn and Minnie Pearl. Minnie Pearl said, "I prayed you guys would get that. I'm glad to see some justice done."

The celebrated Playboys had another sentimental experience when they played an outdoor concert at the state Capitol for *Austin City Limits'* tenth season, with guest vocals by George Strait and Willie Nelson. In 1986 Governor Mark White designated August 30 as "Bob Wills and His Texas Playboys Day" in Texas. When the Playboys returned to tape another *Austin City Limits*, they ended the show with the tribute "The Playboys' Promise," a song written about keeping Bob Wills's music alive. Their raw emotions were difficult to hide.

Michael and I traveled to Fort Worth for the Original Texas Playboys' last performance. We stayed with Diane and her husband, Dick, giving me an opportunity to visit with her and her children, Amy, Andy, and Bobby. Several relatives believed Diane and I shared a resemblance—she looking more like the Wills side of the family while the other children looked more like their mother, Betty. At bedtime Diane and I were surprised to find we were wearing matching nightgowns, obviously sharing the same taste in clothes. I asked her if they would come to Tulsa, but Dick said, "Not unless you can get Diane on an airplane." Fear of flying—another similarity. My grandmother Emma Wills would not fly. Even my father refused to fly again after his first flight in 1935 when the band flew in a private plane for a performance in Waco, Texas. Millions of miles across the country from booking to booking for fifty years in show business were traveled on the ground. Was a phobia passed down through the genes?

On November 16, 1986, we witnessed the Playboys' final performance at the Will Rogers Auditorium. The concert afforded a touching end for the four remaining Playboys from the early Tulsa Band—Leon, Smoky, Eldon, and Joe Frank. They had previously agreed to disband when a member died, and pianist Al Stricklin had recently died from cancer. At the end Leon said, "It will never end in our hearts," as he choked back tears.

"We never played anything the people didn't understand. We never played over their heads. Bob taught us to play from our insides to their insides," said Smoky.

Joe Frank added, "When Bob walked into the room, the atmosphere of the room changed altogether."

Eldon continued, "Bob was dynamic. His capability to control the crowds was unbelievable. He could walk up to the microphone before a loud, noisy group and soon you could hear a pin drop. I've been able to survive in the music business because I worked for Wills. We feel like Bob is still here when we play these old tunes."

Leon concluded, "Bob inspired us to be better musicians the way no one else could. You just wanted to please him. Bob's fiddle had soul. It had feeling. It communicated with people. I can't think of a greater blessing that could have happened to me in my life than when Bob asked me to play a chord before he called out 'Take it away, Leon' on 'Steel Guitar Rag' so many years ago." Leon died in Tulsa two years later at age seventy-one.

Above: Kris Kristofferson at Willie Nelson's Fourth of July Picnic in the Cotton Bowl, Dallas, Texas in 1978 *(Courtesy Rosetta Wills).*

Left: Gary Busey at Willie Nelson's Fourth of July Picnic in the Cotton Bowl, Dallas, in 1978 *(Courtesy Rosetta Wills).*

Chad Arnett and Reneé
Arnett with their mother
Rosetta Wills, Tulsa,
Oklahoma, in 1985
(Courtesy Rosetta Wills).

Tulsa artist Jack Miller's
1982 sketch of Rosetta Wills
standing next to Bob Wills's
photo at Cain's *(Courtesy
Rosetta Wills).*

Alvin Crow (fiddle) and Chad Arnett (drums) on the Cain's stage in 1988
(Courtesy Rosetta Wills).

Left to right: Johnnie Lee Wills, Bob Wills, and Jesse Ashlock performing at 1973 Bob Wills Day in Turkey, Texas, *(Courtesy Frank Rosser and Ed Aubry).*

Left to right: Johnnie Lee Wills, Leon McAuliffe, Bob Wills, and Sleepy Johnson (fiddle) performing at the 1973 Bob Wills Day in Turkey *(Courtesy Frank Rosser and Ed Aubry).*

Left to right: Johnny Gimble (fiddle), Johnny Rodriguez (vocals), and Willie Nelson at Spicewood, Texas, ranch in May 1995 *(Courtesy Rosetta Wills).*

Willie Nelson and Rosetta Wills at Spicewood ranch in May 1995 *(Courtesy Rosetta Wills)*.

Cindy Wills and Rosetta Wills at the postal stamp unveiling ceremony held at the Broken Spoke in Austin on September 28, 1993 *(Courtesy Rosetta Wills)*.

Chapter 13

Bob Inside Austin City Limits

A new book of Willie Nelson's lyrics along with two new
CD releases make a case for Willie Nelson as a musical
alchemist, with the apparent ability to transmute almost
anything with a meter and a melody into his brand of Texas
gold. In Nelson's era in the cycle of popular music, only Ray
Charles, Elvis Presley, Bob Wills, and perhaps Van Morrison
demonstrated an equivalent gift for assimilating and
transforming any type of music that crossed their paths.

> —JOHN T. DAVIS,
> "WHAT PEOPLE LIKE,"
> AUSTIN-AMERICAN STATESMAN

In the mid-seventies, *Austin City Limits*' edited version of a "live" mix compared to Texas Playboys' recording sessions in the thirties, before the invention of tape machines, when engineers etched a performance directly on the master disk. What went on the air in Austin was essentially a polished translation of the rough mix captured by the audio engineer. When the music started, he only had onstage microphones to mix into the multitrack recorder. He got an adrenaline rush when he knew there would be no remix, that he had to get it all the first time. According to Clifford Endres's book *Austin City Limits*, Willie Nelson feels this directness contributed an excitement that faded when more sophisticated techniques came into being.

Back in 1936 during the Brunswick recording session in Chicago, Art Satherley finally perceived the value in Bob's spontaneity. From then on, "Uncle Art" became bothered if Bob didn't holler. Major hits came out of that session, with the majority of the numbers ("Steel Guitar Rag," "Trouble in Mind," "Bring It on Down to My House," "Sugar Blues," and "Basin Street Blues") more analogous to Dixieland jazz and black blues than traditional fiddle tunes. Three other numbers recorded in Chicago but unissued at the time later became favorites ("I've Got the Wonder Where She Went Blues," "Just Friends," and "There's No Disappointment in Heaven").

O. W. Mayo recalled that they got off to a bad start when a Chicago taxi driver, observing Jesse Ashlock's big white hat and cowboy attire, yelled, "Where's your horse?"

Jesse whirled around and shouted, "A jackass will do. Come on!"

Mayo calmly said, "Now listen, boy, you're in Chicago now. We don't wanna do a round with these bunch of cabbies."

They had to record at night because Sammy Kaye's band had scheduled the studio during the day. Once they cut one side, they had to make a duplicate as a backup. If something happened to the original, they produced the record from the backup.

"What happened in Chicago never happened anywhere else," Smoky said. "We were way late in the night, almost three o'clock. We had a much better studio than we had in Dallas. There was a great big clock up there on the wall you could look right at all the time. I forgot what tune we were workin' on, but we had one cut made. All we had to do was make another one just like it and we'd be done. Okay, so I just kept the rhythm goin' real quiet back there so we'd have the same speed. Oh, boy, we started off doin' good when Bob looked up at that clock. We had 'bout ten seconds to go when Bob hollered, 'Ahh-ha, it won't be long now!' That *was not* on the first one. Oh, hell, it was close to six o'clock in the morning before we got it made again."

In 1990 an *Austin City Limits* TV camera captured Michael and me for an instant, startling our friends at home who recognized us in the audience. I had met the young performer's sister one night in a Tulsa bar where she played guitar for Gus Hardin and heard his mother had recorded "San Antonio Rose" in the fifties. Garth Brooks's first self-titled debut album already had three hit singles.

At this early stage in his rapidly ascending stardom, a candid moment occurred that would surely never repeat itself in public. As the technical crew took time out during the taping to fine-tune their camera angles, the band playfully dove into a ballad about good ole Oklahoma boys harvesting the illegal weed down on the farm. As the musical tale described the departure of the empty-handed "narcs," Garth raised his middle finger in the proper defiant gesture to close the final verse. But then suddenly he spied a young girl sitting with her parents on the front row. His face turned red as he stammered out a profusely maudlin apology. During this docile show he didn't swing from anything or destroy any guitars.

I had clipped John Wooley's 1988 *Tulsa World* review on Garth:

On hot solo after hot solo, the musicians mirrored Garth Brooks' energy and sense of fun. As Brooks sold song after song with his authentic country voice and never-let-up attitude, they were there, providing exactly the kind of licks he needed, and indulging in a little horseplay as well. Odd as the mixture may seem, it was like watching Bob Wills front Paul Revere and The Raiders.

When associate producer Susan Caldwell introduced me to Garth after the show, I asked him if he had read Wooley's review. "What did you think the part about Bob Wills meant?" He shrugged his shoulders and shyly grinned. "I don't know. I didn't understand it. Did you?"

Veteran blues and jazz guitarist Gatemouth Brown, who has performed on *Austin City Limits,* also plays a breakdown fiddle. In a 1992 interview astute Austin music critic Michael Point quoted Brown about his early roots:

People thought it was sort of strange for a black blues player to be playing country music, but I never could understand that. They must have forgotten that I was raised in Texas around all that music. Bob Wills is as much an influence on my music as anyone, and if people would just listen they'd know that.

The final taping for *Austin City Limits'* nineteenth season brought together three sensational songwriters—Willie Nelson, Lyle Lovett, and Rodney Crowell. The acoustic format allowed them to play songs they don't usually perform. Willie's idea for the impromptu songwriters' showcase created a successful show. After performing their own compositions most of the show, Willie then said, "Hey, let's do some Bob Wills stuff," and began strumming "Stay a Little Longer."

In 1987 the Austin City Council decreed April as Western Swing Month and promoted events all around town. The Driskill Hotel fashioned a Bob Wills display in the lobby. Bob's "star" in the sidewalk outside still heads up the Sixth Street Walk of Stars. Al Dressen's Super Swing Revue with former Texas Playboys hosted the awards ceremony at the Paramount Theater. My father was the very first inductee into the new Texas Western Swing Hall of Fame. In 1997 at the tenth annual celebration, Cousin Dayna Wills and I accepted the awards for inductees Luke Wills (the only living brother), Johnnie Lee, and Billy Jack. Also included were Bill Boyd (posthumously) and two surprise inductees, former Texas Playboy Gene Gasaway and steel guitarist Tom Morrell.

In 1990 the Friday night "Gathering" initiated the festivities with several former Playboys attending. Smoky Dacus, Joe Frank Ferguson, Eldon Shamblin, Leon Rausch, and Laura Lee Owns McBride (a posthumous inductee who died in 1986) were all inducted into the Texas Western Swing Hall of Fame that year. Johnny

Cuviello (inducted into the Texas Western Swing Hall of Fame in 1992) and Steve Hathaway, who wrote the liner notes for a new release of Bob's 1946 Anaheim radio show on an album, flew in from California. At the awards banquet, we joined our friends Michelle Ramzur and Paul Glasse (a great mandolin player who studied under Tiny Moore.)

After Bob asked Johnny Cuviello to join the band in 1946, Johnny ordered a new drum set with "Bob Wills Texas Playboys" printed on it along with his initials. "I think Bob was really surprised and happy when he saw it. I was the first guy that did it, the first to put his name on the drums. After that a lot of other drummers did it, but I've got a picture on the bandstand with Bob and my drums." Johnny's zealous drumming is an anticipated "Turkey Treat" each year.

In 1945 Bob, Cliff Sundin, and Clifton Johnsen (known as Cactus Jack to his radio audience) formed the Tiffany Music Company. They produced a series of syndicated radio programs for sale to radio stations across the nation. Sundin, an Oakland songwriter, helped finance the business so Bob would record some songs he had written. (In 1984 a friend gave me a well-preserved copy of the sheet music, "Stars and Stripes on Iwo Jima," listing Bob Wills, Cliff Sundin, and Clifton Johnsen as the composers.)

Cactus Jack's sales ability, coupled with Bob's previous radio achievements, marked the venture as a potential success, but somehow the plan failed. The sixteen-inch vinyl discs contained three to five different songs per side, beginning and ending with the Texas Playboy Theme. Scripts for the local deejays of the subscribing stations to read between tracks were also included. The band recorded over 370 selections in 1946 and 1947 but released only fifty disc sets. The band at that point featured Joe Holley, Louis Tierney, Johnny Cuviello, Eldon Shamblin, Junior Barnard, Noel Boggs, Herb Remington, Roy Honeycutt, Tiny Moore, Millard Kelso, Alex Brashear, Luke and Bill Jack Wills, with Tommy Duncan, Evelyn and Dean McKinney (of the McKinney Sisters), and Tommy "Spike" Doss on vocals. The transcriptions, along with other promotional material, were stored in Cliff Sundin's basement until his death in 1981. The liner notes highlight interesting quotes from musicians who played in the sessions.

"Ah, yes, Tiny," Bob used to say, "play that mandolin, 'the biggest little mandolin in the world.'" Tiny said, "This was the way we sounded on many dances we played. In not tryin' for the 'perfect take,' we had a relaxed but drivin' quality that's hard to get on a record. No pressure at all during these sessions—only fun." (Tiny Moore died in 1986 at age sixty-seven.)

"Ah, let's hear you, boy! That's Herby," Bob used to holler. Herb Remington played steel with Bob from 1946 till 1950. When he was twenty years old, he auditioned to play in Uncle Luke's band, but Bob liked Herb's playing so much, he sent Roy Honeycott to Luke's band and "kept the kid." Herb's first gig was a spirited Battle of the Bands with Spade Cooley at the Santa Monica Ballroom. Herb and Bob co-wrote "Boot Hill Drag," which validated Herb as an accomplished steel guitarist. "Noel Boggs and Roy Honeycott played steel before me. If you treated Bob with respect and you did a job for him, that's all he required. He didn't want some genius jazz player. He wanted someone who would fit in and do the job. He was a great person who treated me with the highest caliber of respect. We had fun doin' those Tiffany sessions. We were too tired to be uptight. We recorded those when we got home from a long tour and were really worn down. You know, they say if you get a bunch of tired and hungry musicians together, they play better than ever." Herb now leads the Playboys II band in concerts throughout the country.

"All right," Bob used to shout, "that's my man Jody!" Left-handed fiddler Joe Holley joined Bob's California band in 1944 and continued to travel with him until 1961. In 1987 Joe Holley died at age seventy. He summed up the Tiffany sessions when he said, "Everything was spontaneous, or in Bob's words—'Not cut and dried.'"

The Tiffany Transcriptions were finally released on compact discs in the eighties, with nine volumes now available through Rhino Records. (Volume two includes "San Antonio Rose," "Faded Love," Take Me Back to Tulsa," "Ida Red," "Right or Wrong," "Time Changes Everything," "Steel Guitar Rag," "Stay a Little Longer," and "Maiden's Prayer.") Although my father recorded for several major record labels, the Tiffany recordings are among fans' favorites since they closely simulate a live dance sound. Gone is the big band that sported the large horn section. Instead, electric instruments featured Eldon Shamblin and Junior Barnard on guitars, Tiny Moore on mandolin, and Herb Remington on steel guitar. Bob surrounded himself with young, innovative musicians during this time. Some even believe they were the best who played with him. Or perhaps the fact that the recordings sat in a basement for thirty-five years greatly intrigued the fans— buried Wills treasure unearthed.

Over fifty years after the McKinney Sisters sang on the Tiffany recordings, I sat at a table near the Broken Spoke stage listening to Dean and Evelyn on vocals with Louise Rowe, Bob's only female instrumentalist, on her bright red upright bass. (Louise was inducted into the Texas Western Swing Hall of Fame in 1992.) Several generations whirled around the floor as Louise plucked and the sisters harmonized on "Rose of Old Pawnee." The three ladies, along with other former Texas Playboys, are now performing across the country as the Hall of Fame Touring Band. Dean joined us at our table during their break. "I think Herby, Eldon, and Tiny did the best section work Bob ever had. It was so musically correct with Bob's distinctive touch. The quality on the transcriptions is amazing since we just gathered 'round a mike in a room without all the fancy stuff that's available today."

Smoky and Joe Frank came out to the Spoke one night when Leon Rausch was singing. Hanging out with these fun-loving former Texas Playboys delights me. Smoky hugged me, saying, "The thing I remember about you, Sweetheart, you was a hell of a cute kid!" His husky voice told outrageous stories as mild-mannered Joe Frank nodded in agreement. Smoky quit the band only two months before they went to California to film the movies. "Bob just couldn't understand that, you know. I said, 'Look Bob, I have no desire to go to the picture show and see myself with a set of drums tied to a tree.'"

Smoky, a few years older than the other guys in the band, felt a need to learn a trade so he wouldn't end up playing beer joints on the edge of town in his old age. He fondly recalled his six years with the band. "Hell, we had to like each other 'cause we spent about twenty hours out of twenty-four together. Shoulder to shoulder." His voice got quiet when he talked about his feelings for my father. "Bob Wills was better to us than we had any idea at the time. I know now he was one of the greatest individuals I ever knew. He was fair-minded and everything else. We didn't realize how good he was to us at the time. You think about it different later on."

Joe Frank played with Bob from 1936 until 1940, when he moved to Fort Worth and started playing with the Light Crust Doughboys. "I'm the only one who left Bob to go play with the Doughboys. All the others left the Doughboys to go with Bob. Just count 'em—that fiddle player Jesse Ashlock, old Sleepy Johnson—golly, the whole dadgum bunch." Joe Frank also missed his big opportunity to appear on the silver screen. "O. W. called me and wanted to know if I could go to California, but I told him I couldn't go on account of I was tied up with the Doughboys. Had the midnight show at the Worth Theater. Had the big band down at the Texas Den. And I had a young kid still in the crib. But in 1951 I called Bob. I was workin' at a club downtown, had a quartet with a piano, two girls and myself. It was gettin' out of hand so I called Bob and asked him if there was any way he could use me and he said, 'Hell, yes, come on.' Joe Andrews was playin' bass and singin' so I just played bass and let him sing or sometimes I'd sing and he'd play bass."

When Leon saw me, he grabbed me up in a bear hug proclaiming, "She's got the Ole Man's eyes." When he started singing with Bob he wrote the lyrics on 3 x 5 cards. Bob's bent toward spontaneity frowned on this, and after each song, he politely asked, "Leon, do you think we could throw that little card away now?" After they played the tune a few more times, he asked again, "Leon, have you about got that tune now?" Leon said, "Bob wasn't happy until all my little 3x5 cards were gone."

"You know," Leon continued, "I came down here to Austin with Bob almost thirty years ago, back in the sixties when Bob played the Spoke for the first time.

Your daddy was a taskmaster. He wanted his music done right and there was noth-in' wrong with that. He knew what he wanted to hear and he knew how he want-ed it to sound and what kind of beat he wanted."

Leon paused for a moment before breaking out in another big grin. "I remem-ber how close he was to us boys. I've worked with lots of people on the road and met a lot of people and I've never seen any band leader or group leader or what-ever, Grand Ole Opry stars even, that treated their band like Bob did. You wanted to listen to every word he said. You wanted to watch every move he made. He had a magnetism, an aura, like Elvis.

"Anyway," he continued, "He knew how he wanted us to act. For one thing, he didn't want us to act up, like send your food back in a restaurant and make an ass of yourself and stuff like that. He made it very plain to us that we was to act like gen-tlemen. When we went into a place of business, it reflected directly on him, especially if he was in the building. They all knew who Bob was. Bob would say, 'I can act up, but if I do, it's my business, but you're not to act up and get me in trouble.'

"We was to act like gentlemen and he wanted us to dress like we was traveling instead of just bums," he added. "He was very strict about that. He didn't like long sideburns and wanted us all to be well groomed and have a clean shirt on. You know, I don't think there is a thing wrong with this because he wanted us to look good, have a certain image. If we were gonna go in a restaurant to eat, Bob would say, 'You're not gonna wear that, are you?' When we got out of that bus, we had to have a clean shirt on and act like we had some sense."

Leon paused before he winked at me and rambled on. "Bob loved to sit up in bed, drink coffee, and talk, telling wild tales all night. We'd cover almost eight hun-dred miles a day and Bob always took along his coffee pot. He would tell us about the days people would line the highways between Texas and Oklahoma when he was travelin' to put on a show. Bands were all local back then and people would almost break the windows of the car tryin' to shake their hands."

Bob's band toured—another first.

Leon later introduced me to Dwight Adair, who had purchased the movie rights for Charles R. Townsend's *San Antonio Rose* and was currently negotiating with Japanese investors about producing a movie. Years earlier a California friend had sent me a *Los Angeles Times* article reporting that Seadra/Caribou Films had bought the rights to the biography and were negotiating with Jack Nicholson to play the role of my father (years before Nicholson's roles in the *Batman* movies). But it never happened.

Jody Nix, a fan ever since he played the drums onstage with Bob at age four, has one of Bob's fiddles. Jody said, "We call it the Old Doughboy fiddle 'cause Bob started playin' it when he was with the Light Crust Doughboys. My daddy Hoyle inscribed on the back of it, 'Played and owned by Bob Wills from January, 1930, until June, 1965.' Your daddy even signed it 'Bob Wills—always keep it, Jody,' so I can't ever sell it 'cause he said to always keep it. I've recognized it in old pictures of the Doughboys. I had it restored in 1988 and carry it with me on the road most of the time."

During the late fifties and the sixties Bob played dates with Hoyle Nix's West Texas Cowboys. Jody added, "They played those Battle Dances in our part of the world several times a year. Both bands would play five nights in a row all over West Texas in Midland, Abilene, Lubbock, and, well, just all over West Texas. I remember the night Bob sang 'Sittin' on Top of the World' at our club, the Stampede, in Big Spring. I think that was his last stage performance before his stroke. Then I remember in September of 1973 when Bob sat in with daddy's band, holding his fiddle with his left hand while daddy drew the bow for him. Bob got frustrated and just took the microphone and sang a few verses from Bessie Smith's 'Down Hearted Blues.' Yeah, ole Bob was the best. He loved my daddy and my daddy loved him." The dilapidated Bob Wills's Flex Flyer tour bus rests in permanent, melancholy retirement next to Hoyle's bus at the Nix ranch.

When Austin's time-honored honky-tonk the Broken Spoke (akin to Tulsa's Cain's) celebrated thirty years of being in business, musicians Don Walser and Jerry Jeff Walker attracted a throng large enough to attract the attention of the city's fire marshall. Owner James White didn't want to fix the roof that he claims "Bob Wills fiddled through," but he did. Jerry Jeff's 1973 *Viva Terlingua* album recorded live at Luckenbach remains a masterpiece. It includes Ray Wylie Hubbard's infamous "Up Against the Wall Red Neck Mother" and Gary P. Nunn's "London Homesick Blues" (the *Austin City Limits* theme song).

James and Annetta White had christened the place after the movie *Broken Arrow* starring Jimmy Stewart. After my initial tour of the so-called tourist trap area containing Bob Wills memorabilia among other treasurers, I gave James something unique for his collection—my father's half-smoked cigar that Grandma Parker had saved from his first visit in my mother's home. He phoned the *Austin American-Statesman* and the stogie's photo actually made the paper. When he ran my name in his advertisement reading "Coming Friday, Chris Wall, Kimmie Rhodes, & Rosetta Wills (in the spirit of Bob Wills)," I prayed people wouldn't expect a fiddler.

Hats worn by Willie Nelson, George Strait, Alvin Crow, Lyndon B. Johnson, and my father rest in glass cases and musicians' photographs plaster the walls. An enormous clone of the album cover for Willie Nelson and Leon Russell's *One for the Road*, painted by a local artist, peeks out from behind dusty shelves in a far back corner below the low-ceilinged dance floor. Despite several inquiries, James won't quote me a monetary value for the painting that he wouldn't sell me anyway.

James appears nightly in a white cowboy hat and his Texas-Ranger-uncle's smooth yellow leather vest after he parks his 1954 white Cadillac Coupe de Ville a few feet from the front door. John T. Davis declared in the *Austin American-Statesman*, "James has honed his nightly benediction, touting the merits of pretty girls and good country music and decrying the revisionist evils of Grey Poupon and hanging ferns, into a gem of a performance piece." "Little Hunk 'a Heaven" (Becky Jenkins) rolls an authentic wagon wheel with a broken spoke around the dance floor's edge during the nightly sermon.

Former Lubbock legends Butch Hancock and Jimmie Dale Gilmore, who perform at the Broken Spoke, also gave unquestionably fine acoustic performances on Sunday evenings in Butch's Lubbock Or Leave It art gallery in downtown Austin. When Gilmore performed on the *Tonight* show, Jay Leno asked, "Is that a Bob Wills sound?" He responded, "Well, nearly." Leno then asked, "Are you a Bob Wills fan?" Being from Texas automatically solicits these questions. Even though Gilmore was influenced more by Hank Williams than Bob Wills, he grew up in West Texas, where, he said "Bob Wills was the epitome of music."

When the Spoke hosted Jimmie Dale's annual birthday party, many talented musicians played—Joe Ely, Butch Hancock, Kevin Welch, Kelly Willis, Champ Hood, and Don Walser, to name a few. When growing up in Lubbock, Joe Ely said he saw Bob Wills play at the Nat Ballroom in Amarillo, where the dance floor was built over the swimming pool. Familiar heartbeats throbbed when I met Kevin Welch, whose rendition of Dylan's "Maggie's Farm" captured Michael's attention. A name I didn't recognize also appeared on the bill—Arthur Alexander. His main purpose was to plug his new album, *Lonely Just Like Me*, his first newly recorded material in two decades.

Following the reunited Flatlanders' explosive set (Jimmie Dale Gilmore, Joe Ely, and Butch Hancock), Alexander was introduced as the only man in history to have written songs recorded by Bob Dylan, the Rolling Stones, and the Beatles. After a false start and a couple more numbers, his performance of his own "Every Day I Have to Cry," a song I soon recognized, fired the crowd, and brought him back for an encore of his "You Better Move On." Only three months after this wildly successful comeback performance (his first in fifteen years), he died of heart failure in Nashville at the age of fifty-three.

Alvin Crow's show that replicated Bob's sound with Leon Rausch on vocals and Erick Hokkanen on second fiddle drew a sellout crowd that formed a long line down the block. Their recreation of the Wills fiddle style pleased the dancers, who shouted and stomped enthusiastically after each tune. Alvin assembled the band so it actually had the feel and sound the way he remembered it when he was a kid. "When I saw Bob, he was very energetic, there was nothin' laid back about it—it was like a rock 'n' rock show."

Alvin asked me to help judge a local fiddlers' contest with him and Danny Levin (formerly a member of Asleep at the Wheel) at the Green Mesquite outdoor restaurant one Sunday afternoon. Chad, Cindy, Michael, and I cheered our fiddlin' friends Merry Findley, Mike Henderson, and Rod Moag, who competed in the event. Merry even won first prize.

But sometimes Alvin's alter ego takes possession and he sheds his country image for one of a rock 'n' roll star. He puts his fiddle in its case, takes off his cowboy hat, and joins Lubbock guitarist Jesse Taylor in an electrified revival of Buddy Holly favorites. One night I walked into Headliners East during his rock thing. "Oh, hey, Rosetta just came in. Guess that calls for a Bob Wills tune." He unpacked his fiddle and played "Faded Love."

At the Broken Spoke Alvin graciously invited Cousin Dayna Wills onstage to sing a chorus of "Faded Love" with him when she visited Austin. The night before I had introduced her to Asleep at the Wheel's Ray Benson, who also called her to the bandstand when he sang "Milk Cow Blues." "Dayna, take that sun lookin' good goin' down." She did, way down in Ray's baritone key. She was more prepared for her next song, "Sugar Moon," in her tenor key. Her Austin visit also gave her the opportunity to sit in with Don Walser and the Cornell Hurd Band, whose latest CD *Cool and Unusual Punishment* featured guest artists Johnny Bush, Chris O'Connell, and Tom Morrell.

When my mother visited from Tulsa, we took her to hear Don Walser yodel and view her photo next to the cigar in the Spoke's glass case. Don opened for Johnny Cash's Austin show. When Johnny Cash won his 1995 Grammy (for best contemporary folk album) he said, "I'm a fan of the traditional stuff—George Jones, Jimmie Rodgers, Hank Snow, Bob Wills—that's still the country music I think was the best. . . . I don't listen to a lot of modern country music."

Don Walser announced, "Bob Wills's daughter and her mother are here tonight. They're over there, right at that table. You be sure to stop by and talk to them. Get an autograph if you want." Don recorded a song he wrote for Bob, "The Party Don't Start Until the Playboys Get Here," on an earlier CD, and his latest features one of Bob's big band songs, "Whose Heart Are You Breaking Now," with a full-scale horn section. Don fulfilled a dream when he opened for the 1997 Bob Wills Birthday Bash at Cain's in Tulsa. "Bob Wills has always been my hero all my life. I've had two goals in my life: to play the Cain's Ballroom and to play the Grand Ole Opry. Now, half of my dreams have come true."

An astute ABC executive who recognized Don's talent sent a crew to film several of his performances at different Austin venues. The condensed tape became a six-minute segment primed for Primetime's fifteen million viewers in February 1996. As Charles Young wrote in *Playboy* magazine in January 1995:

> I'd rate this guy the Pavarotti of the plains. I never even suspected that I liked yodeling until I heard Don Walser last year in Austin at a Mexican restaurant and had one of those life-changing esthetic epiphanies: Yodeling is better than sex, I thought, and have backed off only slightly since.

Mark Rubin, bassist for the Bad Livers, has referred to Don Walser as God's Own Yodeler. John Conquest, the *3rd Coast Music* editor with the heavy English accent, feels Barbara Clark's epigram encapsulates the meaning of life, the universe, and Austin: "I have heard Don Walser yodel, therefore I am." He nurtures the Wills legacy and I relished his reference to royalty in his "Honest John" column:

> I've been rewarded with the friendship and encouragement of so many musicians and music lovers that naming any seems invidious, but I have to mention . . . my favorite fan, Miss Rosetta (as in Rosetta Wills)—hey, royalty reads it, to hell with the peasants. . . . What I try to offer is integrity.

Don Walser and Hank Thompson were interviewed on Crook and Chase's Nashville show. Don frequently sings Hank's classic "Girl in the Night" for me and made sure to mention that to Hank when they met on the show. A young acquaintance told me that Don dedicated the song to me in a Monday night gig around three o'clock in the morning. "I'm gonna do Rosetta's favorite song for her, but I guess she's not here." (I sure as heck wasn't.)

Hank once told a deejay in a radio interview, "Bob Wills helped me develop my musical style. He's a hero, but we didn't copy him. He always wanted people to dance, not watch him. He didn't realize what a showman he was. Or how magnetic he was. Bob was the one you watched even when Tommy Duncan was singin'. Bob would get that smile and fiddle goin' and his hollerin' fit perfectly."

Ever since Henry's Bar & Grill closed, Don Walser has been looking for a home, pickin' and singin' in country places like the Broken Spoke, where everyone's a Bob Wills fan, and alternative-rock places like Emo's, where nobody knows who Bob Wills is. He tells the audience about Bob and western swing before he plays these tunes so the kids will understand. An uninformed young man asked my daughter, Reneé, "Who's Bob Wills? I heard he was your grandfather."

"Why, he's the King of Western Swing," she explained.

"Oh, yeah, I know him. I heard him at Emo's down on Sixth Street the other night."

Chapter 14

The Final Tribute

The only people for me are the mad ones—the ones who are mad to live, mad to talk, mad to be saved, desirous of everything at the same time—the ones who never yawn or say a commonplace thing, but burn, burn, burn like a fabulous Roman candle exploding like a spider across the stars, and in the middle you see the blue centerlight pop and everybody goes "awwwww."

—Jack Kerouac,
On the Road

1993—the year of glory.

As I waited to accept an award for my father's 1996 induction into the Country Music Association of Texas Hall of Fame, I recalled the night the Broken Spoke had hosted another event—the 1993 stamp party.

"What do you think your father would think about bein' on a stamp?" asked Jim Swift, the Austin Channel 36 News reporter.

"He'd be shocked. He was a humble person who never would have expected this. When deejay Ken Hightower asked him, 'What does it feel like to be a living legend?' he answered, 'Well, I don't feel any different than I did when I lived down between the rivers. I don't know if every man can say that, but I truly feel just as humble, to folks, as I did when I first started.'"

I thought about other candid comments my father made about himself. When Carole and I took Bobby and Chad to see him at the motel, he was getting older and slowing down. He said, "I've helped myself a lot, but I tend to get a little nervous these days. I'm just like an old racehorse. If you put him at the gate, he's gonna run. I may not win nothin' but I'm gonna run." Living legends aren't supposed to feel insecure, but if they do, they aren't supposed to tell anyone.

His candor often made interviewers uncomfortable. He told Hightower, "You know, in '48 when I traveled cross-country with ole Al Dexter and Tex Ritter, when we stopped in a town, they'd take their little records to the deejays. But I wouldn't do that. My dad always taught me not to push myself in on nobody and I thought I would be pushin' myself in on you guys. I was wrong. Somebody oughta told me."

"Bob, you're not going to retire anytime soon, are you?"

"Man, I wanna keep eatin'. I've made a lot of money, but I've lost a lot of money."

In closing the interview Bob said, "It was wonderful and nice of you to have me on your show. I hope I haven't talked too much and messed up your show. You reckon I have?" Yes, my father's honesty surprised and delighted.

Texan Eddie McDonnell believed that if Elvis Presley deserved a stamp, then Bob Wills deserved a stamp. He circulated petitions for months before sending eight thousand names to U.S. Representative Larry Combest from Lubbock, who had lobbied for a stamp honoring Buddy Holly. (Oklahoma boosters circulated petitions to send to U.S. Congressman Glenn English.) The Postal Service's Citizens Stamp Advisory Committee, which considers three thousand requests yearly, approved a Bob Wills stamp that was unveiled in Nashville and in Turkey, Texas, on Saturday, September 26, 1993.

Casey Monahan and Deb Freeman of the Texas Music Office helped the Broken Spoke host a second unveiling the following Tuesday. Bob had played the Broken Spoke three times between 1966 and 1968. James White remembered, "Bob was my first big-time act to play here. I'll always remember the day he opened up the front door. There he was! He had on his cowboy hat, cigar in his mouth, and was carryin' his fiddle. Everyone in the place and at the bar looked his way. The whisperin' began, the nudgin' elbows, sayin', 'There he is. There's Bob Wills.' He was real easy to get along with and told me to just let him know whatever I needed him to do. The night I walked Bob Wills up to our bandstand is definitely a night to remember."

Diane attended the unveiling in Nashville and my half-sister Cindy flew in from Dallas for the Austin ceremony. City councilman Max Nofzinger read proclamations from the Austin City Council and Governor Ann Richards that decreed September 28 as Bob Wills Day. Austin Postmaster Jack Johns presented commemorative stamp plaques to Cindy and me, and also gave me the large stamp poster on display in the foyer.

After the ceremony Alvin Crow and His Pleasant Valley Boys filled the dance hall with Wills's music. My brown-eyed beauty Reneé, Paul, and Justice Dempsey Diamond, my three-month-old grandson, joined us for the ceremony. When Carmel, Paul's mother, visited from New York last summer, she wanted an authentic taste of a Texas honky-tonk. Shortly after I introduced her to James at the Broken Spoke, we joined others sitting in rickety chairs at a long, wobbly table. The couple across from us struck up a conversation, and when my father's name came up as it often does in these settings, I told the young man in the cowboy hat I was

Bob's daughter. He instinctively reached for my hand and kissed it. I don't usually evoke that reaction, but in Texas you can expect anything. Afterward Carmel told Reneé in her unmistakable Scottish accent, "Your mother is certainly spirited!"

When Reneé and Paul visited New York, they met a man in an Upper Nyack pub who worked for Columbia University. As soon as he learned they lived in Austin, he asked, "So, you're from Texas. I'm a big Bob Wills fan. Have you ever heard of him?"

"Yes, as a matter of fact, he's my grandfather."

"Oh, my God! You know he's an icon!"

1993—the year of sorrow.

In March Diane phoned to tell me that Betty had died. I vicariously experienced the sorrow Diane, Carolyn, and Cindy felt when they accepted a memorial plaque dedicated to their mother at the 1993 Bob Wills Day. But grief became my reality—painful feelings defying imagination—when my son Chad died only two months later.

Paul had rushed Reneé to Brackenridge Hospital on June 1 after her premature labor started (two months early). We prayed for it to stop since each additional day in the womb had an effect on the baby's survival. Chad and I visited her each day, discussing boys' names. He informed his friends in his apartment complex that Reneé's choice of Justice was the most perfect name possible, the same commanding way he made Bob's version of "Basin Street Blues" (where all the light and dark folks meet) the complex's anthem. I wonder now if Chad knew the letters JUS were on his license plate.

On June 11, 1993, Justice was born. Michael and I arrived at the hospital around six o'clock in the morning. I immediately phoned Chad, but no answer. I called every thirty minutes all morning, but still no answer. Feeling apprehensive, I drove to his apartment that afternoon, fearing his Lupus had flared again. He opened the door dressed in boxer shorts with his long, wet hair piled high in a towel. "Hi, Mom." I can still hear his voice.

Tragedy struck less than two weeks later, on June 23. Lavern and Cheryl drove me to Chad's apartment at breakneck speed, reassuring me he would be okay. Yes, he was in a coma; however, the paramedics had revived his heart, though he couldn't breathe without the respirator. We chased the screaming sirens down Fifteenth Street to the Brackenridge Emergency Room door. The ambulance and Lavern ran all the red lights, never slowing for any intersection.

The emergency room personnel moved as if in slow motion. Tension mounted as we silently stared at the floor in the waiting room. The doctor told us that a blood clot in Chad's lungs might have broken loose. My grandson, two weeks old and two months premature, lay in the Neonatal Intensive Care Unit. My twenty-six-year-old son lay in the Adult Intensive Care Unit. Calm down. Calm down.

Chad will be fine. This is only another close call, another incident in Chad's chaotic life since the Lupus diagnosis. This wasn't the first time I had followed a screaming ambulance to an emergency room.

But his life was gone before the ambulance made it to the hospital. No brain activity registered on the sensitive instrument. For a long time I stood silently by his bed, repulsed by the sight and sound of the grotesque equipment covering his face. I whispered in his ear, "It's okay. Mom's here. I love you." He lingered in a coma for twelve tormenting hours before he died. Twenty-six years of instinctive maternal protectiveness for nothing. I became a black hole, a vacuum incapable of being filled, and would never feel whole again.

Several weeks after his funeral I sat in my sunroom made of rustic beams and glass, watching the restless squirrels rush madly from tree limb to tree limb. I longed to feel the joy I had known before Chad's death. The sun shone brightly through the green trees full of chirping birds as the stifling hot air offered no hope of rain to relieve the intense July heat. In the background the radio droned on about the weather. No rain for forty-eight days, close to breaking the Austin record. I closed my eyes and my mind's eye once again saw the tremendous lightning bolts and heard the violent storm's crashing thunder that occurred in the early morning hours after Chad's service. I sat up abruptly as I realized that was the last time it had rained. I hurriedly found a calendar and counted the days—forty-eight days. I mumbled to myself, "It may never rain again."

My attention returned to *Where Two Worlds Touch*, a book on spirituality. Despite reading books, seeing a therapist, and praying for understanding, my grief overwhelmed me. The next chapter on synchronicity (coincidences of an extraordinary nature) told a story about a father who lost his nineteen-year-old daughter. His grief raged on for months after her death without any relief. He thought often about how much his daughter loved butterflies. After walking for a long time at the beach, he returned to find his car surrounded by a hundred orange and black butterflies. From that moment on his grief lessened.

I slowly put down the book, looked outside into the heavily wooded area, and cried aloud as tears streamed down my face. "Oh, Chad, where are my butterflies? Where's my sign?" Suddenly a booming noise on the roof startled me. I leaped from the couch, fearing a storm had come up. Then I saw a huge limb fly past the patio door and land in an upright position as if a miniature tree had sprung from the ground. The limb had broken off from a tall tree high above the deck. My eyes traveled up near the top where the clean split looked as if a gigantic knife had sliced it in one quick chop. Glorious green leaves filled the ten or fifteen small branches. It fell within inches of latticework and hanging plants without disturbing anything.

The limb had no explainable reason for breaking away. No storm. No wind. I slowly walked back into the house feeling deeply touched. I later questioned an arborist about the falling of the limb. "It's impossible for a live limb to break away on a calm day," he said. But perhaps nothing is impossible.

Thanksgiving. Christmas. Holidays. A cheerless, dismal time after a death in the family. I ached to hug Chad again, eat turkey, and play Monopoly. On Chad's birthday, I woke up in pain from a dreadful abscessed tooth—a prime example of the mind-body connection. Reneé brought me Shel Silverstein's book *The Giving Tree* and rekindled my spirit with her note in the back:

> *Mom,*
> *Chad has come to you now to sit down and rest. You were and still are the best giving tree any child could hope for. I am blessed that my life was molded and shaped by someone with a soul as kind as yours. I am also blessed to have known the love of a brother. Chad knew love—you taught him that, and that is the greatest gift of all parents' gifts.*
> *I love you very much, Mom.*
>
> *Reneé*

Good-looking Chad, the talented drummer with Bob's dark brown eyes, stole hearts with his alluring smile. He claimed all those Bob Wills fans at the capitol landed him his job as a Senate messenger.

His honed wit kept us laughing at his outrageous Elvis Presley, Keith Richards, and Mick Jagger imitations. At his ninth-grade talent show, the young girls squealed each time he threw the drum sticks in the air, whirling them effortlessly. His drum teacher Lewis choked back tears at his funeral as he whispered to me, "Chad was such a showman." Chad's Tulsa grandparents had a full drum set etched in marble on his gravestone. Only a week before he died, he told me, "Mom, I've been practicin' my drums and think I'll start a band here in Austin. After all, I'm Bob Wills's grandson."

"This may be the most important song I've ever written," Don Henley said before he sang "Heart of the Matter" at his exceptional Erwin Center concert. His insightful lyrics about forgiveness took me back to a Sunday afternoon visit with my father after he suffered his first stroke in 1969. Betty had rented an apartment near Hillcrest Hospital, where he began the arduous task of rebuilding his health through physical therapy. Late afternoon near dusk we stopped by the furnished apartment. A musty smell greeted us when we entered the living room. With no personal possessions and no pictures hanging on the walls, the room had an empty, detached feeling. The last few rays of sunlight peeking through the half-open venetian blinds cast shadows on the brown shag carpet.

Propped up on the couch, unable to move freely, he reached out to hug me, his eyes sparkling. He seemed happy to see us and tried with difficulty to hold two-year-old Chad. Although always affectionate, this time he was different. His haunted eyes and passionate grip on my hands unmasked the gravity of his feelings. I felt the vibrations from his heart—the harmony between the message he was sending me and his innermost feelings.

I remembered what the musicians who traveled in the car with him had told me. "Rosetta, he feels so guilty 'bout you. When he's drinkin', he always talks 'bout you." More guilt. I experienced a poignant moment with him when I truly understood he longed to make up for his past mistakes. Since we are all fallible human beings, good people often do bad things. Our reality is not just to "forgive and forget" because the real test lies in forgiving what one can never forget. I will probably never understand why my father let me grow up without getting to know me, but forgiving does not require total understanding. I can partially understand what influenced him and why he made some of the choices he made. You can't make someone love you and you can't make someone forgive you. But love is the true power behind forgiveness. So I'm thinking about forgiveness. Forgiveness.

A symposium on Texas Country Music held at Austin's La Zona Rosa devoted part of the program to "The Wills Legacy: Past and Present." More newspaper clippings for my scrapbook. An informal panel with Eldon Shamblin, Dr. Charles Townsend, Joe Nick Patoski, Alvin Crow, John Morthland, and Curley Hollingsworth discussed Bob's music and western swing. Big, brawny Eldon giggled when he asked his customary question, "Rosetta, remember that time I tuned your piano?"

"I'll never forget it."

"You know, I thought people would forget about Bob when he died. I didn't think any of us would ever play western swing again. I thought it was all over."

"So did I, Eldon, but I guess we were wrong."

Evie Ashlock called a few weeks later. "Rosetta, have you seen Willie's new CMT video about western swing? It has a lot of film clips from your daddy's old movies in it."

"Yeah," I replied. "It's called 'Turn Me Loose and Let Me Swing.' I taped it the other night. Hey, did you know Willie sings 'Rosetta' on one of his CDs? But he doesn't sing the 'God Bless You, Honey' part. I guess that's just somethin' my daddy added."

Epilogue

Yes, my father left me a legacy. Even the protagonists of Robert James Waller's book *Border Music* dance to "Faded Love" and champion Bob's well-established phrase "Take it away, Leon."

A recent record store ad confirmed my father's enduring reputation as his face jumped out at me from the cover of 1973's album, *For The Last Time,* midpage next to Jimmy LaFave's new release, *Road Novel,* while right below was Jimmie Vaughan's *Strange Pleasures* and above was Tracy Byrd's *No Ordinary Man.* Another ad for featured CDs positioned *Bob Wills: Essential 1937–1945* between Bob Dylan and Miles Davis.

The interest in my father's music continues to grow as yet another generation rediscovers him. In the mid-eighties MCA, Rhino, UA, MGM, and other labels offered album collections of his early recordings. (Columbia had issued anthologies in 1973, 1976, 1982, 1987, 1992, and 1997.) The bins in the record stores are now bulging with reissues of old material on compact discs like *George Jones Sings Bob Wills* (1963) and Merle Haggard's *Best Damn Fiddle Player in the World* (1970).

A recent superb three-CD boxed set on Liberty, *Bob Wills—Encore,* includes the version of "Rosetta" that he recorded in 1963. The live, improvised "St. Louis Blues" and other reissued tunes make the set a collector's gem. Dr. Townsend's liner notes state that my father sold more records on Brunswick's Vocalion label in 1936 than any of the other 192 artists in Vocalion's catalog.

Billboard didn't establish a preferred country recordings list until 1944, calling it *Most Played Juke Box Folk Records.* Although Eddy Arnold dominated the 1944–49 *Billboard* charts, he was followed closely by Ernest Tubb, Bob Wills, Red Foley, and Gene Autry. In Bob Millard's *Country Music: 70 Years of America's Favorite Music,* he named seventeen Bob Wills's hits during the ten-year span of 1936–46 on his list of Most Important Records from 1923 through 1992:

- **1936:** Spanish Two-Step
- **1937:** Steel Guitar Rag; Trouble In Mind; Right or Wrong; Get Along Home, Cindy
- **1938:** Maiden's Prayer
- **1939:** San Antonio Rose (no lyrics)
- **1940:** New San Antonio Rose (with lyrics)
- **1941:** Take Me Back To Tulsa

1942: My Life's Been a Pleasure; Please Don't Leave Me

1943: Home in San Antone; Miss Molly

1944: You're From Texas; We Might As Well Forget It

1946: New Spanish Two-Step; Roly Poly

While my lists start with *Billboard* chart data, they are tempered by a feeling that what matters is whether a song actually sold a lot of records, launched or changed a career, had significant impact on the genre over the long run, or if it is *still remembered*—something that contemporaneous annual charts, however scientifically compiled, cannot know.

In the nineties country music is bigger than ever, as evidenced by *Billboard*'s charts when they changed their formula to use bar coding at the point of sale in 1991 to create an accurate list. The Garth Brooks phenomenon surprised everyone when his *Ropin' the Wind* made its debut at number one on the pop charts-a first for a country album.

But in the opinion of guitar genius Chet Atkins, as quoted by Nicholas Dawidoff in *In the Country of Country,* nineties' Nashville has strayed too far from its original, soulful country sound:

> To young folks right now, country music just means some guy with a tight ass and a white hat. But to the older people—Johnny Cash, Merle Haggard, Bob Wills—they're important to the older people. But I'm not good at talking about that. I'm just a guitar player. Right now we're in a curve with everything sounding alike, but somebody will come along and get us back where we need to be.

Becky, Broken Spoke's "Little Hunk 'a Heaven," brought me a 1994 collector's edition of *Life* magazine titled "The Roots of Country Music," and asked me, "Did you know your father is listed as number seven of the hundred most important people in country music history?" The issue stated:

> To all the music, the Playboys brought their own unique signature, underscored by Bob's constant squawks and hollers, comments, and dance calls. No matter how brilliant the musicianship became (and make no mistake, the Playboys represent the zenith of country music virtuosity), *they never stopped havin' fun.*

Feel good, feel happy.
Dance all night. Dance a little longer.
Never stop havin' fun.

Bibliography

Books

Clark, Roy, with Marc Eliot. *My Life in Spite of Myself*. New York: Simon & Schuster, 1994.

Cooper, Daniel. *Lefty Frizzell*. New York: Little, Brown & Company, 1995.

Dawidoff, Nicholas. *In the Country of Country*. New York: Pantheon Books, 1997.

Endres, Clifford. *Austin City Limits*. Austin: University of Texas Press, 1987.

Ginell, Cary, with Roy Lee Brown. *Milton Brown and the Founding of Western Swing*. Champaign: University of Illinois Press, 1994.

Guralnick, Peter. *Lost Highway*. New York: Harper & Row, 1989.

_____. *Last Train to Memphis*. Boston: Little, Brown, & Company, 1994.

Horstman, Dorothy. *Sing Your Heart Out, Country Boy*. Nashville: County Music Foundation Press, 1996.

Jenkins, Dan. *Baja Oklahom*. New York: Atheneum, 1981.

Jennings, Waylon, with Lenny Kaye. *Waylon: An Autobiography*. 3d ed. New York: Warner Books, Inc., 1996.

Leigh, Keri. *Stevie Ray: Soul to Soul*. Dallas: Taylor Publishing Company, 1993.

McWhorter, Frankie, as told to John R. Erickson. *Cowboy Fiddler in Bob Wills' Band*. Denton: University of North Texas Press, 1997.

Marschall, Rick. *The Encyclopedia of Country & Western Music*. New York: Simon & Schuster (Exeter Books), 1985.

Millard, Bob. *Country Music: 70 Years of America's Favorite Music*. New York: HarperCollins, 1993.

Nelson, Willie, with Bud Shrake. *Willie*. New York: Simon & Schuster, 1988.

Perkins, Jr., John E. *Leon Rausch: The Voice of the Texas Playboys*. Arlington: Swing Publishing Company, 1996.

Richards, Tad, and Shestack, Melvin B. *The New Country Music Encyclopedia*. New York: Simon & Schuster, 1993.

Savage, William W., Jr. *Singing Cowboys and All That Jazz*. Norman: University of Oklahoma Press, 1983.

Sheldon, Ruth, *Hubbin' It: The Life of Bob Wills*. Privately published, 1938.

Stricklin, Al, with Jon McConal. *My Years with Bob Wills*. San Antonio: Naylor Company, 1976.

Tosches, Nick, *Country: The Biggest Music in America.* New York: Dell Publishing Company, 1977.

Townsend, Charles R. *Stars of Country Music: Uncle Dave Macon to Johnny Rodriguez,* edited by Bill Malone and Judith McCulloh. Urbana: University of Illinois Press, 1975.

_____. *San Antonio Rose.* Urbana: University of Illinois Press, 1976.

Ward, Ed, Geoffrey Stokes, and Ken Tucker; introduction by Jann S. Wenner. *Rock of Ages: The Rolling Stone History of Rock and Roll.* Englewood Cliffs, N.J.: Rolling Stone Press/Prentice-Hall, 1986.

White, Timothy. *Rock Stars.* New York: Stewart, Tabori & Chang, 1984.

Williams, Richard, *Dylan: A Man Called Alias.* New York: Henry Holt and Company, 1992.

Willoughby, Larry. *Texas Rhythm, Texas Rhyme.* Austin: Tonkawa Free Press, 1990.

Articles and Periodicals

Carmack, George. San Antonio newspaper article.

Davis, John T. "What People Like." *Austin American-Statesman,* August 17, 1995.

Hentoff, Nat. "Record Review." *Cosmopolitan,* 1976.

_____. "The Timeless Fiddler." *Wall Street Journal,* June 5, 1992.

Hirshberg, Charles, and Robert Sullivan. "100 Most Important People in the History of Country." *Life Collector's Edition: The Roots of Country Music,* September 1994.

Kienzle, Rich. "Milton Brown." *The Journal,* June 1992.

_____. "Bob Wills, The California Years." *The Journal,* February 1993.

_____. "Bob Wills, The Tulsa Years." *The Journal,* June 1996.

_____. "Art Satherley, Columbia's Pioneer A&R Man," *The Journal,* August 1996.

McLeese, Don. "Roots Are Keys to Innovations." *Austin American-Statesman,* January 3, 1991.

Millburg, Steve. "Taking It to the Limits." *Southpoint,* April 1990.

Nelson, Willie. "A Tribute to Bob Wills." *Country Music,* August 1974.

Patoski, Joe Nick. "Wills' Testament." *Texas Monthly,* September 1976.

Raphael, Judy. "Time Travel in Tulsa." *New Country,* November 1994.

"The Roots of Country Music." *Life Collector's Edition: The Roots of Country Music,* September 1994.

Rowland, Mark. "Dance All Night, Stay a Little Longer." *Musician,* March 1993.

_____. Review of Asleep at the Wheel's "Tribute to the Music of Bob Wills and the Texas Playboys." *Musician,* December 1993.

Simmons, Michael. "Billy Jack Wills and His Western Swing Band." *Fiddler,* Summer 1996.

Tosches, Nick. "The Strange and Hermetical Case of Emmett Miller." *Journal of Country Music* 17 (no. 1).

"Transition." *Newsweek,* May 26, 1975.

"Twenty Things You Never Knew About the Grand Ole Opry." Author and publication information unknown.

Young, Charles. *Playboy,* January 1995.

Audio Recordings and Liner Notes

George-Warren, Holly. *Not Fade Away.* MCA Records, 1996.

Groom, Dewey. *A Tribute Album to the King of Western Swing.* Star Image Corporation, 1982.

Henry, John, and Guy T. Miller, hosts. "Hadacol Hillbilly Hoedown," part of *Saturday Bandstand.* KAKC (1300 AM), Tulsa radio interviews, 1991.

Hightower, Ken. *Bob Wills: I Love People.* Western Heritage Records, 1976.

Ivey, William. *The Bob Wills Anthology.* Columbia Records, 1973.

Johnston, Buck Wayne, host. Interview next to Bostonia Ballroom, El Cajon, California, 1967.

McEntire, Reba. *Reba McEntire: Live.* MCA Records, 1989. Recorded live at MCallum Theater in Palm Desert, California, April 2–4, 1989.

McEuen, John. "Bob Wills: The Country Music Legend." *Hall of Fame Album.* United Artists.

Tiffany Transcriptions, Vol. 1–9. Rhino Records, early 1980s.

Townsend, Charles R. *Bob Wills: Encore.* Liberty Records, 1995.

Warren, Lawson, and Hugh Cherry. *The Bob Wills Story.* Great Empire Broadcasting, 1989. Mike Lynch and Mike Oatman, executive producers.

Videotapes

Frank, Jack. *Oklahoma Magazine.* PBS, Tulsa. 1992.

Rhodes, Garydon. *Fiddlin' Man: The Life and Times of Bob Wills.* 1993.

Wooley, John. *Still Swingin': The History of Bob Wills and Western Swing Music.* 1994.

Miscellaneous

Parker, Mary Lou. Seventeen letters Bob Wills wrote to Parker in 1938 and 1939.

Thomason, Ruth. "Journal of Bob Wills and His Texas Playboys Radio Shows on KVOO in 1940."

Wills, Rosetta. Scrapbooks containing numerous newspaper clippings from the 1930s, 1940s, and early 1950s.

Taped Interviews with the Author

Tommy Allsup

Robbie Jo Wills Calhoun

Mary Lou Parker Cloud

Johnny Cuviello

Smoky Dacus

Don Dennis

Casey Dickens

Joe Frank Ferguson

Steve Hathaway

Curly Lewis

Dean McKinney

Sue House Morrow

Jody Nix

Leon Rausch

Herb Remington

Eldon Shamblin

Snuffy Smith

Corky House Stout

Harvey Tedford

Dayna Wills

Irene Wills

Lorene Wills

Luther J. Wills

Appendix

To order the *Western Swing Newsletter:*
Steve Hathaway, Editor
1733 Cheney Drive
San Jose, CA 95128-1947
Phone: (408) 947-1947
Fax: (408) 777-1030

Western Swing Societies

Canadian Western Swing Society
Contact: John York
3565 Camridge Street
Vancouver, BC, V5KIM3, Canada
Phone: (604) 299-2301

Fresno Western Swing Society
Contact: Joe Sausage
Phone: (209) 226-3298 or (209) 229-5767

International Western Swing Association
8210 East 71st Street, suite 130
Tulsa, OK 74133-2908
(800) 541-3190
Voicemail or fax: (918) 682-1234
e-mail: westswing@aol.com

Sacramento Western Swing Society
Membership Chair: Flo Carpenter
PO Box 60203
Sacramento, CA 95860
Phone: (916) 487-0760
Fax: (916) 487-1383

Seattle Western Swing Society
Contact: Lou Bischoff
Phone: (206) 823-5336

Visalia Area Western Swing Society
Contact: Chuck Masters
Phone: (209) 747-1200

INDEX